First Nations Sacred Sites
in Canada's Courts

Law and Society Series
W. Wesley Pue, General Editor

A list of the books in this series appears at the end of this book.

Michael Lee Ross

First Nations Sacred Sites in Canada's Courts

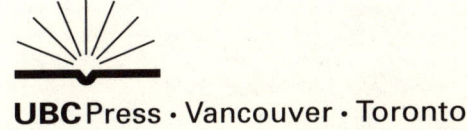

UBC Press · Vancouver · Toronto

15   14   13   12   11   10   09   08   07   06   05   5   4   3   2   1

Printed in Canada on acid-free paper

Library and Archives Canada Cataloguing in Publication

Ross, Michael Lee, 1956-
    First Nations sacred sites in Canada's courts / Michael Lee Ross.

    (Law and society, ISSN 1496-4953)
    Includes bibliographical references and index.
    ISBN 0-7748-1129-3 (bound); ISBN 0-7748-1130-7 (pbk.)

    1. Native peoples – Legal status, laws, etc. – Canada. 2. Native peoples – Land tenure – Canada. 3. Native peoples – Canada – Claims. 4. Native peoples – Canada – Religion. I. Title. II. Series: Law and society series (Vancouver, B.C.)

KE7715.R68 2005   346.7104'32'08997   C2005-900195-X
KF5660.R68 2005

Canadä

UBC Press gratefully acknowledges the financial support for our publishing program of the Government of Canada through the Book Publishing Industry Development Program (BPIDP), and of the Canada Council for the Arts, and the British Columbia Arts Council.

This book has been published with the help of a grant from the Canadian Federation for the Humanities and Social Sciences, through the Aid to Scholarly Publications Programme, using funds provided by the Social Sciences and Humanities Research Council of Canada, and with the help of the K.D. Srivastava Fund.

Printed and bound in Canada by Friesens
Set in Stone by Brenda and Neil West, BN Typographics West
Copy editor: Francis Chow
Proofreader: Stacy Belden

UBC Press
The University of British Columbia
2029 West Mall
Vancouver, BC V6T 1Z2
604-822-5959 / Fax: 604-822-6083
www.ubcpress.ca

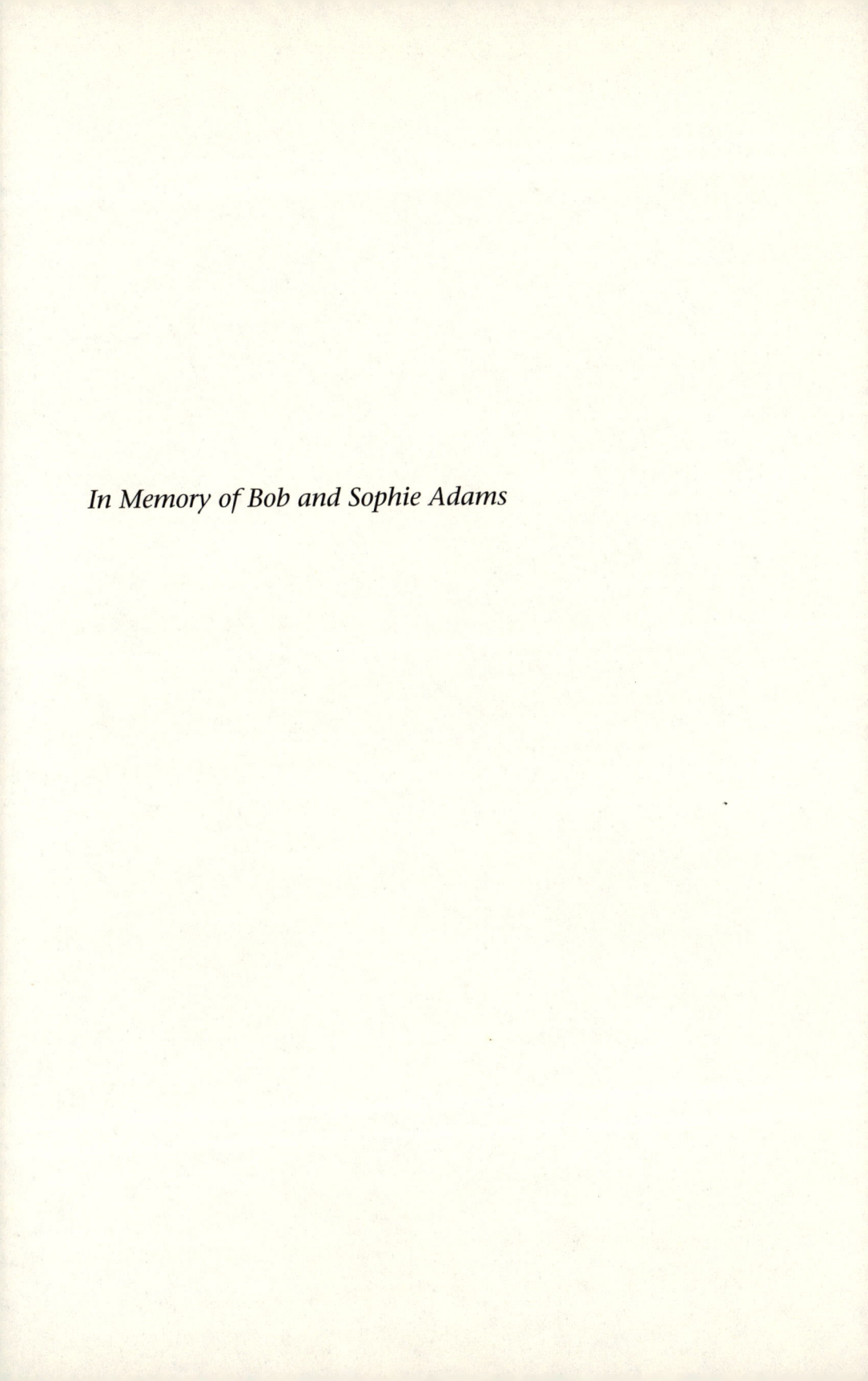

In Memory of Bob and Sophie Adams

Contents

Acknowledgments

Customarily, acknowledgments sections serve two purposes. First, since both the writing of a book and the thinking that underlies the writing, although activities of individuals, are intertwined with the efforts of others in larger, supervening collective enterprises, authors use acknowledgments sections to make known those persons and institutions on whom their work – from its origins to its publication – has most depended. Second, since it is only natural to feel especially grateful towards those who have contributed most to their projects, authors also use acknowledgments sections to express their gratitude. As *First Nations Sacred Sites in Canada's Courts* was thought through and written over the space of two years, in several places, and in various circumstances, I have had the benefit of the contributions of many. It pleases me considerably, then, to be able to acknowledge some of them here, both by making them and their contributions known and by expressing my lasting gratitude.

The beginnings of this book's basic ideas are traceable to a two-week visit to Calgary, Alberta, in the summer of 2001. Thanks to Gary and Cecilia Brisebois, who convivially shared their home with me, I was often free to let my curiosity run wild in the archives of the Glenbow Museum. This book is but one of the unlooked-for fruits of those investigations. I am much indebted to the Glenbow's archivists and staff for their virtually unlimited patience in responding to my doubtless seemingly endless questions and requests for documents. I am yet more indebted to Gary and Cecilia. Were it not for their unfailing friendship and unhesitating generosity, not only might this book not have been conceived but also, once conceived, it might not have come to see the light of day.

The impetus to develop and first articulate my thoughts in writing was provided by Professor Robert Paterson of the University of British Columbia's Faculty of Law. To fulfill a requirement for his justly popular seminar on cultural property, which I attended in the spring of 2002, I chose to write a paper on First Nations sacred sites. Portions of that paper live on in this book. I am grateful, then, to Professor Paterson for encouraging me to pursue the topic, for indulging me during the writing process, and, finally, for offering his invaluable comments.

I must not, however, neglect to thank my other former teachers at Hot Springs High School in Montana (especially Merle Farrier), the University of Alberta (especially Kweku Garbrah, Brian Inglis, and Peter Schouls), the University of St. Thomas in Houston (especially Patrick Lee), the University of Toronto (especially Joseph Boyle, Calvin Normore, Joseph Owens, John Rist, and Robert Tully), and the UBC Faculty of Law (especially Maurice Copithorne, June McCue, Daniel Préfontaine, and Annie Rochette), many of whom have in one way or another helped to shape ideas in this book. Most especially, I want to thank Professors Wesley Pue and Michael Jackson of the UBC Faculty of Law. Most of my academic training has been in philosophy and thus I am at home in the world of abstractions and theories. Nonetheless, because the legal profession has little appetite for things theoretical, and because this book is intended partly for lawyers, I hesitated to include a theoretical chapter. As it happens, Chapter 1, my theoretical chapter, is the most crucial chapter of this book, lending it analytical depth and argumentative power. Simply put, were it not for Professor Pue, who – a *rara avis* in the legal academy – champions the importance of theory in the study of law, this book either would not be or, what is worse, would be far less than it is. Although more general, Professor Jackson's contribution is no less real. Through his teaching and by his lawyerly advocacy, he exemplifies what it means to be steadfastly committed to justice, whether it is justice for First Nations peoples or for others. To reduce it to a single word, what *First Nations Sacred Sites in Canada's Courts* is ultimately about is justice. This reflects in no small part Professor Jackson's influence.

I began researching my topic in earnest and writing during the summer of 2002. All of my early – as well as some of my later – research and writing was done at the University of British Columbia. Although I availed myself of several campus libraries, I relied most on the UBC Law Library. I cannot praise enough its librarians (especially Shauna Barry and Sandra Wilkins) and staff for their day-to-day friendliness, their ready yet respectfully unobtrusive helpfulness, and, not least, their sense of humour.

I spent most of the fall of 2002 and the first months of 2004 on the Flathead Reservation in Montana. Thanks to the hospitality of Marcia Pablo, director of the Tribal Preservation Department of the Confederated Salish and Kootenai Tribes, I was privileged to occupy my mornings and afternoons writing in the forest calm of her home at the foot of the Mission Mountains in the Flathead Valley. Marcia's encouragement was present at every stage of this book's development. (Indeed, I chided her more than once for encouraging me to undertake a task meant only for the foolhardy.) Marcia's knowledge of First Nations/Native American cultural and sacred sites is remarkable. Her knowledge of her own Salish and Kootenai peoples' sacred sites (on both sides of the forty-ninth parallel) is intimate and profound. I am most grateful to Marcia for sharing her knowledge, her abundant good sense and her humour, and for patiently serving as my reality check.

I returned briefly to Vancouver in November 2002 to complete my research and the book's first draft. I was able to stay conveniently close to the UBC campus thanks to Dobrin Kalchev, a physicist at TRIUMF (Canada's national laboratory for particle and nuclear physics), who let me use his apartment while he was away in Geneva. When I returned yet again in late spring 2004 to complete the last of my revisions, Dobrin generously shared his quarters with me. I count myself fortunate to have found such a good friend, someone who combines equally a scientist's understanding of how things are and a poet's eye for how they ought to be.

From the middle of January through March 2003 and intermittently during the remaining months, I made revisions while lending a hand at my family's ranch in the upper Peace River area of northeastern British Columbia. The early revisions were completed in fits and starts during the annual life-and-death drama of calving season. I am grateful to my northern Rosses, especially to my father, Donald Lee, and my brothers, Bryan Keith and Steven Kenneth, for making it possible to postpone my return to "the real world" and thus to continue my writing projects.

During the writing of *First Nations Sacred Sites in Canada's Courts*, I profited enormously from discussions with friends, whether over coffee – as is my wont – or by long-distance phone calls or e-mails. In particular, I wish to thank Aaron Bruce, Lee Schmidt, Thomaz DaGroomes, Andrea Hilland, Erik Lund, Len Marshall, John Rickert, Dawana St. Germain, and Jonathon York for patiently listening to my sometimes faltering thoughts, sharing their insights, and being friends good and true.

Although it goes almost without saying, I welcome hearing from others with serious interests in the topic of this book and invite them to reach me by e-mail at michaelleeross@yahoo.ca.

I have also profited greatly from the thoughtful criticisms and suggestions made by the two persons assigned by UBC Press to read and report on my manuscript. While I did not agree with every criticism or follow every suggestion, I agreed with and followed most. The few that I did not agree with or follow were not dismissed lightly. Thanks to their selfless willingness to labour in anonymity, *First Nations Sacred Sites in Canada's Courts* is a significantly better book than it would otherwise have been. My hope is that as they read this final version, they will recognize their contributions and sense my appreciation in its pages.

And as I have mentioned UBC Press, I cannot forget to thank Randy Schmidt, editor for the Press. Randy skillfully shepherded both me and my manuscript through the longer-than-anticipated publication process. He maintained what I have come to know is his characteristic intelligence and good cheer in the face of unforeseeable trials. He also helped in subtle but important ways to improve some of the ideas in this book. I hope that he too will recognize his contributions and sense my appreciation in these pages.

Finally, no one has sacrificed more or better understands what I have sacrificed to see this project through to its completion than Marlene Pablo Ross, my constant friend, my trusted confidant, my wisest advisor, my faithful companion in my peripatetic way of life, my lovely and loving wife. Thank you.

First Nations Sacred Sites in Canada's Courts

Introduction: What First Nations Peoples Have at Stake

On the final day of August 2001, the Inter-American Court of Human Rights, the western hemisphere's highest human rights tribunal, delivered a landmark decision on the rights of indigenous peoples in international human rights law.[1] In its decision in *The Mayagna (Sumo) Awas Tingni Community v. Nicaragua*, a case originating in Nicaragua, the Court affirmed, on the one hand, the collective rights of indigenous peoples to the free and full enjoyment of their lands and resources in accordance with their customary laws, practices, and values, and, on the other, the corresponding duties of states within whose boundaries they live to formally recognize, give effect to, and respect those rights. As a key step in its reasoning, the Court described the importance of the land to indigenous peoples as follows:

> Indigenous groups, by the fact of their very existence, have the right to live freely in their own territory; the close ties of indigenous people with the land must be recognized and understood as the fundamental basis of their cultures, their spiritual life, their integrity, and their economic survival. For indigenous communities, relations to the land are not merely a matter of possession and production but [have] a material and spiritual element which they must fully enjoy, even to preserve their cultural legacy and transmit it to future generations.[2]

Essentially, the Court recognized that to be indigenous is, collectively speaking, to be in a special relationship with the land.[3] By so doing, the Court committed itself to the proposition that anything that undermines indigenous peoples' special relationship with their lands threatens "their cultures, their spiritual life, their integrity, and their economic survival" or, in other words, threatens their existence *qua* indigenous.

The Court also, it should not be overlooked, identified what it is that makes indigenous peoples' relationship with their lands special. What makes it special or distinctive is that it includes, in addition to the ordinary possessory and productive aspects, "a material and spiritual element." The Court was saying, then, that the existence, survival, and, not least, well-being of indigenous peoples depend not only on their ownership and occupation of their lands but also, more crucially, on their material and spiritual connections to the same.[4]

The Court did not elaborate on the material and spiritual aspects of the special relationship. Nonetheless, a few general characterizations are ready to hand. For instance, the material aspect of the relationship certainly includes not only a physical presence but also a physical dependence on the land – the land (including its plants and animals), then, is understood as physically sustaining. The spiritual aspect of the relationship is exemplified by indigenous peoples' widespread belief that the land is a gift given into their care. Because indigenous peoples commonly refer to the spiritual realm to explain the (believed) facts that the land has been given to them and that they have been charged with caring for the land,[5] their relationship with the land as a gift is a spiritual relationship. Clearly, the Court was correct in stating that indigenous peoples' relationship with their lands has both material and spiritual aspects.

Just as there is far more to the material aspect of the relationship than what I have mentioned, so too there is far more to the spiritual aspect. Here I want to mention just one more common feature. For indigenous peoples generally, the land is never merely physical. It is permeated by the spiritual.[6] The land is, therefore, never spiritually desolate. Because indigenous peoples look upon the land as permeated by the spiritual, their relationship with their lands must always have a spiritual aspect.

Before turning my discussion in a less abstract direction, I want to delve just a little further into indigenous metaphysics. Indigenous peoples generally hold not only that the world is permeated by but also that it is enveloped by the spiritual.[7] The world is enveloped by the spiritual because it is not, physically speaking, self-sufficing. To put it another way, the world is not the source of its ultimate significance. Not surprisingly, indigenous peoples look to the spiritual realm for the ultimate significance of their lands, of their relationship with their lands, and consequently of themselves. Their relationship with their lands is therefore fundamentally and irreducibly spiritual.[8]

It is a testament to the care with which the Inter-American Court of Human Rights crafted its words that the statement quoted above aptly describes the importance of the land (including waters[9]) to the First Nations (or Native American) peoples of Canada and elsewhere in North America.[10] Being First Nations is, indeed, a collective way of being in a relationship with the land. First Nations peoples' relationship with the land includes not only the usual possessory and productive aspects but also material and spiritual aspects. Thus, anything that undermines their relationship with the land, and especially their material and spiritual connections to the land, threatens "their cultures, their spiritual life, their integrity, and their economic survival."

As with other indigenous peoples, First Nations peoples' relationship with the land is fundamentally and irreducibly spiritual.[11] But more can and, for my purposes, should be said about their spiritual relationship with the land. The spiritual connection First Nations peoples have to the land is a connection not only to the land as a whole but also to particular portions of the land. First Nations peoples do not view the land as spiritually homogeneous or uniform. Although the land as a whole has spiritual significance, certain portions of it have their own special spiritual significance. First Nations sacred sites are paradigmatically places of special spiritual significance. For First Nations peoples, their sacred sites are places of the greatest convergence of the physical and spiritual. First Nations peoples are, therefore, spiritually connected to particular portions of the land through their sacred sites.

It is clear, then, that their sacred sites are crucial to the existence, survival, and well-being of First Nations peoples, for their sacred sites distribute their spiritual connection to particular portions of the land. Without their sacred sites to distribute their spiritual connection to the land, First Nations peoples would be left with a mere shell of their spiritual relationship with the land. Absent the spiritual connection to particular portions of the land afforded by their sacred sites, First Nations peoples would have only their spiritual connection to the land as a whole to sustain their spiritual relationship with the land. Such a diminished spiritual connection, lacking specific anchors in the land, would be tenuous and, hence, vulnerable to modernity's onslaughts. Thus, what endangers First Nations sacred sites endangers their spiritual relationship with the land. Furthermore, because the spiritual aspect is an integral aspect of their overall relationship with the land, what endangers their sacred sites endangers their overall relationship. Finally, because to be First Nations is to be in a special relationship with the land, what endangers their sacred sites ultimately puts their existence, survival, and well-being in jeopardy. Their sacred sites are therefore crucial to their existence, survival, and well-being.

A different argument supports a similar conclusion. First Nations spirituality and religion are rooted in the land. Sacred sites are their taproots. First Nations sacred sites serve a variety of spiritual and religious functions (as places, for example, associated with creation events, utilized for cleansing rituals, or suitable for vision quests), all fixing First Nations spiritual and religious beliefs and practices in the land. Whatever endangers their sacred sites threatens to uproot and thus to harm their spirituality and religion. But their spirituality and religion are integral parts of First Nations cultures. Thus, whatever endangers their sacred sites undermines their cultures.[12]

Moreover, because other cultural elements (such as history, ethics, law, and politics) are intricately interwoven with their spirituality and religion, First Nations sacred sites often serve other cultural functions (as historical sites or places for political deliberation, for example). Again, whatever endangers their sacred sites undermines their cultures. First Nations sacred sites are therefore crucial to First Nations cultures.

Thousands of First Nations sacred sites in Canada and elsewhere in North America have been destroyed or seriously damaged. Thousands more are under imminent threat of the same. Throughout Canada and the rest of North America, First Nations peoples' access to and use of their remaining sacred sites are often hindered or even denied. It is against this grim background that First Nations peoples are fighting to maintain or regain access to, to use, to protect, and to preserve their sacred sites. In light of the foregoing analysis, it is clear what First Nations peoples have at stake in their fight for their sacred sites – in a word, everything. For starters, the possibility, not to mention the actuality, of their well-being is at stake, for their well-being as First Nations peoples is impossible without their sacred sites. Short of this but more fundamentally, their very being as First Nations peoples is at stake. To put it plainly, their fight for their sacred sites is a fight for their collective lives.

Not surprisingly, then, given what is at stake, First Nations peoples have occasionally taken their fight for their sacred sites to the courts. For First Nations peoples living within Canada's boundaries, the legal weapon of choice has been Canada's constitutional commitment to recognize and affirm Aboriginal and treaty rights. Normally, when First Nations peoples have taken their fight for their sacred sites to Canada's courts, they have tried to leverage their constitutional rights into protection for their sacred sites. This book is about how Canada's courts have responded.

In Chapter 1, I sketch the outlines of a general theory of sacred sites. The theory's key explanatory concepts include a distinction between a sacred site's surface and deep symbolism, a distinction between a sacred site's practical religious and theological/cosmological significance, and the notions of a sacred site's status and its ethic. The theory proves its explanatory worth throughout Chapter 5 and intermittently in Chapters 3, 4, and 6.

I must emphasize here that Chapter 1 contains only the *outlines* – indeed, only the *partial* outlines – of a general theory of sacred sites. A full-blown general theory would require a book of its own. To reiterate, this book investigates how Canada's courts – Canada's appointed guardians of the law – have dealt with sacred site claims of First Nations peoples. To whatever extent a theory of sacred sites emerges in this book, it is wholly in service of that larger purpose.

In Chapter 2, I describe the historical and legal context in which First Nations peoples carry their fight for their sacred sites to Canada's courts.

I divide my discussion into four sections. In the first, I explain why First Nations have had to fight for their sacred sites. In the next, I discuss the potential of Aboriginal and treaty rights as a means whereby First Nations may gain a measure of constitutional protection for their sacred sites. Although I conclude that Canada's Aboriginal rights regime is moribund, I suggest that the British Columbia Court of Appeal's decisions in *Taku River Tlingit First Nation v. Tulsequah Chief Mine Project* (January 2002) and *Haida Nation v. British Columbia (Minister of Forests)* (February 2002) may breathe new life into it. (I discuss these decisions and their implications for First Nations sacred sites in Chapter 4.) In the third section, I touch upon the use of interim measures and other negotiated agreements to protect sacred sites. Finally, I discuss the obstacles First Nations peoples face in having their interests in their sacred sites fairly translated into legal language and ritual and, so translated, fairly interpreted by the courts.

In Chapters 3 and 4, I set forth and discuss nearly a dozen court cases in which First Nations peoples have attempted to leverage their constitutionally guaranteed Aboriginal and treaty rights into protection for their sacred sites. (The cases were chosen for their *legal* significance, for what they tell us about the courts, about the law. They are not necessarily the foremost cases on what First Nations peoples or anyone else may consider the most important religious or spiritual issues.) I have sorted the cases into two groups based on whether the First Nation in question has employed what I call the Meares or the Haida litigation strategy. Chapter 3 is concerned with cases based on the Meares strategy and Chapter 4 on cases based on the Haida. Regarding the cases based on the Meares strategy, I first show how the strategy developed, then demonstrate that it has largely failed to protect sacred sites, and finally explain why it has failed. Regarding the cases based on the Haida strategy, I again show how the strategy developed and then discuss its potential for protecting sacred sites. On the latter point, I argue that First Nations sacred sites have the potential to test most severely the limits of, on the one hand, the Crown's constitutional duties towards First Nations peoples as articulated by the British Columbia Court of Appeal in the *Taku River* and *Haida* cases and, on the other, a reviewing court's ability to assess whether the Crown has fulfilled those duties in undertaking an activity that affects a sacred site.

My discussion of the cases in Chapters 3 and 4 is extended and detailed, for two reasons. First, judicial remarks bearing directly on First Nations sacred sites are few, fragmentary, and unsystematic, even in those cases explicitly concerned with First Nations sacred sites. This means that if we are to gain a good sense of the courts' thinking on the subject, logical gaps must be filled in, unstated (often extralegal) assumptions stated, implications drawn, and positions teased out. Undertaking these analytical tasks required a relatively detailed and long discussion. The second and more important reason is that readers, I believe, should be able to conveniently test my conclusions – especially as they are critical of the courts – against what the courts have actually said and done. Most readers, I assume, do not have easy access to cases. Moreover, some of the cases I refer to are difficult and/or costly to access. Thus, most readers, I assume, will have to – or, as a matter of convenience, will want to – rely on my presentation of the cases to form their judgments as to whether my conclusions are fair or not. Obviously, the usual case summaries with which legal textbooks are replete and to which lawyers are professionally habituated would not have sufficed.

In Chapter 5, I draw my main conclusions about how First Nations sacred sites have fared in Canada's courts. My conclusions are mostly critical. I assess the performance of the courts by examining the results and the judiciary's reasoning about First Nations sacred sites. I conclude that First Nations sacred sites have fared poorly on both counts. In support of the latter conclusion, I argue, among other things, that the courts' efforts to gain an understanding of First Nations' perspectives on their sacred sites have been deplorably inadequate, that the courts have failed to treat First Nations sacred sites fairly, and that their unfair treatment of First Nations sacred sites betrays a bias against First Nations peoples and their sacred sites.

Chapter 6 contains my final remarks. There I do two things. First, I suggest ways in which Canada's courts could improve on their treatment of First Nations sacred sites. Second, I show that Canada too has something significant at stake in the fight of First Nations peoples for their sacred sites. What Canada has at stake is nothing less than its national soul.

1
The Outlines of a General Theory of Sacred Sites

Sacred sites are a universal human phenomenon. Their universality is not an expression of uniformity, however. Different peoples or groups consider different places sacred. Consequently, what one group counts as sacred another may not. The Ganges, for instance, is sacred to Hindus but not to Muslims. Different peoples or groups sometimes consider the same places sacred but for different reasons. Jerusalem, for example, is a city sacred to Jews, Christians, and Muslims but not for precisely the same reasons.

These differences suggest, among other things, that we should accept the following as facts: first, that sacred sites are not naturally sacred, and second, that the sacredness of sites depends upon their symbolism. I can give grounds for accepting the first by means of a simple comparison. Darkening clouds are harbingers of rain. Moreover, they are natural harbingers of rain. It is in the natural order of things – the order available for scientific investigation – for darkening clouds to bring rain. Because of this, anyone with sufficient intelligence and experience of the elements can grasp the connection between darkening clouds and rain. The connection is thus recognizable the world over. It is not so with sacred sites. A person might long wander King Island, an island near Bella Coola, for instance, without ever learning that Ista, a rainforest valley located on the island, is sacred. Yet the Nuxalk people, whose territory includes King Island, treasure Ista as sacred. It is not that the imaginary King Island wanderer would have failed to perceive subtle hints of Ista's sacredness but rather that there are no such hints to perceive. There are no such hints because Ista, although truly sacred, is not naturally sacred.

This brings me to the second suggested fact, that is, that the sacredness of sites depends upon their symbolism. Granted that sacred sites are not naturally sacred, it makes good sense to think that they must be symbolically sacred. Consider the previous example. Ista would not be sacred to the Nuxalk people if it did not represent or symbolize to them more than what it is naturally. Among other things, what Ista symbolizes is the place where the first woman, Ista, descended to earth and where Nuxalk laws originate. Ista's symbolism is recorded in Nuxalk *smayustas*. (The word *smayusta* refers to origin stories, songs, dances, and more.) It is not in the natural order of things – the order available for scientific investigation – that the Ista valley is any of these things, but in the symbolic order. Simply put, if the Ista valley did not symbolize these (or other similar) things to the Nuxalk, it would not be sacred to them.[1]

The role of symbolism is, however, a little more complicated than I have portrayed it. In the Ista example, there are really two layers of symbolism at work, a surface and a deep symbolism. I have dealt only with Ista's deep symbolism. Let me explain. If the Nuxalk did not represent or symbolize it as sacred, in their *smayustas*, for instance, Ista would not be sacred to them. This is the surface layer of Ista's symbolism, simply representing Ista as sacred. It so happens that Ista's surface symbolism is grounded in a deeper symbolism as the place where the first woman descended to earth (and so on). Thus, the Nuxalk look upon Ista as sacred (its surface symbolism) because they look upon it as the place where the first woman descended to earth (its deep symbolism).

Although all sacred sites have surface symbolism, not all have deep symbolism. A site may, for instance, be considered, and therefore represented as, sacred simply because certain religious ceremonies are performed there. It would have no deep symbolism, and so another place might be found equally suited to the same purposes. Indeed, the site might even cease to be considered sacred if the ceremonies stop or are moved elsewhere.

Whether a sacred site has deep or only surface symbolism does not alter the second fact, that is, that the sacredness of sites depends upon their symbolism. This fact, it should be noted, serves to explain why sacred sites (and other sacred things) are never sacred *simpliciter* but are always sacred *to* someone. (Statements to the effect that "such and such is sacred" are elliptical ways of saying that "such and such is sacred to someone.") Sacred sites, like other sacred things, symbolize more than what they are naturally. Yet sacred sites, like all sacred things, cannot symbolize or represent anything unless they symbolize or represent it *to* someone. Thus, sacred sites are always sacred *to* someone because their sacredness depends upon their symbolism.

Sacred sites serve other than ordinary purposes or functions. Often they are places set aside for religious activities, such as offering, cleansing, or seeking enlightenment. Often too they are places serving important theological/cosmological functions within the worldview of a particular people or group. When serving such functions, sacred sites become, by virtue of their deep symbolism, integral to the articulation of larger, often spiritual, realities and relationships. Sometimes sites are selected for practical religious purposes because of their theological/cosmological significance. Sometimes, however, sites possess theological/cosmological significance without serving any practical religious use. To some, these sites are the most sacred. It seems generally true that a site that serves either a practical religious or a theological/cosmological function (or both) is a sacred site, for these functions do appear to be reserved to sacred sites.

Sacred sites may also serve other functions not reserved to them. They may, for example, serve social/cultural functions. They may also serve to anchor a community's identity in a place, unify it politically, and focus its collective efforts. While such functions probably always accompany sacred sites, they may also accompany other sites. A shopping mall, for example, might anchor a community's identity in a place without being considered a sacred site. Moreover, the social/cultural functions of sacred sites seem to be merely derivative, that is, they seem to be effects or by-products of their practical religious and/or theological/cosmological functions. The Ka'ba in Mecca, for example, serves to unify Muslims – and thus serves a social/cultural purpose – because of its practical religious purpose and theological significance. To Muslims, its sacredness derives from its latter functions, not its former. Finally, sacred sites may also serve mundane purposes. A church, for example, can serve as a place for the local PTA to meet in addition to serving as a place of worship.

Besides serving special functions, sacred sites enjoy special status. Generally, sacred sites possess a status higher than that of other sites. To many people, temples, synagogues, churches, or mosques are sacred, while banks are not. For such people, temples, synagogues, churches, or mosques have higher status and therefore command greater respect than banks.

There are, however, degrees of sacredness. Hence, one sacred site may have greater status than another. The Ganges, for example, is not the only river sacred to Hindus but it has the greatest status as the most sacred. The degree of sacredness, and therefore the particular status that attaches to a sacred site, appears to correspond to the value assigned to its particular function(s). Ista, for instance, is particularly sacred to the Nuxalk and therefore holds a high status among their sacred sites. The fact that it is their origin site, and thus serves a highly significant and unique theological/cosmological purpose, makes Ista especially valuable (or, better, precious) to the Nuxalk people. Because they so value Ista's place in their lives as their origin site, they accord it a very high status. The fact that Ista also serves various crucial social/cultural functions, such as anchoring Nuxalk identity in their territory, further adds to its value and hence its status.

Sacred status calls for a special etiquette or ethic.[2] Sacred sites are not to be treated like others. Indeed, different sacred sites may call for different treatment. The crucial distinction is between what is and is not appropriate, a distinction that depends upon a site's practical religious and/or theological/cosmological significance.[3] To deal with a sacred site inappropriately is to risk desecration. At its most extreme, desecration destroys a site's sacredness.

A sacred site's ethic may encompass not only a person's outward behaviour but also his or her interior state of mind or soul. Some sacred sites are to be visited or used only by those who have been properly trained and/or are morally or otherwise worthy. In such places, an untrained or unworthy person's mimicry of words or actions or, in some cases, mere presence – however respectfully intended – may constitute sacrilege. A site's ethic determines what counts as proper training and worthiness.

It is not uncommon for knowledge of sacred sites to be guarded. There are basically two levels of knowledge of a sacred site. At the first level, one knows only that a site is sacred. At the second, one knows why it is sacred. At the second level, one's knowledge may be superficial or deep. Generally, a sacred site's ethic determines whether knowledge of it is to be guarded and to what extent. Thus, a site's ethic may require that all knowledge of it is to be kept hidden from all but a few. Or it may allow its location to be widely known but not its significance. Or it may even allow its significance to be widely known but not its location. Sometimes it is not so much the ethic of a place that requires knowledge of it to be kept secret or confidential as it is the threat of desecration by people, usually from outside the community, who lack the requisite respect.

Before I close this chapter, I want to deal briefly with what I consider a fundamental mistake regarding sacred sites. The mistake is this. It is sometimes suggested that we can believe that a site is sacred only if it is sacred to us. I cannot, then, according to this position, believe that a site is sacred unless it is sacred to me. What this position implies is that if a site is sacred to you but not to me or if a site is sacred to me but not to you, I must judge you wrong.[4] This position projects truth's appearance by confusing *someone believing a site is sacred* with *a site being sacred to someone*. Although it is true that a site cannot be sacred to me unless I believe it is sacred, it is not true that I cannot believe that a site is sacred unless it is sacred to me. In other words, believing that a site is sacred is a necessary but not a sufficient condition for a site to be sacred to me. This is because being sacred to someone is not only a matter of believing something is sacred. It is also a matter of accepting the grounds (that is, the practical religious and/or theological/cosmological grounds) for counting the site as sacred, according the site its proper status relative to other sites, and being morally bound by its ethic. And so I can believe, for example, that Ista is sacred without it being sacred to me and therefore without having to conclude that the Nuxalk people are wrong to believe in its sacredness. For I can believe that Ista is sacred without having to accept (literally or otherwise) that the first woman did descend to earth there, without having to accord it a higher status relative to other sites, and without feeling bound by its ethic.

Conceivably, Ista could become sacred to me (or to any non-Nuxalk person). Even so, unless I were to become sufficiently incorporated into Nuxalk society, I would be exceedingly foolish to think that Ista's being sacred to me is the same as Ista's being sacred to a Nuxalk person. *Qua* sacred to the Nuxalk, Ista is not merely one place physically related to other places within Nuxalk territory; it is a place that has been assumed into a historically conditioned and collectively maintained network of Nuxalk symbols, values (including priorities), and practice. In short, it occupies a "place" within Nuxalk culture. Unless I share that culture, then, Ista cannot be sacred to me in the same way it is sacred to a Nuxalk person.

2
The Context in Which First Nations Carry Their Fight to the Courts

Like other indigenous peoples in the Americas and elsewhere, Canada's First Nations have found it increasingly necessary to fight, sometimes literally[1] as well as metaphorically, for their sacred sites and specifically to fight to maintain access to them, to use them unhindered, to protect them from desecration and destruction, and to preserve them for their future generations. In the past two decades, First Nations have carried their fight into the Canadian courts. How they have fared when they have done so is an issue I will deal with mainly in the next three chapters. Here I want to sketch the historical and overall legal context in which they have proceeded and still must.

The Predicament and Its Origins
As a starting point, it is well to keep in mind why First Nations peoples have to fight for their sacred sites and why they are finding it increasingly necessary to do so. The simple explanation is that their sites are not only under threat but *increasingly* under threat. But the simple explanation raises further questions: Why are they under threat? Why are they increasingly under threat? The answers are fairly obvious. Their sacred sites are under threat, first, because First Nations peoples have lost control over their sites' fate and, second, because those who claim control are posing a threat. They are increasingly under threat because those who claim control pursue an agenda of socioeconomic development that makes ever-expanding demands on the land and its resources.

It would be false to say that First Nations have lost control over all their sacred sites. Generally speaking, First Nations peoples still maintain control over sacred sites located on-reserve. It is sacred sites located off-reserve that, again generally speaking, fall outside their control.

During a period of intense colonization and settlement of Canada from roughly the end of the eighteenth century into the early twentieth century, the British and their Canadian successors took it upon themselves to ensure that some lands were set aside or reserved for Indians.[2] Indian reserve boundaries were established in one of two ways. Sometimes they were established by mutual agreement or treaty ("by treaty" including those established later pursuant to treaty) and other times by Crown imposition. In this regard, British Columbia is a striking contrast to Ontario and the other western provinces. Most of the reserves established during this period in Ontario, Manitoba, Saskatchewan, and Alberta were established by treaty.[3] In British Columbia, however, most were established by Crown imposition.[4]

Section 92(13) of the *British North America Act*[5] gave the provinces exclusive jurisdiction over "Property and Civil Rights." The act did, however, designate certain classes of property as falling exclusively within federal jurisdiction.[6] Most significantly for present purposes, section 91(24) gave Parliament exclusive jurisdiction over "Indians and Lands reserved for the Indians."

Since 1876, Parliament has exercised its jurisdiction over "Indians and Lands reserved for Indians" primarily through *Indian Act* legislation.[7] Although the federal Crown claims title to reserve lands,[8] and thus those lands are alienable only to it, the land is collectively owned by the band for whom it is reserved. And while the power of First Nations peoples to deal with reserve lands as they collectively see fit is closely circumscribed by the *Indian Act* and other legislation, for the most part they have maintained control over their on-reserve sacred sites.

A decade or so ago, Aboriginal peoples (Indian, Inuit, and Métis peoples) made up 3.5 percent of the total population of Canada. There were then 2,242 reserves in Canada belonging to nearly 600 Indian bands.[9] Well over half of the reserves, over 1,600, were in British Columbia. Yet, despite these numbers, Canada's reserves covered only 2.5 million hectares (6.5 million acres) in total. Keeping to the ten provinces, where most First Nations peoples live, reserves amounted to less than 0.5 percent of the total land.[10] Today, although the Aboriginal population has steadily grown, matters are only marginally better land-wise. As of 2001, there were 2,666 reserves belonging to 612 bands and covering slightly over 3 million hectares (about 7.6 million acres).[11] Again, keeping to the ten provinces, since over 99 percent of the total land is off-reserve, thousands of First Nations sacred sites are located on public and private lands now under the control of others.

Section 35(1) Rights

This does not mean that the provinces, private owners, or the federal government exercise absolute control over all sacred sites located off-reserve on provincial public, private, or federal lands. First Nations peoples do sometimes have a say. Relevant legislation, regulation, and policy sometimes call for First Nations input in decisions having the potential to adversely affect access to, use of, or the integrity of their sacred sites.[12] A duty of administrative fairness can sometimes require First Nations input in shaping such decisions. Aboriginal and treaty rights, however, have the potential to give First Nations peoples their greatest say in how off-reserve sacred sites are dealt with.

Existing Aboriginal and treaty rights have enjoyed constitutional protection in Canada since 1982. Section 35 of the *Constitution Act, 1982*[13] states:

1   The existing aboriginal and treaty rights of the aboriginal peoples of Canada are hereby recognized and affirmed.
2   In this Act, "aboriginal peoples of Canada" includes the Indian, Inuit and Métis peoples of Canada.
3   For greater certainty, in subsection (1) "treaty rights" includes rights that now exist by way of land claims agreements or may be so acquired.
4   Notwithstanding any other provision of this Act, the aboriginal and treaty rights referred to in subsection (1) are guaranteed equally to male and female persons.

An Aboriginal or treaty right is considered existing if it existed as of 1982.[14] (Since the issue of whether or not an Aboriginal or treaty right is existing will seldom come up in my discussion, I shall dispense with the participle except where clarity or accuracy requires.)

Treaty Rights
Whether or not a First Nation has treaty rights of access, use, protection, or preservation in relation to its off-reserve sacred sites depends on the terms of the treaty. The most significant case to date on treaty rights to use and, by implication, to access off-reserve sacred sites is the Supreme Court of Canada's *R. v. Sioui* decision.[15] *Sioui* involved four Huron men from the Lorette Indian Reserve in Quebec who, after having entered Jacques-Cartier Park (a provincial park near the reserve) to practise certain ancestral customs and religious rites, were convicted of cutting down trees, camping, and making fires in areas not designated for such purposes. The Quebec Court of Appeal, in a 2-to-1 decision, overturned the conviction.[16] The Attorney General of Quebec subsequently appealed. The Supreme Court of Canada, in a unanimous decision, dismissed the appeal. The Court found that the Hurons at Lorette had entered into a treaty with the British in 1760 that guaranteed their right to carry on their customs and religious rites at places within the "territory frequented by the Hurons at the time, so long as the carrying on of the customs and rites is not incompatible with the particular use made by the Crown of this territory."[17] The Court held that the appellant, the Attorney General of Quebec, had failed to

establish that the exercise of Huron rites and customs was incompatible with the Crown's occupation of the land in the form of a park.

There are several features of the *Sioui* case and the Supreme Court's decision deserving remark. First, the Hurons involved apparently could not argue long-standing ancestral territorial rights. Their pre-contact ancestral lands are in Ontario. About 1650, they removed to the Quebec area. "In 1760," after signing the aforementioned treaty, "they were settled at Lorette on land given to them by the Jesuits eighteen years earlier."[18] Second, the Court found that the Lorette Reserve is not territory sufficient to accommodate certain traditional Huron customs and religious rites.[19] Third, it recognized that the Hurons were following their customs and performing their religious rites "near Lorette on territory which they feel is suited to such purposes."[20] Finally, the Court never explicitly said that the site(s) on which the Hurons were exercising their treaty rights is (are) sacred. Presumably, however, the facts that religious rites were being – and for generations had been – performed there and that the area was suited to performance of those rites qualified the area (or portions thereof) as sacred to the Hurons of Lorette.

To date, there are no Canadian cases involving the assertion of a treaty right to the protection and/or preservation of an off-reserve sacred site *qua* sacred.[21]

The Aboriginal Rights Approach
Assertions of Aboriginal rights regarding off-reserve sacred sites have as yet arisen only – except in a few criminal cases and then only tangentially[22] – in interim or interlocutory injunction proceedings or judicial review petitions. (I will be discussing some of these in the next two chapters.) An action devoted to proving a specific Aboriginal right of access, use, protection, or preservation with regard to an off-reserve sacred site has yet to come before the courts.

There are various reasons why no such action has come before the courts. Besides such obvious ones as the time, cost (for many First Nations, the cost is prohibitive), and risk involved in bringing such an action to court, one of the key reasons surely has to be the limitations of an Aboriginal rights approach generally. Its limitations are most evident in two respects, namely, the test for Aboriginal rights and the doctrine of infringement.

The Supreme Court of Canada set out the test for Aboriginal rights in *R. v. Van der Peet*.[23] There the Court, in a seven-to-two decision, dismissed the appeal of Dorothy Van der Peet, a Sto:lo woman, of a British Columbia Court of Appeal decision restoring her conviction of selling ten salmon caught under an Indian food fishing licence contrary to provincial fishing regulations. The appellant unsuccessfully argued that she had an Aboriginal right to sell the fish, that the fishing regulations infringed her constitutionally protected right, and therefore that the regulations were – or, more accurately, the allegedly offending section was – invalid. The Court introduced its test for determining whether or not a claimed right is an Aboriginal right, and hence protected by s. 35(1) of the *Constitution Act, 1982,* as follows:

> In order to be an aboriginal right an activity must be an element of a practice, custom or tradition integral to the distinctive culture of the aboriginal group claiming the right.[24]

This test, the "integral-to-a-distinctive-culture" test, is premised, as the Court noted, on prior identification of the nature of the right claimed.[25] A court's assessment of a claim to an Aboriginal right proceeds, then, in two main stages. First, it must identify the nature of the right claimed, then it must decide whether or not the right claimed is integral to the claimant's distinctive culture. If and only if the right claimed is integral to the claimant's distinctive culture is it an Aboriginal right.

From the point of view of someone who is considering advancing an Aboriginal rights claim in a court of law, the potential for things going seriously awry at the first stage may be unacceptably high. For starters, the court may misidentify, and consequently mischaracterize, what is being claimed. In addition, there is a requirement that the characterization of the claimed right must be "cognizable to the non-aboriginal legal system."[26] The claim is thus to be made cognizable through the mediation of the common law.[27] The fact that a claim to an Aboriginal right must be refracted through the common law lens increases the risk of initial misidentification, for what the claimant claims need not match what the court through its reliance on the common law identifies.[28] A further concern about this first stage stems from the fact that a court cannot identify the claimed Aboriginal right independently of describing it. But descriptions may be specific, general, or something in between, and every one, moreover, equally true of whatever it describes. The concern is that the level of abstraction (generality/specificity) at which a court decides to describe a claimed Aboriginal right can determine whether or not the right passes the integral-to-a-distinctive-culture test and therefore qualifies as an Aboriginal right. A too general description can mean that an otherwise qualifying right will fail to pass the test. A too specific description, supposing it passes the test, can render the claimant's right of narrower compass than he or she is entitled to, or even a practical nullity.[29]

Anyone considering advancing an Aboriginal rights claim in court will also have concerns about the second stage of the court's analysis. Here the claimed right may fail the integral-to-a-distinctive-culture test. It may fail on one or more of several grounds, including the following: by not being integral to the claimant's culture,[30] by not being continuous with pre-contact practices, customs, and traditions,[31] by not being distinctive,[32] or by having arisen "solely as a response to European influences."[33] It is possible, then, for a court to find, for instance, that a claimed right is integral to a claimant's culture but nonetheless not an Aboriginal right because it is not a distinctive part of that culture. Conversely, it is also possible for it to find that the claimed right is distinctive but not integral.

A further limitation of the Aboriginal rights approach to protecting First Nations interests, including interests attached to off-reserve sacred sites, is provided by the doctrine of infringement. The doctrine was set forth by the Supreme Court of Canada in *R. v. Sparrow*.[34] *Sparrow*, which was decided six years earlier than *Van der Peet*, was the Court's first opportunity to examine the import of s. 35(1) of *Constitution Act, 1982*. There the Court, in a unanimous decision, ordered a new trial for Ronald Sparrow, a Musqueam man, who had been convicted under the federal *Fisheries Act,*[35] of fishing with a drift net exceeding the length permitted by the band's food fishing licence. The Court adopted the British Columbia Court of Appeal's finding that Mr. Sparrow had an existing Aboriginal right to fish for food purposes (including for social and ceremonial activities).[36] It remained, then, for the Court to decide whether the federal drift net restrictions interfered with and, moreover, represented a *prima facie* infringement of the Musqueam people's constitutionally protected Aboriginal right to fish for food purposes,[37] and if so, whether they did so justifiably. Because the findings of fact at trial were not sufficient for the Court to make a decision on these issues, it ordered a retrial.[38]

The doctrine of infringement takes its start from the proposition that Aboriginal rights – rights *recognized* and *affirmed* by s. 35(1) of the *Constitution Act, 1982* – are not absolute.[39] Because they are not absolute, it is possible for legislation and accompanying regulations to infringe Aboriginal rights without being thereby constitutionally invalidated.[40] Neither are the Crown's powers of infringement absolute, however. The Crown's relationship to Aboriginal peoples is a fiduciary one. Therefore, it owes them a fiduciary duty.[41] The Court in *Sparrow* found that "the words 'recognition and affirmation' [in s. 35(1)] incorporate the fiduciary relationship ... and so import some restraint on the exercise of sovereign power."[42] The restraint imported is that s. 35(1) permits the Crown to infringe Aboriginal rights if, but only if, it does so justifiably. To be justified, an infringement must be, first, "in furtherance of a legislative objective that is compelling and substantial," and, second, "consistent with the special fiduciary relationship between the Crown and aboriginal peoples."[43] Although its precise articulation and attendant degree of scrutiny depend upon the nature of the particular Aboriginal right potentially infringed, the Crown's fiduciary duty always includes duties to consult and to seek accommodation.[44]

The Supreme Court of Canada's test for Aboriginal rights (*Van der Peet*) and its doctrine of infringement (*Sparrow*) are largely responsible for First Nations peoples' manifest disenchantment with court-established Aboriginal rights. When other factors such as time, cost, and risk are added in, the disincentives outweigh the incentives for bringing Aboriginal rights cases to court. It is unsurprising, then, that no First Nation has brought an action devoted to proving an Aboriginal right of access, use, protection, or preservation with regard to an off-reserve sacred site.

If, despite the current negatives, a First Nation decides to pursue an Aboriginal rights claim in the courts, it will most likely, provided it has not previously surrendered its lands by treaty, seek a declaration of Aboriginal title.[45] One of the advantages of having a recognized Aboriginal title as opposed to a set of other recognized land-centred Aboriginal rights is that Aboriginal title brings with it a right to engage in a broader range of activities:

> Aboriginal title is a right in land and, as such, is more than the right to engage in specific activities which may be themselves aboriginal rights. Rather, it confers the right to use the land for a variety of activities, not all of which need be aspects of practices, customs and traditions which are integral to the distinctive cultures of aboriginal societies.[46]

Despite its advantages over other Aboriginal rights, Aboriginal title carries similar limitations with regard to the tests for Aboriginal title[47] and justifiable infringement. Its limitations are most evident with regard to infringement. In *Delgamuukw v. British Columbia,* Chief Justice Lamer gave a litany of legislative objectives that could justify infringing Aboriginal title:

> In my opinion, the development of agriculture, forestry, mining, and hydroelectric power, the general economic development of the interior of British Columbia, protection of the environment or endangered species, the building of infrastructure and the settlement of foreign populations to support those aims, are the kinds of objectives that are consistent with this purpose (that is, s. 35's purpose of reconciling "the prior occupation of North America by aboriginal peoples with the assertion of Crown sovereignty") and, in principle, can justify the infringement of aboriginal title.[48]

Given that each of these legislative objectives qualifies as "compelling and substantial," few infringements of a First Nation's Aboriginal title could ever fail the first part of the Supreme Court's two-part test for justifiable infringement.[49]

A declaration of Aboriginal title can, nonetheless, afford a First Nation a measure of control it would not otherwise enjoy over its off-reserve sacred sites falling within its recognized territory. A declaration of Aboriginal title would put the Crown on notice that it cannot sanction infringements involving either interference with a First Nation's access to, use of, and even management of its sacred sites or activities threatening the physical integrity of its sites without sufficient justification.

Although true, the above way of putting the matter nonetheless exaggerates the measure of control over sacred sites afforded by a declaration of Aboriginal title. The right in land that Aboriginal title confers is a uniform right, that is, the basic right is the same for all places within the recognized territory. The rights that attach to sacred places by virtue of Aboriginal title differ in no way from the rights that attach to non-sacred places. Different rights for different places requires Aboriginal rights over and above Aboriginal title and its accompanying package of rights. Consequently, although a declaration of Aboriginal title can afford First Nations a measure of control they would not otherwise enjoy over their off-reserve sacred sites, it affords nothing more than what it affords for any of their recognized off-reserve lands.

The irony of the overall situation should not escape us. The Aboriginal rights of Canada's indigenous peoples were elevated to constitutional status in 1982, yet today, over twenty years later, virtually none of those constitutionally protected rights has legal effect.[50] Most significantly, despite all the attention that has been given to Aboriginal title, no Aboriginal community's Aboriginal title has yet been recognized. Consequently, because they have not established their Aboriginal rights in the courts – a case-by-case process[51] – Aboriginal peoples are precluded from simply taking claims of violations of their constitutional rights to court to have them adjudicated straightaway. This is in stark contrast to the constitutionally enshrined rights of Canadians generally, which are listed in the *Canadian Charter of Rights and Freedoms*.[52]

Canada's Aboriginal rights regime has become moribund.[53] Nonetheless, the British Columbia Court of Appeal is attempting to breathe new life into it. In a pair of recent decisions, first in a majority decision at the end of January 2002 involving the Taku River Tlingit First Nation[54] and again in a unanimous decision near the end of February 2002 involving the Haida Nation,[55] the Court held that a First Nation's asserted Aboriginal rights (including Aboriginal title) could secure a measure of interim legal effect in the period prior to being either conclusively established in a court of law or assumed into a negotiated treaty. Provided that a First Nation has an adequate *prima facie* case to a claim for Aboriginal rights, the Crown has corresponding enforceable legal and equitable duties to consult in good faith and to seek a workable accommodation of those rights prior to deciding to undertake an infringing activity.[56] The scope of the former duty and the strength of the latter "will be proportional to the potential soundness of the claim for aboriginal title and aboriginal rights."[57] The Court of Appeal's stated (proximate) aim in taking this step is to provide, via the judicial review process, an alternative framework to the interlocutory injunction process for balancing competing interests on an interim basis.[58] As it explains,

> the interlocutory injunction process is not necessarily suitable for balancing competing interests in every case. If there are obligations with respect to consultation and accommodation between the parties which are in effect as binding legal obligations before title is declared, then the exercise of those obligations may provide an alternative framework to the interlocutory injunction in the period preceding final determination of aboriginal title or rights by treaty or by a Court of competent jurisdiction.[59]

It is too soon to say how well the Court of Appeal's alternative framework will serve its stated aim. It is also too early to say whether its efforts to resuscitate Canada's Aboriginal rights regime will succeed.

If the British Columbia Court of Appeal's efforts do succeed, First Nations peoples who can make an adequate *prima facie* case for the relevant Aboriginal rights will be able to regain a measure of control over their sacred sites. They will not regain as much control as they would, should they eventually either establish those Aboriginal rights in a court of law or negotiate a stronger set of treaty rights. For the interim, however, it would be more control than they would otherwise exercise.

Interim Measures and Other Similar Agreements

For those First Nations and other Aboriginal peoples who are involved in treaty negotiations but who have not yet reached a final agreement with the federal and provincial or territorial governments, it is often possible to negotiate temporary agreements designed to protect certain of their interests in the interim. These interim measures agreements, as they are called, are increasingly seen – especially in British Columbia, where treaty negotiations have stalled[60] – as an indispensable means for "building treaties incrementally over time."[61] Interim measures agreements can serve a variety of purposes,[62] including temporarily protecting the integrity of and access to sacred sites.[63]

The negotiation of interim measures agreements is not limited to those First Nations and other Aboriginal peoples who are involved in treaty negotiations. Although originally conceived in broader terms,[64] interim measures agreements were initially available only to Aboriginal peoples participating in treaty negotiations. That, however, has proven to be an unnecessarily restrictive and insufficiently pragmatic approach. A large number of Aboriginal peoples, mostly First Nations peoples, who have valid claims to Aboriginal title, are not involved in treaty negotiations. Many, mainly First Nations in British Columbia, have chosen not to participate in treaty negotiations at this time.[65] Others, particularly First Nations in the Atlantic provinces, do not yet have a treaty process available to them.[66] Consequently, a more expansive and pragmatic approach to interim measures agreements has developed. Such agreements may now serve not only as aids to existing treaty negotiations but also as steps towards future participation in treaty negotiations. It is possible, then, for First Nations and other Aboriginal peoples who are not yet involved in treaty negotiations to negotiate interim measures agreements protecting the integrity of and access to sacred sites.

Despite the fact that interim measures agreements typically do not give rise to legal rights, they may afford some First Nations peoples a measure of protection for their off-reserve sacred sites in the interim leading to the conclusion of a final agreement. At the very least, they may serve as an interim alternative to litigation or confrontation.

Interim measures agreements are not the only negotiated options for protecting sacred sites. Accordingly, even those First Nations who have previously signed treaties with the Crown may, provided there is willingness on the part of one or more of the corresponding levels of government, negotiate agreements for the protection of their off-reserve sacred sites.[67] As with interim measures agreements, the negotiation of such agreements would provide an alternative to litigation or confrontation.

The Translation/Interpretation Gauntlet

In any dispute that comes before the courts, litigants are faced with a two-sided communication problem. On the one hand, they have to encapsulate and present their concerns, interests, and positions in legal language and ritual; on the other hand, it is up to judges to interpret those translated concerns, interests, and positions as they will (within fairly wide parameters). The litigant whose concerns, interests, and position can be fully encapsulated and presented in legal language and ritual is exceedingly rare. There is, then, at the outset a translatability problem. Litigants, moreover, must deal with the difficulty of ensuring that what is translatable is faithfully translated. Even then, if a litigant succeeds in more or less faithfully translating his or her concerns, interests, and position into legal language and ritual, a judge may still interpret those translated concerns, interests, and position in ways other than how they were intended. So long as the judge operates within the court's (fairly broad) interpretive parameters, such misinterpretation is difficult to impossible to challenge on appeal.

I have already briefly touched upon the fact that First Nations peoples have to run this translation/interpretation gauntlet any time they argue

Aboriginal rights before the courts. As daunting as the challenge is generally, it is even more daunting if their arguments concern sacred sites specifically. There are numerous reasons for this. Here, however, I will mention only a few.

To begin with, sites sacred to First Nations are usually not sacred to those most responsible for the translation and interpretation of their concerns, interests, and position into and within a legal/judicial context. First Nations lawyers make up a small portion of the profession. Not all of them represent First Nations clients. Only rarely are First Nations lawyers members of the First Nations they represent. Hence, it is unlikely that a site that is sacred to the First Nation will also be sacred to its counsel. Similarly, First Nations people make up a small portion of the judiciary. It is highly improbable, then, that the site sacred to the litigating First Nation will also be sacred to the judge.

The question is this: How confident should a litigating First Nation be that its concerns, interests, and position regarding one of its sacred sites will be fairly translated into and interpreted within the legal/judicial context currently on offer? The answer that ultimately, if not immediately, suggests itself is: "Not very."

Lawyers and judges are as prone as others to confuse *someone believing a site is sacred* with *a site being sacred to someone*. Whether they are religious, irreligious, or anti-religious is unlikely to make a difference. Any lawyer or judge who makes this mistake and who is presented with a First Nations site that is not sacred to him or her must, *a priori*, disbelieve the site's sacredness. While it is true that they may still be willing, given sufficient evidence, to believe that the First Nation believes that the site is sacred, they must, nonetheless and again *a priori*, believe that the First Nation is mistaken. For because the site is not sacred to them, they disbelieve its sacredness, and because they disbelieve its sacredness, they judge the contrary belief (the First Nation's belief) false. If a First Nation's claims of sacredness are prestamped FALSE in the minds of those most responsible for translation and interpretation, it will be more difficult for its concerns, interests, and position regarding its sacred site to be fairly translated into and interpreted within the legal/judicial context.

Lawyers and judges are also as prone as others to extend their skepticism about a First Nation's bases for counting a site sacred to the site's sacredness. As before, whether they are religious, irreligious, or anti-religious is unlikely to matter. Some First Nations sites are sacred because of their practical religious use. Others are sacred because of their theological/cosmological significance. Still others are sacred for both reasons. Almost all lawyers and judges are likely to be skeptical about the religious underpinnings of the site's use and/or its theological/cosmological significance.[68] It does not follow *logically* that they must then also be skeptical about the site's sacredness. But if they are skeptical about the former, it will be hard for them to avoid entertaining the thought that if the First Nation got it wrong about the grounds for a place's sacredness, it must have it wrong about its sacredness.[69] If, therefore, those most responsible for translating and interpreting them into and within a legal/judicial context are skeptical towards a First Nation's bases for counting a site sacred, it will be more difficult for them to fairly translate and interpret them.

Supposing that lawyers and judges avoid committing either of the above mistakes, the status they finally assign to a First Nation's sacred site in the translation/interpretation process is unlikely to match the original status accorded by the First Nation. A site's sacred status differentiates it from other sites. Its degree of sacredness situates it relative to other sacred sites. Thus, a sacred site's status is gauged relative to the status of other sites, sacred and non-sacred. A sacred site's status is situational. The translations and interpretations rendered by lawyers and judges are not, however, well suited to preserving situational complexities. At best, they preserve situational fragments. Thus, a First Nation's sacred site will lose some of its situatedness in the translation/interpretation process. Having lost some of its situatedness, it is unlikely that the site's assigned status will match its original status.

Perhaps more serious, however, is the new status it will gain. Lawyers and judges must, like everyone else, work from the familiar when encountering something new. Since they will not (except rarely) be familiar with a First Nation's sacred site before it becomes a subject of litigation, they will have to draw comparisons with familiar sites. The result will be, in terms of the translation/interpretation process, a conceptual relocation of the site. This relocation – or, one might not unfairly say, dislocation – cannot help but affect the site's status. And obviously, the lawyers' and judges' own prior views about the sacred sites with which they are familiar will come into play. The best that a litigating First Nation can hope for, it would seem, is that its sacred site is ultimately accorded a status analogous to its original status.

Of course, the process of translating into and interpreting within a legal/judicial context a First Nation's concerns, interests, and position regarding a sacred site involves more than a mere *conceptual* relocation of the site. It involves a *cultural* relocation. Thus, it involves the site's relocation within an alien network of symbols, values (including priorities), and practice. Considered this way, the chances that a First Nation's sacred site will ultimately be accorded a status with the legal judicial context analogous to its original status seem slim indeed.

This, then, is the context in which Canada's First Nations have had to fight for their sacred sites. They have had to fight for them because of the predicament that most of their sacred sites are off-reserve and therefore largely outside their control and because those who claim control pose the threat. As the threat has grown, First Nations have found it increasingly necessary to take their fight to the courts. But, to build on the metaphor, the legal weapons at their disposal have proven of limited efficacy. Indeed, the initially most promising legal weapon, Aboriginal rights, is currently of doubtful efficacy. Those First Nations who, in spite of the limited to doubtful efficacy of the legal weapons at their disposal, have carried their fight for their sacred sites to the courts have had to run the translation/interpretation gauntlet just described. It is small wonder, then, that, although their sacred sites are among the things most precious to them, First Nations have only recently – rarely and usually in desperate situations – taken their fight to Canada's courts. What has happened when they have done so is what I discuss next.

3
In Canada's Courts:
The Meares Strategy

In the two decades since Canada constitutionally recognized and affirmed their Aboriginal and treaty rights in s. 35(1) of the *Constitution Act, 1982,* First Nations have primarily utilized two litigation strategies in their efforts to leverage those rights into at least temporary control over their off-reserve sacred sites.[1] The first – and, as it happens, the first of the two to be so utilized – is the interlocutory strategy. Following this strategy, a First Nation asks the court for interlocutory relief (usually an injunction halting resource or other development) to safeguard access to, use of, or the integrity of a sacred site pending a determination of its Aboriginal or treaty rights at trial. For reasons that will soon become apparent, I will call this the *Meares strategy.* The second, more recently evolved strategy involves judicial review. Following this strategy, a First Nation tries to protect a sacred site by challenging the administrative approval of a (typically resource-related) project or activity that threatens the site's practical religious use or integrity. Although the challenge may involve the claim that the Crown's decision maker violated administrative law principles, what is distinctive about this strategy is the fact that it challenges the decision on fiduciary and constitutional grounds. Again, for reasons that will become apparent, I will call this the *Haida strategy.*

In this chapter, I discuss the Meares strategy; in the next, the Haida strategy.

The Meares strategy was first tried and eventually succeeded in *MacMillan Bloedel v. Mullin* (*Meares Island* case) in the mid-1980s. In the roughly four years following, the strategy was re-employed successfully in two similar cases. Despite its early and impressive successes, the strategy has, throughout the 1990s to the present, failed to yield further similar successes. In the final portion of this chapter ("What Went Wrong?"), I discuss some possible reasons for this outcome.

Early Success
Meares Island is a small, scenic island (8,500 hectares or 22,100 acres) lying just off the west coast of Vancouver Island, at the heart of Clayoquot Sound,

a short boat ride northeast of Tofino. The island is mountainous and mostly blanketed by an ancient rainforest, with some trees older than a millennium and a half. The island lies within Nuu-chah-nulth traditional territory. Members of two of the fourteen Nuu-chah-nulth bands, the Tla-o-qui-aht (Clayoquot) and Ahousaht, inhabit two small Crown-imposed reserves on the island's west coast. The rest of the island is virtually uninhabited.

The province granted the first logging lease on Meares Island during the opening decade of the twentieth century. In the 1950s, MacMillan Bloedel acquired the then available leases. By the 1980s, it held rights to ten lots totalling 3,593 hectares (8,875 acres), or about 42 percent of the island.[2] With licence in hand, MacMillan Bloedel was set to commence building roads and facilities on Meares Island near the end of November 1984. It had decided to dedicate the first year of its five-year plan to log the island to clear-cutting three lots on the island's east side.

The Nuu-chah-nulth, residents of Tofino, and others had anticipated MacMillan Bloedel's actions. Organization to prevent the logging of Meares Island was well underway by the beginning of the 1980s. On 21 April 1984, the Tla-o-qui-aht Band, in a well-publicized ceremony on the island, declared Meares Island a Tribal Park.[3] At the end of September, the Nuu-chah-nulth Tribal Council unanimously pledged its full support to the Tla-o-qui-aht and Ahousaht bands in their efforts to prevent the impending logging.[4] When the first of MacMillan Bloedel's work crews was sent to the island on 21 November 1984, it was met by sea and land blockades – the first logging blockade in Canadian history.[5] Although the crew was eventually permitted, through the intervention of the Royal Canadian Mounted Police (RCMP), to land, it was prevented from proceeding inland to begin its work and so returned to Tofino.

Two days later, on 23 November 1984, MacMillan Bloedel, after being issued a writ based on its claim for damages for unlawful obstruction of its operations, applied for a restraining order. Four days later, on 27 November, the Nuu-chah-nulth countered. Moses Martin, a defendant in the first action, and Corbett George, chiefs of the Tla-o-qui-aht and the Ahousaht bands, respectively, filed their own writ and thereby initiated declaratory proceedings against the province, seeking a declaration of Aboriginal title to Meares Island. That same day, the Nuu-chah-nulth applied for an order restraining MacMillan Bloedel's operations pending trial.

Argument in the British Columbia Supreme Court commenced on 7 January 1985. Mr. Justice Gibbs delivered his decision two and a half weeks later, on 25 January. He ultimately decided to refuse the Nuu-chah-nulth's requested interlocutory injunction and to grant MacMillan Bloedel's.

Gibbs J. grounded his decision in a lengthy survey of the law on interlocutory injunction petitions. Put simply, he concluded that to succeed, such petitions must satisfy two basic criteria. The first is that the claim on which the petition for interlocutory relief is based, the claim made in the action, must be a serious or fair question to be tried. The second criterion is that the balance of convenience – or, as some would say, inconvenience – must favour granting the relief sought. If a petition fails to satisfy the first criterion, it is to be denied. If it satisfies the first but not the second, it is also to be denied. Thus, the first criterion is the first of two basic tests that courts apply. As a general rule, courts will not complete the second test, the balance of convenience test, unless they form a doubt that monetary damages would be an adequate remedy for the harm the petitioner will likely suffer should the injunction be refused and should he or she later succeed at trial. That is, they will not go through the process of comparing the potential harm to all parties concerned if they do not find it likely that the petitioner will suffer irreparable harm. The general rule does, however, allow for exceptions. Other factors that courts may take into account in applying the second test include the effects that granting or refusing the injunction may have on the local, regional, and provincial economies, a resulting change in the status quo, and public interest.[6]

As the MacMillan Bloedel and Nuu-chah-nulth petitions were mutually exclusive, Gibbs J. had three basic options before him: he could grant MacMillan Bloedel's request and refuse the Nuu-chah-nulth's; he could grant the Nuu-chah-nulth's request and refuse MacMillan Bloedel's; or he could refuse both requests. Because taking the third option would allow the Nuu-chah-nulth and their sympathizers to continue making "it impossible, or at best difficult and dangerous, for MacMillan Bloedel to carry out logging operations"[7] and thus would be nearly tantamount to granting the Nuu-chah-nulth's request, Gibbs J. concluded that the first two options were his only live options.

Since one of the two petitioners would have to be granted an injunction, the decision came down to determining which of the two held the stronger position. On both of the fundamental issues – whether the petitioner raises a serious question for trial and whether the balance of convenience favours granting the injunction to the petitioner – Gibbs J. found that MacMillan Bloedel held the stronger position.

On its face, MacMillan Bloedel's case against those responsible for blockading its operations was strong. It held the requisite documents (title, permits, licences, etc.) legally entitling it to log Meares Island. Although the defendants to the first action challenged the company's tenure, arguing that the right to log the island had lapsed or expired almost six decades earlier, Gibbs J. held that, given the presumption of regularity accorded to past acts of public officers, MacMillan Bloedel's case remained strong. Thus, he held that MacMillan Bloedel's petition for an injunction was based on a claim that not only raised a serious question for trial but that, moreover, had good prospects of succeeding.

In contrast, Gibbs J. held that the Nuu-chah-nulth's case had little or no merit and so did not raise a serious question for trial. The Nuu-chah-nulth's case depended on their claim to Aboriginal title. He concluded that their case was bound to fail at trial because they had not made out – and likely could not make out – an arguable case for Aboriginal title.[8] He rested his conclusion on two distinct lines of reasoning, one based on his analysis of the law, the other on his estimation of the supporting evidence. As for the law, Gibbs J. held that supposing Nuu-chah-nulth Aboriginal title ever existed, it either had been extinguished by colonial ordinances or proclamations[9] or, if it had not been so extinguished, survived as a burden on the provincial Crown's underlying title. If, contrary to his own view, it survived as a burden on the province's title, it had been, in any case, Gibbs J. said, subsequently incidentally impaired by provincial legislation of general application (specifically by the *Forest Act*[10]) so as to allow the province the lawful power to dispense of the so-burdened Crown land and resources on Meares Island accordingly.[11] As for the evidence supporting the Nuu-chah-nulth's claim to Aboriginal title, Gibbs J. found that the affidavits contained only opinions purporting but no facts proving that Nuu-chah-nulth people occupied Meares Island exclusively at the time of England's assertion of sovereignty in 1846.[12] Having decided that it suffered from these (fatal) legal and (crippling) evidentiary weaknesses, Gibbs J. concluded that the Nuu-chah-nulth's case did not present a serious question for trial.

Judged by the first basic test a petitioner must meet to obtain an interlocutory injunction, MacMillan Bloedel's position seemed far and away the stronger. Normally, the chambers judge would have proceeded to ask whether MacMillan Bloedel would likely suffer irreparable harm were its request for an injunction denied. If the answer were no, the judge would simply have denied its request and that would have been an end to the matter. (Since the Nuu-chah-nulth's petition had failed the first test, there would not have been any need to conduct a parallel inquiry.) But the *Meares Island* case was not a normal case and Gibbs J. had already decided that in the circumstances one of the two petitioners would have to be granted an injunction. Thus, despite the fact that neither petitioner had, in Gibbs J.'s estimation, proved irreparable harm, he proceeded to inquire into which of the two the balance of convenience favoured.

At the end of the day, Gibbs J. found that several factors tipped the balance in MacMillan Bloedel's favour, namely, "the interference with the conduct of business operations, the potentially disastrous consequences [which would follow granting an injunction to the Nuu-chah-nulth] ... the propensity of the opponents of logging to take the law into their own hands, and the laches of the Indian Bands."[13] As to the "potentially disastrous consequences" of which he spoke, Gibbs J. had earlier commented as follows:

The issue of an injunction to the Indian Bands at this stage [in the litigation] would represent, and be interpreted as, some recognition, even though only pending trial, of an overriding aboriginal title. It would be looked upon as a precedent and would spawn a rash of similar applications throughout the province.

And such a course of action would not necessarily be restricted to proposed logging operations. Based upon a claim of the breadth of that made in the prayer for relief in the second [i.e., the Nuu-chah-nulth's] action, similar challenges could be made to any resource or wildlife harvesting authorized by the provincial Crown in the land claims areas. It is the prospect of the havoc which wholesale challenges would create in the financial, business and public activities in this province which has led me to conclude that it is urgent and imperative that I reach a decision based upon the relative strength of each party's case and grant one or other of the applications.[14]

As for the "laches of the Indian Bands" of which he spoke, he had this to say: "The Indian Bands have slept on the rights they assert for months and years. In an affidavit [chief] Moses Martin [who was a defendant in the first action and a plaintiff in the second] swore: 'Since June 25, 1981, we have taken the position that MacMillan Bloedel Limited is not to log our land known as Meares Island.' But he waited until November 27, 1984 to seek a declaration of his rights, at a time when MacMillan Bloedel's plans were on the eve of being implemented."[15] Taking these factors together, Gibbs J. concluded that the balance of convenience heavily favoured MacMillan Bloedel.

Although they failed to prove the point to Gibbs J.'s satisfaction, the Nuu-chah-nulth bands had submitted evidence that they would suffer irreparable harm if MacMillan Bloedel were granted an injunction. Among other things, the Nuu-chah-nulth claimed that they would suffer irreparable harm in the form of "interference with food gathering and medicine gathering, interference with cultural and historical links with the past, destruction of trees which are involved in traditional native practices, and destruction of culturally modified trees and archeological sites."[16] The Nuu-chah-nulth failed to prove irreparable harm mainly because, Gibbs J. explained, their evidence was too general. The affidavits failed to identify specific geographical locations lying within MacMillan Bloedel's licence area. The affidavits failed, moreover, to show that the company's logging operations would seriously circumscribe any of the Nuu-chah-nulth's aforementioned activities. Indeed, Gibbs J. went on to note, MacMillan Bloedel was legally obliged to, among other things, protect the environment and manage the heritage resources within its area of operations on Meares Island. As long as it met those obligations, he concluded, its interference with Nuu-chah-nulth activities and practices would be minimal. And, in any case, he added, since MacMillan Bloedel's 1985 harvest would cover only 2 percent of Meares Island, at the end of roughly a year's time – the time he thought it should take the Nuu-chah-nulth to bring their case to trial if they proceeded with dispatch – little of the island would have been affected.

Gibbs J. ultimately concluded that MacMillan Bloedel's position was the stronger, on the grounds of presenting a serious question for trial and on a balance of convenience. He therefore decided to grant MacMillan Bloedel's request for an injunction against the protestors and to refuse the Nuu-chah-nulth's against the company's operations.

Both the protestors and the Nuu-chah-nulth immediately appealed. The British Columbia Court of Appeal, with five justices sitting, heard arguments near the end of February 1985. The Court delivered its judgment on 27 March 1985. It unanimously and curtly dismissed the protestors' appeal. To the surprise of many, however, the Court split three to two in favour of allowing the Nuu-chah-nulth's appeal and granting them an injunction preventing MacMillan Bloedel's logging, road building, and other site preparation on Meares Island. It left MacMillan Bloedel's original injunction against the protestors in place but modified it to accord with the new order restraining its operations.[17]

Four of the five judges gave separate reasons for their judgments. Justices Seaton, Lambert, and Macfarlane agreed in allowing the Nuu-chah-nulth's appeal, while Justices Macdonald and Craig agreed in denying it. Lambert J.A., the only one not to give separate reasons, simply stated his agreement with Seaton J.A. Macfarlane J.A., declaring his "substantial agreement," chose to amplify several of Seaton J.A.'s points but to deviate subtly on one crucial point. In what follows, I will summarize the reasons of Seaton and Macfarlane JJ.A. first and those of Macdonald and Craig JJ.A. second.

Like his fellow judges, Seaton J.A. held that the chambers judge had erred in concluding that the Nuu-chah-nulth's claim to Aboriginal title did not raise a serious question for trial. Specifically, he held that Gibbs J. had wrongly concluded, first, that the Nuu-chah-nulth's claim had no hope of success at trial and, second, that the affidavit evidence did not suffice to show that there was a serious question to be tried. On the first point, most importantly, he observed, claims of Aboriginal title cannot be treated globally[18] and are therefore too difficult to be rejected summarily. Moreover, he pointed out, land and resource-related rights other than Aboriginal title could also be at stake. As he explained, "[t]he question is made more difficult in this case by the range of rights that the Indians might have and the nature of the logging that MacMillan plans. The proposal is to clear-cut the area. Almost nothing will be left. I cannot think of any native right that could be exercised on lands that have recently been logged. It follows that rights far short of outright ownership might well warrant retaining the area until after trial."[19] Such complexities simply could not be gauged adequately on an interlocutory application. Taken together with what Seaton J.A. considered, contrary to the chambers judge's finding, "a substantial body of evidence" supporting the Nuu-chah-nulth's claim,[20] these considerations made it manifest, he concluded, that there was a serious question to be tried.

Seaton J.A. also disagreed with the Gibbs J.'s application of the balance of convenience test. He disagreed both with the chambers judge's specific finding that the Nuu-chah-nulth had failed to prove irreparable harm and also with his overall assessment that the balance of convenience favoured MacMillan Bloedel.

MacMillan Bloedel, Seaton J.A. agreed with the chambers judge, would not suffer irreparable harm if the Nuu-chah-nulth were granted an injunction. As the area to be logged on Meares Island amounted to roughly 1 percent of its total tree farm licence in the surrounding area, the timber on Meares was relatively economically insignificant to the corporation's operations in the region. The timber, moreover, would still be there to be harvested if the Nuu-chah-nulth's case failed at trial. Meares Island had become important to MacMillan Bloedel not because of its timber but because of the larger symbolism it had acquired. As Seaton J.A. explained:

> Meares Island is important to MacMillan Bloedel in this way. MacMillan Bloedel has gone through all of the necessary steps to obtain permission to cut. If it is stopped here there is a worry that it will be stopped elsewhere. Meares Island has become the front line in the dispute over Indian title. It has also become central to the dispute between the logger and those who favour the preservation of wilderness areas.
>
> Meares Island is important to MacMillan Bloedel not because of its trees, but because it is where the line has been drawn. It has become a symbol.[21]

Meares Island had also acquired larger symbolism for the Nuu-chah-nulth people. As Seaton J.A. explained, "the Indians have pressed their land claims in various ways for generations. The claims have not been dealt with and found invalid. They have not been dealt with at all. Meanwhile, the logger continues his steady march and the Indians see themselves retreating into a smaller and smaller area. They too have drawn the line at Meares Island. The Island has become a symbol of their claim to rights in the land."[22] Basically, the Nuu-chah-nulth had come to the position that if they could not maintain their rights to and on Meares Island, they had no hope of maintaining them elsewhere. Thus, for them Meares Island had taken on a critical symbolism.

But Meares Island's importance to the Nuu-chah-nulth was, Seaton J.A. observed, more than symbolic. It held both a record of their past in the form of shell middens, fish traps, canoe skids, and culturally modified trees and also the natural resources (especially cedar trees) still required for a multitude of sustenance and other uses. Furthermore, he noted, a living society, with its own unique structure, was interwoven with the island, its heritage sites, and its resources. Hence, for the Nuu-chah-nulth people, Meares Island possessed more than ordinary symbolic, material, and social/cultural importance.

So interpreted, the evidence clearly proved that the harm that the Nuu-chah-nulth would suffer should their petition for interlocutory relief be denied and should they subsequently succeed at trial would far outweigh the harm that MacMillan Bloedel would suffer. It clearly proved, moreover, that the harm suffered by the Nuu-chah-nulth would then be irreparable. The fact that MacMillan Bloedel's logging operations for 1985 – its start-up year on the island – would have a greater impact on the island than the whole of its prior history of commercial logging was itself a strong indicator that the harm would be irreparable.[23] In consequence, Seaton J.A. concluded, "[b]oth justice and convenience demand that the proposed logging not take place while the Indians' claim is being actively pressed in litigation."[24]

A further factor to be considered in the assessment of the balance of convenience supported the same conclusion. The Nuu-chah-nulth's claim to Aboriginal title to, and other rights in and on, Meares Island would have to be substantiated at trial. That would require establishing not only past occupation but also past use. Establishing the extent of past use of the island's trees would, however, pose a serious problem. As things then stood, only one study had been conducted on the Native use of Meares Island trees. The study was confined to a limited area and its findings extrapolated therefrom to the rest of the island. The report suggested, among other things,

that in the area MacMillan Bloedel proposes to log in the next years, there are many trees that have had bark taken from them. Other trees were cut down generations ago. A number of the logs on the ground and a few standing trees have had planks taken from them. Some logs and some trees are notched. Some trees have been felled and the first step toward making a canoe completed.

The material indicates that the natives have used this area over a long period. Many of the bark-stripped trees within the area being examined could be dated. The trees show use in the twentieth century, the nineteenth century, the eighteenth century and in the seventeenth century. A stump was found from which the tree had been felled in 1685 or earlier. Bark had been stripped from another tree in 1642.[25]

The problem was that the report gave an incomplete picture of past timber use on the island. Thus, if logging were allowed to go forward before a full study could be completed, evidence that might have been used to support the Nuu-chah-nulth's claim at trial would likely be lost forever. Such a loss would be irreparable.

Although Seaton J.A. was satisfied both that the Nuu-chah-nulth would suffer irreparable harm if their petition was not granted and that the balance of convenience strongly favoured the Nuu-chah-nulth's interests over MacMillan Bloedel's, he was obliged to take other larger, public interests into account. The chambers judge had been especially concerned that granting an order to restrain MacMillan Bloedel's operations on Meares Island could have a cascade effect, giving rise to a series of similar petitions across the province and thus shutting down the province's forest and other resource-dependent industries. Seaton J.A. disagreed that such a scenario was a serious possibility, explaining that

> Meares Island has attained an [sic] unique importance. I have already said
> that it has become a symbol for each side in the contest between the forest industry and the Indians. I have also said that to prevent or postpone
> logging on Meares Island will not have a significant economic impact.
> When other areas are considered, they will be considered in light of this
> decision. They will be seen as an addition to the Meares Island restriction
> and in consequence, the balance of convenience may be seen to have
> shifted to favour the industry.[26]

In effect, Seaton J.A. was saying that the chambers judge's concern rested on a misunderstanding of the shifting nature of the balance of convenience. Despite whatever precedential value that the *Meares* case might acquire, courts would still have to assess the balance of convenience anew on each subsequent application. The mere appearance of the feared cascade effect could then, in the right circumstances, suffice to tip the balance against First Nations petitioners.

Seaton J.A. held, then, that the claim on which the Nuu-chah-nulth's petition for interlocutory relief was based raised a serious question for trial and that the balance of convenience favoured granting their petition.

Macfarlane J.A. agreed with Seaton J.A. that questions of Aboriginal rights (including title) are of such difficulty and complexity that they can be decided only on full trial, and thus that the Nuu-chah-nulth's claim raised a serious question for trial. He went on to add that given that it raised a serious question, there was no need on the part of the chambers judge to consider further its probability of success. In any case, he noted, "[u]sing the [Supreme Court of Canada's decision in the] Calder case[27] as a standard the least that can be said is that there is an even chance of success at trial."[28]

Like Seaton J.A., Macfarlane J.A. observed that the apprehension that granting the Nuu-chah-nulth an injunction on Meares Island would precipitate a rash of like petitions threatening the province's forest and other resource industries was based on a misunderstanding of the judicial process.[29] Unlike Seaton J.A., he also responded to the chambers judge's assertion that the Nuu-chah-nulth had slept on their rights. To the contrary, he noted, "[t]hey have made their rights known, they have participated in [multiparty] discussions [from 1981 to 1983] which might have led to a resolution of their problem and they have left legal action as a final resort. Their conduct also must be viewed in the light of the recognized desirability to work out this problem without going to court, and, ideally, by negotiation."[30]

As to whether the Nuu-chah-nulth would suffer harm should MacMillan Bloedel be permitted to log Meares Island, Macfarlane J.A. adopted the position that the Nuu-chah-nulth's point of view deserved serious consideration. As he put it simply, "I think this island must be viewed as a special place so far as the Indians are concerned."[31] How special could be surmised by keeping in mind that "the claim by the Tribal Council to which they [i.e., the Tla-o-qui-aht and Ahousaht bands] belong to Aboriginal rights extends beyond Meares Island and encompasses a large part of Vancouver Island. But we are only concerned here with Meares Island, and particularly with two percent of it that MacMillan Bloedel plans to log in the next year. It is with respect to that small part that they claim an injunction, on a temporary basis, to prevent logging."[32] In other words, the Nuu-chah-nulth's limited request for injunctive relief implied their belief that whereas monetary compensation might be acceptable for harm they might suffer elsewhere on account of logging and other activities, it would be inadequate in the case of Meares Island. From the Nuu-chah-nulth's point of view, then, the value of maintaining Meares Island as it was transcended money. Although acknowledging the Nuu-chah-nulth's sentiments, Macfarlane J.A. refused to pronounce that the Nuu-chah-nulth would suffer irreparable harm. Instead he allowed that the limited nature of the Nuu-chah-nulth's request gave the Court room to treat the harm as sufficient to tilt the balance of convenience in their favour. As he explained, "[i]f an injunction were being sought with respect to the whole area the economic consequences of granting an injunction would probably weigh heavily against making the order. But small, isolated, special sites may be dealt with differently than most of the terrain."[33] Unlike

Seaton J.A. (and Lambert J.A.), then, Macfarlane J.A. did not find that the Nuu-chah-nulth would suffer irreparable harm if the logging went forward. Nonetheless, like Seaton J.A. (and Lambert J.A.), he did conclude that the balance of convenience favoured their petition.

Although they agreed with the majority that the chambers judge had erred in holding that the Nuu-chah-nulth's claim did not pose a serious question for trial, Macdonald and Craig JJ.A. parted company with regard to the balance of convenience.

Macdonald J.A. premised the core of his reasons for judgment explicitly on the assumption that, because of their comprehensive nature, Aboriginal claims would be settled ultimately through negotiation, not litigation. The assumption meant, he contended, that courts should refrain from granting interlocutory or permanent injunctions in cases involving claims of Aboriginal title and other rights. The reason they should refrain from granting such requests was, he urged, that by granting them, courts would be granting something other than ordinary interlocutory or permanent injunctions. Usually, an interlocutory injunction comes to an end after the case has been settled at trial. Usually too, if the case succeeds, a permanent injunction is issued in similar terms at trial's end. The *Meares* case did not, he suggested, represent the usual situation. For starters, no one could say how long it would take to go to trial. Its resolution, moreover, would take place only at the Supreme Court of Canada. An interlocutory injunction granted pending trial would likely stand until the case was settled at the highest level. Given the length of time that such an injunction would likely stand, the harm that the Nuu-chah-nulth would suffer if their petition were denied did not, Macdonald J.A. implied, compare favourably with the harm that MacMillan Bloedel (and others) would suffer if the restraining order were issued.[34] As well, a permanent injunction granted at trial's end would – even if still standing after a Supreme Court of Canada decision – be anything but permanent. For whatever the litigation's eventual outcome, it would ultimately take successful negotiations to settle the issues in a comprehensive fashion. Whether the permanent injunction would figure into the final settlement, and thus whether it would really be permanent, would be up to the parties negotiating rather than the courts. The fact that the Nuu-chah-nulth but not MacMillan Bloedel would be a party to those negotiations would, Macdonald J.A. also implied, serve to offset any harm that they might suffer by being refused first an interlocutory and later a permanent injunction.[35]

Finally, Macdonald J.A. shared the chambers judge's concern that an injunction granted in the *Meares* case would cascade into a series of similar petitions, endangering the province's forest and other industries. He remained unconvinced of Seaton J.A.'s assurance that the Meares Island situation was unique. Meares was "unique only," he wryly stated, "in the sense that every individual situation is unique as to its details and particulars."[36] Granting an injunction in the *Meares* case would create a precedent. With that precedent in hand, he added, "[l]egal ingenuity will have no trouble formulating and bringing before the Court application with respect to situations which, in their essentials, will make this judgment indistinguishable."[37]

Craig J.A. agreed with Macdonald J.A.'s reasons for holding that the chambers judge was right to refuse an injunction on the balance of convenience. His main contribution to the dissent was to explain why he thought that the injunction's refusal would not yield irreparable harm. He noted that the proposal to log Meares Island had been carefully scrutinized over a number of years by many groups and agencies. The area where the logging was to take place was determined to be "the 'least sensitive area' in terms of environment."[38] Additionally, he reiterated – what the chambers judge had noted – that MacMillan Bloedel had had "very stringent conditions" placed on its operations rendering "[t]he possibility of any environmental damage ... very slight."[39] In Craig J.A.'s view, what this implied was that the Nuu-chah-nulth were unlikely to suffer irreparable harm if their request for an injunction were refused and they later succeeded at trial. Thus, like Macdonald J.A., he concluded that the Nuu-chah-nulth's appeal should be dismissed.

Within roughly four years of the British Columbia Court of Appeal decision in the *Meares Island* case, two similar cases arose in which First Nations peoples pressed for and were granted interlocutory injunctions to prevent or stop logging on their lands pending a decision on their rights at trial. The first case, *Hunt v. Halcan Log Services*[40] or the *Deer Island* case, also involved an island off the east coast of Vancouver Island. The second case, *Westar Timber v. Ryan,*[41] involved a portion of land within Gitksan and Wet'-suwet'en traditional territory in northwestern British Columbia and was closely connected to the *Delgamuukw* case. I will begin with the first case.

Hunt involved a small island, Deer Island, lying about a kilometre off the eastern shore of northern Vancouver Island, within Beaver Harbour across from Fort Rupert. The island falls within the Kwakwak'wakw (Kwakiutl) people's traditional territory. Deer Island acquired wider fame in the early twentieth century as the site where Edward Curtis filmed the movie *Land of the Headhunters* or *Land of the War Canoes* and cast local band members as actors. The Kwakwak'wakw have three reserves extending to the shore of Beaver Harbour.

Until 30 April 1986, MacMillan Bloedel claimed ownership of Deer Island. On that date, it sold the island to Halcan Log Services for $250,000. Halcan, a small logging company, purchased the island expecting to gross over $1.25 million for its harvested timber. After obtaining the requisite provincial permit, Halcan commenced its logging operations on 24

November 1986. The project, a clear-cutting operation, was scheduled to take about thirty days. The following week, on 1 December, Halcan's workers were met by a large group of Kwakwak'wakw people who had come to the island to – apparently peacefully – demand that the logging stop. Halcan acceded.

Halcan immediately initiated an action based on its claim of ownership and possession of a permit entitling it to log the island. Pending trial, it asked the court to grant it an injunction restraining the Kwakwak'wakw and others from trespassing or obstructing its access to and operations on the island.

The Kwakwak'wakw initiated their own action based on claims of both Aboriginal and treaty rights. Their claim encompassed rights "to hunt, to harvest from the fishery on and adjacent to the island, to harvest fruits, berries and medicines, to have access to ancestors' grave sites and to carry out other traditional uses."[42]

Mr. Justice Trainor heard both petitions on 22 December 1986. He delivered his judgment on 6 January 1987. He held that while both parties had raised serious questions for trial, the balance of convenience favoured the Kwakwak'wakw. Accordingly, he granted them an injunction to stop Halcan's operations on Deer Island and refused to grant Halcan's request for an order prohibiting the Kwakwak'wakw from visiting the island and exercising their claimed rights thereon.

The Kwakwak'wakw claim was really two claims. On the one hand, it was a claim primarily of Aboriginal title to Deer Island and secondarily of other Aboriginal rights. On the other hand, it was a claim of treaty hunting and fishing rights. Trainor J. applied the serious-question test to both claims. Regarding the first claim, the claim to Aboriginal title, he found that there was evidence that the Kwakwak'wakw had long occupied the island. Among other things, the Kwakwak'wakw had and still used Deer Island as a burial place and so considered it to be "spiritual or sacred."[43] Likewise, contemporary Kwakwak'wakw continued to depend, as their parents and grandparents had, on the island as a major source of food, especially during winter months, when it became too dangerous to travel to other islands. Regarding the second claim, the claim to treaty rights, Trainor J. found that the Kwakwak'wakw had signed a treaty in 1851, one of the fourteen Douglas Treaties on Vancouver Island. The treaty guaranteed their rights "to hunt over the unoccupied lands, and to carry on ... [their] fisheries as formerly."[44] Given, then, that a reasonable argument could be made that their Aboriginal and/or treaty rights were still in existence when s. 35(1) of the *Constitution Act, 1982* came into force, the Kwakwak'wakw's claim, like Halcan's,[45] raised a serious question for trial.

Turning to the balance of convenience, Trainor J. found that an award of damages would be an adequate remedy for having Halcan's logging operations postponed should it be decided at trial that Deer Island and its timber were the company's to do with as it saw fit. The Kwakwak'wakw's situation was different, however. As Trainor J. explained, "[i]f the logging is not stopped as a result of these proceedings and Halcan removes the timber and sells it pursuant to the contract it has, then success at trial by the Kwakiutl Indian Band would put on this court the nearly impossible task of assessing damages for the loss of aboriginal and treaty rights I have described. In my view, refusing to grant the injunction could result in irreparable damages."[46] In support of his conclusion, the chambers judge quoted from Seaton J.A.'s judgment in the *Meares Island* case, first, as to the material, symbolic, and social/cultural importance of the island and its resources to the First Nations people who claim the island and, second, as to the need to preserve the as yet undocumented evidence of their use and occupation for purposes of trial.

Because Halcan claimed ownership of Deer Island, there was a larger concern to be considered in weighing the balance of convenience that was not present in the *Meares Island* case. The land to be logged on Meares Island was provincial Crown land. Deer Island was private property. The larger concern, as counsel for Halcan submitted, was that "to refuse to prohibit trespassers on the island would cast doubt on title under the [province's] *Land Title Act*."[47] Trainor J. conceded the point but, following Seaton J.A.'s lead in the *Meares* case,[48] added that he was not swayed. "If there is doubt on tenure," he ended, "that should be removed by full consideration in the trial process."[49]

Having determined that the balance of convenience favoured the Kwakwak'wakw, Trainor J. issued an order enjoining Halcan from logging on Deer Island. He then brusquely rejected Halcan's motion to enjoin the Kwakwak'wakw from trespassing on the island in the interim, saying that "[t]o grant the order sought would be to prohibit the Kwakiutl from having access to the island to visit burial grounds and carry out traditional ceremonies. It would also stop them from exercising the rights they claim to hunt, harvest roots, berries and fish on and around the island. To permit a continuation of those activities during the interim period until trial will cause no harm to Halcan."[50]

To understand *Westar Timber v. Ryan*, it helps to know a little about the beginnings of the *Delgamuukw* case. *Delgamuukw* was initiated on 23 October 1984 by a group of thirty-nine Gitksan and twelve Wet'suwet'en hereditary chiefs. Their aim, as summed up by the trial judge, Chief Justice McEachern, was to obtain "a declaration of title or ownership, jurisdiction and other aboriginal rights."[51] The case was, in the Chief Justice's view, "mainly about land."[52] So understood, it was mainly about 58,000 square kilometres (22,000 square miles) of land in northwestern British Columbia, land both rich in natural resources and claimed as traditional territory by the Gitksan and Wet'suwet'en peoples. Because of numerous pre-trial proceedings, the trial did not get under way until two and a half years later, on 11 May 1987. By the time the chambers judge in *Westar* heard the arguments for competing petitions for injunctive relief over four days in mid-October 1988, the *Delgamuukw* trial had been underway for almost a year and a half.[53]

Westar involved three petitions for interlocutory relief based on three distinct actions. The first action was launched on 6 May 1988 by Westar Timber against the same group of Gitksan and Wet'suwet'en hereditary chiefs that had initiated *Delgamuukw*. Westar, a company with substantial sawmill and logging operations in northwestern British Columbia, held provincial permits and licences to build roads and log on Crown land in two areas within Gitksan and Wet'suwet'en traditional territory. The two areas are bisected east-west by the Babine River, with the area immediately to its south, for the sake of convenience, referred to as the *Shegisic* (after the Shegisic watershed) and the area immediately to its north as the *Shedin* (after the Shedin watershed).[54] Westar launched its action after confronting a series of blockades obstructing its attempts to improve the Babine Slide forest access road located in the Shegisic. In an earlier interlocutory proceeding, Westar asked for and was granted an injunction enjoining the defendants from interfering with its work on the road. Westar's plans were to improve the Babine Slide forest access road to the nearest point to the Babine River, build a second road branching from the Babine Slide forest access road to the river, bridge the Babine River, continue the second road north into the Shedin, and commence clear-cut logging in the Shedin in early 1991. Westar had contracted Formula contractors to construct the approaches to and the bridge over the Babine. When Westar and Formula attempted to push their construction beyond the Babine Slide forest access road to the Babine River, they were stopped by a new barricade. With their operations halted, Westar sought a new injunction based upon the first action while Formula launched the second against the same defendants, seeking injunctive relief to allow it to fulfill its contract with Westar. Shortly thereafter, the Gitksan and Wet'suwet'en launched the third action, seeking an order enjoining Westar and Formula from continuing work in the area immediately south of the bridge site, bridging the Babine River, and beginning work in the Shedin.

The Gitksan's and Wet'suwet'en's action and interlocutory petition were not an ordinary action and interlocutory petition. Echoing their writ in the main action, the *Delgamuukw* case, their writ in the action under discussion asked specifically for "[a] declaration that the plaintiffs have rights of ownership and jurisdiction over the lands and resources including all timber thereon covered by Tree Farm Licence No. 51 [i.e., the Shegisic] and Forest Licence A-16A31 Chart Area 52 [i.e., the Shedin]."[55] Obviously, if the Gitksan and Wet'suwet'en succeeded in their main action in obtaining the declaration of ownership of and jurisdiction over their traditional territory, the second action would turn out to have been unnecessary. The second action was simply a fallback position adopted for purely instrumental purposes. The Gitksan and Wet'suwet'en initiated it only because they were held by the British Columbia Court of Appeal to be barred by the *Crown Proceedings Act*[56] in the main action from seeking an injunction against the provincial Crown enjoining it from issuing permits and licences such as those issued to Westar.[57] Since they could not stop the logging by enjoining the Crown in the main action, they had to initiate a parallel action in an effort to enjoin Westar and Formula. The action was launched and the injunction applied for with the understanding that if their petition were granted, the injunction would terminate with the decision in the *Delgamuukw* case.

Mr. Justice Macdonell delivered his reasons for judgment on 20 October 1988. His decision was a compromise. To the Gitksan and Wet'suwet'en, he granted an injunction restraining Westar and Formula from constructing the footings and installing the bridge on the Babine River and from proceeding with any work north of the river. To Westar and Formula, he granted an injunction restraining the Gitksan and Wet'suwet'en from interfering with or obstructing their lawful works south of the Babine. This meant that they could continue with improvements on the Babine Slide forest access road, that they could construct the branching road and the southern approach to the river, and that Westar could carry on its logging of the Shegisic.

Macdonell J. felt no hesitation concluding that both Westar[58] and the Gitksan and Wet'suwet'en had made claims that raised serious questions for trial. In Westar's case, there was a triable question regarding its "right to pursue its business pursuant to licences granted."[59] And patently, since their basic claim was already at trial in *Delgamuukw,* the Gitksan and Wet'suwet'en claim also raised a serious question.

Turning to the balance of convenience, Macdonell J. found that Westar and the Gitksan and Wet'suwet'en had each shown that they would likely suffer irreparable harm if an injunction were granted against them. Westar's argument was this. The company estimated that by 1991, when it planned to begin logging the area, the Shedin would be the source of about 30 percent of the timber supplying two of its mills in northwestern British Columbia. Were their bridge and road construction and, as a result, their logging in the Shedin postponed by an injunction, their counsel argued, "it would not be practically possible to calculate the loss that they may suffer by not having an adequate log supply when needed, as it depends on markets and the impact of loss of markets, the possible shutdown of mills, and the overall financial viability of the company should this become necessary if there were not an alternate log supply. Additionally, the question arises whether the Gitksan [and Wet'suwet'en] could pay damages if assessed."[60] On their side, the Gitksan and Wet'suwet'en argued that the potential loss to them should Westar be allowed to continue was also incalculable, "as there is no way to measure the impact of road building and possible clearcut logging and occupation of the lands they claim should they succeed, as the damage to the environment and the lands and wildlife would be irreparable."[61] The potential for harm appeared most serious in the Shedin, an area that theretofore had remained inaccessible by road and that consequently, unlike the Shegisic, had never been logged. Hence, the Gitksan and Wet'suwet'en argued finally that "the effect of continuing with the road building and logging opens up the whole territory, not only to the logging company, but to the public at large who likely would interfere with their hunting and trapping over the lands they claim, and their exercising any rights over their territory."[62] Macdonell J. found merit in both parties' arguments and so concluded that damages would not likely serve as adequate compensation should either party's petition be granted and the party enjoined later succeed at trial.

Given that the balance of convenience was a wash as far as irreparable harm was concerned, Macdonell J. turned his inquiry to other relevant factors. The factor he settled on as determinative was preservation of the status quo. The question then became, what is the status quo in the given situation? Not surprisingly, Westar and the Gitksan and Wet'suwet'en advanced different versions of the status quo. Westar claimed that the status quo was "that they have rights that they have obtained by licence from the Province of British Columbia to harvest timber and that they are continuing to exercise their rights at this time ... so the status quo is that Westar should be entitled to continue to harvest timber in that area [i.e., the Shegisic] as well as the area of Chart 52 [i.e., the Shedin], which is an extension of the territory over which they have rights."[63] The Gitksan and Wet'suwet'en, in contrast, claimed that the status quo generally was "leaving the land both below and above the Babine as it is, without falling timber until the lawsuit is completed."[64] They claimed, moreover, that the Shedin, more specifically,

is virgin territory without access, and the status quo is to leave it in its natural state until the [*Delgamuukw*] lawsuit is resolved, and that way protect the territories against the potentially devastating effect of clearcut logging on the environment and the animal life and ecology and the deprivation of their right to manage their lands as they choose, including selective forest harvesting. That status quo is that there is no bridge over the river and that the territories are not invaded by hunters from outside the band, and that with a bridge all that will change.[65]

Macdonell J. determined that preserving status quo meant different things for the north and south sides of the river. On the north side, in the Shedin, preserving the status quo meant keeping the area in its present state, not only unlogged but also largely inaccessible to outsiders. On the south side, in the Shegisic, however, it meant allowing Westar to continue logging.

It should be noted that Macdonell J.'s determination was premised on the expectation that the *Delgamuukw* decision would be delivered in sufficient time to allow Westar (proceeding expeditiously) to bridge the Babine, punch its road north, and begin supplying its mills with the Shedin's timber without critical delay should the Gitksan and Wet'suwet'en lose.[66]

Macdonell J. granted, then, two interlocutory injunctions, neither matching exactly what either party had petitioned for. To Westar, he granted an order restraining the Gitksan and Wet'suwet'en from interfering with its road work and logging south of the Babine. This meant that Westar and Formula were free to finish the branch road and south bridge approach to the Babine. To the Gitksan and Wet'suwet'en, he granted an order restraining Westar and Formula from constructing bridge footings, installing the bridge, and constructing any roads north of the Babine. As a condition of his orders, the Gitksan and Wet'suwet'en had to abstain from any further confrontation with Westar's and Formula's workers.

Although the Gitksan and Wet'suwet'en could not have been entirely pleased with the chambers judge's orders, they had, nonetheless, succeeded in at least temporarily protecting the Shedin. Westar and Formula, however, not being similarly appeased, decided – with the province's Attorney General intervening in support – to appeal.

On 9 June 1989, the Court of Appeal gave its reasons for judgment. The Court split two to one in favour of allowing the appeal but only to the extent of varying the injunctions to allow Westar and Formula to construct the bridge footings. Esson and Carrothers JJ.A. set forth separate but concurring reasons and thus formed the majority. Locke J.A. dissented. He favoured allowing Westar's and Formula's appeal in full, and thus removing the interlocutory order restraining their efforts to bridge the Babine, to extend their road north, and to log the Shedin. The basic issue on which the justices split was whether or not the chambers judge had erred in his understanding and application of the balance of convenience test.

The *Westar* appeal was, however, about much more than whether or not the Shedin should be protected pending the outcome of the *Delgamuukw* trial. In granting an interlocutory order protecting the Shedin, the chambers judge had relied on the British Columbia Court of Appeal's decision in the *Meares Island* case. The *Westar* appeal was, on the Attorney General's part, in effect an invitation to the Court to overrule its earlier decision in *Meares*. Despite the split in the Court over how to treat the chambers judge's decision regarding the Shedin, the Court unanimously refused, albeit without making the point explicit, to abandon the *Meares Island* decision.

The task of defending the Court's *Meares Island* decision fell mainly to Esson J.A. In his reasons for judgment, he took pains to fully present and address the Attorney General's attack on *Meares*. The Attorney General's argument was basically as follows. On the authority of the Supreme Court of Canada,[67] in cases raising issues regarding the constitutionality of legislation, "the proper course on an interlocutory injunction application is to preserve the status quo under the existing legislation, and to leave the party who seeks to challenge the legislation to his remedy at trial."[68] To put it another way, the proper course is to adopt a presumption of constitutionality. Although the presumption is rebuttable – and thus an interlocutory injunction may still be granted – it is rebuttable on condition that public interest is given its due weight in assessing the balance of convenience. The *Meares Island* case raised constitutional issues regarding the application of the provincial *Forest Act*[69] to Nuu-chah-nulth territory. The British Columbia Court of Appeal's decision in that case (in retrospect) failed to recognize the necessity of giving due weight to public interest in granting an injunction restraining logging, and thus in rebutting the presumption of constitutionality. The *Westar* case similarly raised issues regarding the constitutionality of the provincial *Forest Act* insofar as it purports to apply to Gitksan and Wet'suwet'en territory. Because the chambers judge relied upon the *Meares Island* decision in granting an injunction restraining Westar from logging in the Shedin, he did not give sufficient weight to the public interest in assessing the balance of convenience, and therefore he too lightly set aside the presumption of constitutionality. Consequently, the Attorney General's submission concluded, the chambers judge had erred in applying the balance of convenience test.

In his response, Esson J.A. acknowledged at the outset that the public interest must be considered in interlocutory applications such as that of the Gitksan and Wet'suwet'en. The need to do so was apparent because, he explained, the forest industry "is the main foundation of the economy of the Province."[70] He then elaborated on his point, saying:

> The forest industry, in its present form, could not exist without huge amounts of timber being cut each year. Much of that timber must be taken from areas which are the subject of Indian land claims. It is ... simply unthinkable that, in order to preserve the "status quo" pending the final determination of those claims, a series of interlocutory injunctions should so cripple the industry as to throw people out of work, reduce the revenues both of the government and industry and thus threaten the very existence of that industry and our existing social arrangements.[71]

However, the Court of Appeal in the *Meares Island* case had, Esson J.A. went on to show (quoting at length from the dissents as well as from the majority), "recognized fully the nature and extent of the public interest involved in applications of this kind."[72] Indeed, he concluded, the Court's decision clearly supported the following pair of propositions: "The first is that the court should not grant an injunction if the economic consequences of doing so would have a serious impact upon the economic health of the province, the region or the logging company. The second is that, notwithstanding the powerful considerations militating against granting the interlocutory relief to those claiming aboriginal rights, such relief may be granted in respect of particular sites which have unique qualities."[73] The latter proposition simply articulated the specific condition that would have to be satisfied before an interlocutory injunction could be granted in similar cases. Hence, the Court of Appeal's decision in the *Meares Island* case did not, contrary to the Attorney General's submission, fail to recognize the necessity of giving due weight to public interest in such cases.[74]

Granted, then, that the chambers judge was justified in relying on the Court of Appeal's decision in the *Meares Island* case, it was still possible that he erred in his application of the balance of convenience test. Accordingly, the appellants submitted that the chambers judge had erred by, among other things, treating the Shedin as unique, concluding that a delay in Westar's operations in the Shedin would not present a realistic problem, and misidentifying the status quo. Esson J.A. responded to each of these claims in turn.

As to the Shedin's uniqueness, Esson J.A. agreed with the appellants that the Shedin differed from Meares Island in a number of respects. For one, while there had been a need to keep Meares Island in its current state in order to preserve unrecorded potential evidence for trial, there was no such need with regard to the Shedin. For another, while Meares Island's timber had long been used for a wide variety of traditional purposes – as indicated by the island's culturally modified trees – the Shedin's timber (seemingly) had not. Nonetheless, the Shedin was, he suggested, relevantly unique in other ways. As Esson J.A. explained:

> If the Gitksan [and Wet'suwet'en] succeed in establishing that they have unextinguished aboriginal rights in respect of the land within the claim area, any declaration of existing rights in 1990 or later will have to take into account what has happened in the last century and more since the white man came to those lands. What the Indians ask for is to be put back into the same relationship which they had with the land before the coming of the white man. What makes the Shedin area different from the area south of the Babine, and even more clearly different from Hazelton and

other communities within the land claim area, is that, after all this time, it remains pristine in that [it] has not been changed by white settlement. It is an area, small in relation to the whole of the land claim area, where it is feasible to contemplate the Gitksan continuing in the same relationship to the land which they enjoyed before the coming of the whites.[75]

Esson J.A. acknowledged that there were likely other similar areas within the Gitksan and Wet'suwet'en land claim area, and therefore that this fact affected the relative significance of the Shedin. He denied, however, that it affected its significance to the point of effacing its status as a unique place within the total land claim area. Thus, he concluded, the chambers judge did not err by treating the Shedin as unique relative to the area south of the Babine.

As to whether a delay in Westar's operations in the Shedin would present a realistic problem, Esson J.A. shared Westar's stated concern that "if the road system in the Shedin cannot be built in 1989 and 1990 so that logging can begin in 1991, there will be a shortfall of 30 per cent or so in the amount of wood required to keep its mills in operation, and the result inevitably will be a substantial curtailment of its production with consequent irreparable damage to it and to the economy of the region."[76] However, he noted that the chambers judge had – unlike the Court of Appeal – the advantage of having sufficient opportunity to fully consider the evidence placed before him, and that the chambers judge's conclusion that a (short) delay in Westar's operations was not a realistic problem was a reasonable inference from the evidentiary record. Thus, he again concluded that the chambers judge did not err by concluding that the delay did not present a realistic problem.

Finally, as to the status quo to be preserved, the appellants had argued that it was "wrong in principle," for the chambers judge, "to treat the status quo as anything other than the established system of forest administration and the rights obtained thereunder by Westar."[77] In reply, Esson J.A. noted simply that the argument was "essentially a repetition or variant of the Attorney General's submission" and was therefore met by the Court's earlier decision in the *Meares Island* case.[78] And so, he concluded, the chambers judge did not err by misidentifying the status quo in applying the balance of convenience test.

Esson J.A. did determine, however, that Westar was entitled to succeed on one point. The chambers judge was wrong, he agreed, to restrain Westar from constructing the footings for the Babine River bridge. The construction of the footings, unlike bridge installation, was, he noted, particularly dependent on seasonal factors. Moreover, their construction would not contribute anything to the irreparable harm that might result from bridging the Babine and constructing the road north into the Shedin. With regard to the construction of the bridge footings, then, the balance of convenience clearly favoured Westar. The appeal should, he held, be allowed to the extent of varying the chambers judge's orders accordingly.

In his concurring reasons, Carrothers J.A. agreed that the chambers judge was unfair in enjoining Westar from constructing the bridge footings but that otherwise he did not err in enjoining the company from extending its operations into the Shedin.

Locke J.A., in dissent, held that the chambers judge had erred in his balance of convenience inquiry by misidentifying the status quo. The status quo was not, he urged, "the state of a piece of land: It is a complete, long-standing, established legal and administrative fabric and system which has obtained in this province for over a hundred years."[79] Since Westar's planned operations in the area, not the pristine state of the Shedin, represented the status quo, the chambers judge erred, Locke J.A. concluded, by not finding that the balance of convenience favoured Westar's plans for the Shedin.

Locke J.A. agreed with Esson J.A.'s analysis of the Court's decision in the *Meares Island* case. And so he agreed that injunctions may, despite countervailing public interest, be granted in extraordinary circumstances. His agreement, he explained, did not, however, extend to the *Westar* case: "It is my view – as has been emphasized by others – that there is always room to grant an injunction in extraordinary cases, and Meares Island is a classic example, but that is not the case at bar. This is a case involving wilderness Crown land, only occasionally traversed by a trapper, unconnected with preservation of evidence or places of worship. No case could be more different."[80] Clearly, Locke J.A.'s focus was very different from Esson J.A.'s. Esson J.A. had focused on the fact that the Shedin was still a pristine portion of Gitksan and Wet'suwet'en traditional territory and thus one of a small number of rapidly vanishing areas where they could maintain their traditional relationship with the land in its full integrity. In his eyes, that made the Shedin sufficiently unique to justify the chambers judge's decision to grant an interlocutory injunction protecting it. Locke J.A.'s focus, however, was on the fact that the area was still wilderness. Conceived as wilderness, the Shedin was disassociated from the Gitksan and Wet'suwet'en, their activities, their purposes, and their needs. Whereas Meares Island had been extensively materially, socially, and culturally integrated into the Nuu-chah-nulth people's life, the Shedin, Locke J.A. implied, remained largely peripheral to Gitksan and Wet'suwet'en life.[81] It therefore lacked, he concluded, the uniqueness that would warrant interim protection.

The interlocutory injunctions granted in the *Meares Island, Deer Island,* and *Westar* cases were not intended to provide more than short-term protection for areas special to the First Nations peoples involved. The *Meares Island* injunction, however, has afforded long-term protection. Within a year and a half of the Court of Appeal's decision to grant the injunction in the *Meares* case in March 1985, MacMillan Bloedel attempted twice to have it dissolved. In September 1985, the Nuu-chah-nulth applied for and obtained an adjournment of their trial. On that occasion, MacMillan Bloedel asked for and was refused the injunction's dissolution. Almost a year later, in August 1986, the company reapplied to have the injunction dissolved and again its application was dismissed.[82] As of summer 2004, the trial remains adjourned (by agreement of the parties) and the injunction in place.[83]

Similarly, the *Deer Island* case never came to trial. In that case, however, the Kwakwak'wakw were claiming treaty as well as Aboriginal rights. In 1992, they filed a specific claim with the federal Indian Claims Commission alleging, among other things, that Deer Island should have been reserved pursuant to the Douglas Treaty. The commission accepted the claim for negotiation, and a settlement agreement was reached. The Kwakwak'-wakw ratified the agreement in March 1997. As part of the agreement, Deer Island became Kwakwak'wakw reserve land.[84]

The outcome in the *Westar* case was significantly different. The Gitksan and Wet'suwet'en had launched their action against Westar and Formula entirely for purposes of obtaining an injunction. The common understanding was that the injunction granted to them would terminate with the close of the *Delgamuukw* trial. However, when the trial decision came down on 8 March 1991, dismissing the Gitksan's and Wet'suwet'en's claims of ownership and jurisdiction, Westar did not apply to discharge the injunction.[85] The injunction was still in place when the Court of Appeal handed down its decision, overturning the trial judgment in part, in June 1993. The Court of Appeal held, among other things, that the Gitksan and Wet'suwet'en did possess unextinguished Aboriginal rights but that they were non-exclusive rights falling short of rights of ownership in and jurisdiction over their traditional territory. The injunction was also still in place when leave to appeal to the Supreme Court of Canada was granted in March 1994. Sometime before the Court of Appeal's decision came down, Westar transferred its forest licence in the area including the Shedin to Skeena Cellulose. In 1995, Skeena applied to have the interlocutory injunction discharged. On 31 March 1995, Mr. Justice Hunter of the British Columbia Supreme Court granted Skeena's application and discharged the six-and-a-half-year-old order restraining logging operations in the Shedin.[86]

Failure

What I earlier referred to as the Meares strategy arose out of the *Meares Island* case and received further articulation in the *Westar* case (particularly in the judgment of Esson J.A.). The Meares strategy, as I am using the term, is a litigation strategy for protecting sacred sites. The strategy consists in petitioning for an interlocutory injunction to protect a sacred site pending a determination of the relevant Aboriginal and/or treaty rights at trial. For the strategy to succeed, the petitioner must, it is commonly believed, establish to a court's satisfaction that the sacred site or surrounding area is sufficiently unique to warrant granting an injunction.[87] Absent sufficient uniqueness, courts will more than likely find that public interest considerations (particularly concerns about negative economic consequences should the injunction be granted) tilt the balance of convenience against the petitioner. While there is no definition of uniqueness or test for what counts as sufficiently unique, courts tend to look at *Meares* as the paradigm.[88]

Sacredness certainly implies uniqueness. One would think, therefore, that some sacred sites should qualify as sufficiently unique to warrant interlocutory injunctive protection. By definition, a place that is sacred serves other than ordinary purposes or functions. What is other than ordinary is unique in a broad sense. Some sacred sites are also unique in a narrow sense, that is, they are one-of-a-kind sites. Must a sacred site be unique in a narrow sense to qualify as sufficiently unique to warrant interlocutory injunctive protection? Meares Island has come to be characterized as unique in a narrow sense. This could be taken to suggest that only sites unique in a narrow sense – whether sacred or not – will qualify. As Esson J.A.'s judgment in *Westar* made clear, however, areas that are unique in a broad sense, such as the Shedin, may also qualify for interlocutory injunctive protection.[89] In certain circumstances, therefore, sacred sites that are unique only in a broad sense should qualify for interlocutory injunctive protection.

Neither Meares Island nor Deer Island nor the Shedin were presented – at least in the court decisions discussed above – as sacred places or sites. Both islands were claimed to have sacred burial sites. The Nuu-chah-nulth's chief concern was the *protection* of their sacred burial sites, while the Kwakwak'wakw's was *access* to their burial sites. The Kwakwak'wakw were undoubtedly also concerned with protection. However, because Deer Island was the logging company's private property and because the company was accusing the Kwakwak'wakw of trespassing, access was their most pressing concern. Although the Nuu-chah-nulth and the Kwakwak'wakw explicitly claimed that Meares Island and Deer Island respectively contained sacred burial sites, neither emphasized the point above others (for instance, their dependence on cedar or the fisheries adjoining the islands). Moreover, neither explicitly argued that their island, taken as a whole, was sacred. In the case of the Shedin, the Gitksan and Wet'suwet'en did not explicitly argue that the area was sacred in whole or in part.[90]

Remarkably, in the handful of cases in which the sacredness of an area has been explicitly asserted or in which the sacredness of sites located therein emphasized, petitions for interlocutory relief based on a claim of Aboriginal or treaty rights have failed. Why they have failed is a question I will discuss below ("What Went Wrong?"). What follows next is a summary of a select few of those cases.

I begin with *Tlowitsis Nation and Mumtagila Nation v. MacMillan Bloedel*,[91] or the *Lower Tsitika Valley* case. The Lower Tsitika Valley watershed is located on northeastern Vancouver Island. It empties into an estuary in Robson Bight, a well-known habitat for killer whales. In 1973, the watershed, along with other portions of northern Vancouver Island, was placed under a development moratorium. Four years later, in 1977, a cabinet committee decided that the watershed's timber could be harvested but only on an integrated resource basis. Thereafter, portions of the watershed were set aside for ecological reserves and other purposes. In the summer of 1989, MacMillan Bloedel, which had acquired rights to four forest cutting blocks in the Lower Tsitika Valley watershed, was permitted to begin road construction into Block 101. The company's plan was to log all four blocks, beginning with Block 101, over a five-year period (1989-94).

As it happens, the Lower Tsitika Valley watershed falls within territory claimed by the Tlowitsis-Mumtagila people. The watershed is an area they hold sacred. The Tlowitsis-Mumtagila had voiced their opposition to the watershed's logging, first in a series of public meetings and eventually to the media. The latter course of action yielded a meeting between their representatives and MacMillan Bloedel but with unsatisfactory results. The road building into Block 101 continued into the late summer of 1990.

On 19 October 1990, MacMillan Bloedel began its falling operations in Block 101. The operations were frustrated by a group of protestors, however. Although the Tlowitsis-Mumtagila did not take part in the protest, they were not inactive. They decided to launch an action seeking, among other things, a declaration of Aboriginal title to and Aboriginal rights in the Lower Tsitika Valley watershed. On 30 October, they applied *ex parte* for an interim order prohibiting logging in Block 101. Although an order prohibiting logging was refused, one restricting logging was granted. On 2 November, with writ issued, the Tlowitsis-Mumtagila filed an application for an interlocutory injunction. On 7 November, argument before Mr. Justice MacKinnon was completed. Two days later, on 9 November 1990, he dismissed the application and vacated the interim order.

In their arguments, the Tlowitsis-Mumtagila placed their emphasis on the sacredness of the Lower Tsitika Valley watershed. The watershed was, they said, an area in which they continued to engage in spiritual practices. In an attempt to communicate the significance of the watershed to MacKinnon J., they described it as being analogous to a Christian church – a sacred place vulnerable to acts of desecration. MacMillan Bloedel's logging, they argued, amounted to a desecration of their sacred place. As such, it would, they continued, interfere with their Aboriginal right to engage in spiritual practices in the area.

Following the lead of the British Columbia Court of Appeal in the *Meares Island* case, MacKinnon J. had little hesitation in concluding that the Tlowitsis-Mumtagila's Aboriginal title and rights claim raised a serious question for trial. The crucial issue, then, was where the balance of convenience lay. Both parties advanced arguments supporting the claim of irreparable harm. The Tlowitsis-Mumtagila argued that MacMillan Bloedel's logging should not continue because it would, among other things, adversely affect the estuary in Robson Bight by causing siltation and excessive noise, disrupt the habitat of the killer whales, and desecrate sacred grounds. Moreover, they submitted, "the area to be logged is very small and alternate licenses can be used by MacMillan Bloedel."[92] MacMillan Bloedel, for its part, argued that it had "[n]o alternate site available where ... [it] could cut logs in a timely manner to supply its mill."[93] Thus, it continued, if its operations in the Lower Tsitika Valley were halted, not only would it lose the time and money it had invested in getting its operations started but many jobs would also be lost. Finally, the company expressed its concern that a decision in favour of the Tlowitsis-Mumtagila, taken together with others, would "affect the right to log any area where someone simply asserts an aboriginal claim."[94]

MacKinnon J. was particularly concerned with the potential loss of employment and its negative economic consequences for the province. Accordingly, he concluded, unless the Tlowitsis-Mumtagila could show that the Lower Tsitika Valley watershed qualified as unique, the status quo should be maintained. And the status quo, he determined, was that MacMillan Bloedel's logging operation was already underway in Block 101.

Had the Tlowitsis-Mumtagila established that the watershed was unique? MacKinnon J. concluded that they had not. As for the assertion of negative effects of logging on the killer whale habitat, he noted that the evidence tendered pointed to numerous studies that suggested otherwise. Also, although the Tlowitsis-Mumtagila had expressed concern in the initial interim proceedings that logging would destroy culturally modified trees needed for evidence at trial, they had not reiterated their concern in the interlocutory proceedings. This meant that the Tlowitsis-Mumtagila's case for uniqueness rested entirely on the claim of the watershed's sacredness. What was purportedly unique, then, about the Lower Tsitika Valley watershed was that logging would, as MacKinnon J. put it, "desecrate ... spiritual grounds."[95]

After observing that the evidence supporting the claim of the watershed's sacred status was slim, MacKinnon J. went on to register his concern over the context in which the Tlowitsis-Mumtagila had asserted it:

The major submissions on behalf of the plaintiffs, the unique feature of this land – is that logging will desecrate their spiritual grounds. This comes largely from the affidavit of Daisy Smith. It is in the form of Indian history as recounted to Daisy Smith by her elders. At the present time, there does not appear to be any physical confirmation of this to be found in the Lower Tsitika Valley.

I am a little concerned as to the timing that this rationale for opposing the logging was made public. The plans to log this area and the opposition of the native Indians has been known for some time.

The native Indians opposed the logging primarily on the grounds that they owned the land or the right to use the land. They were critical of the logging methods used by companies, including MacMillan Bloedel. They also expressed fear that logging would destroy evidence necessary to prove their aboriginal rights. Indeed, in the initial appearance before me, this was the primary reason relied upon for the injunction. No mention appears to have been made to anyone until a few days ago, that this [i.e., the land's sacredness] was their chief concern. They had many opportunities to do so in press releases, discussions with MacMillan Bloedel and at other times.[96]

The point of MacKinnon J.'s remarks is not immediately apparent. It becomes clear only when they are considered in light of the quotation that follows. After the above remarks, he went on to quote from Macfarlane J.A.'s judgment in the *Meares Island* case, where Macfarlane J.A. explained why it was a misunderstanding of the judicial process to think that an injunction in the case of Meares Island would cascade into a rash of similar injunctions. The passage quoted concluded with the sentence: "The bona fides of any particular application will weigh heavily in the balance."[97] What MacKinnon J. was implying, then, by quoting the passage from Macfarlane J.A., was that he held doubts about the bona fides of the Tlowitsis-Mumtagila's application.

The upshot was that the way in which the Tlowitsis-Mumtagila had proceeded had undercut their argument for the Lower Tsitika Valley's uniqueness. It was not – as their counsel would later mistakenly claim on appeal[98] – that the way they had proceeded had, in the chambers judge's estimation, undercut the credibility of the evidence they had tendered in support of the area's sacredness but rather that it had undercut the claim that the area's sacredness (or degree of sacredness) qualified it as unique. The evidence simply did not, MacKinnon J. believed, support the claim. Because they had failed to establish the area's requisite uniqueness, the balance of convenience, the chambers judge concluded, favoured MacMillan Bloedel and the preservation of the status quo. Accordingly, he refused the interlocutory injunction and vacated the interim order.

The Tlowitsis-Mumtagila immediately applied for leave to appeal Mac-Kinnon J.'s order denying an interlocutory injunction. The application was refused. Their seemingly strongest argument was that the chambers judge had erred by rejecting the uncontradicted evidence of the watershed's sacredness, and therefore by assessing the credibility of those who, unobserved by the chambers judge, gave the evidence. MacDonald J.A. disagreed, responding:

> [M]y view is that the Judge did not err in the way that was argued. I do not think that he made an assessment of credibility. If he had done so he would have embarrassed the judge who will eventually try this action. He did not in my view, embarrass that judge either by accepting or rejecting the evidence as to the sacred character of the ground. What he did, and quite properly, was to take into account the circumstances in which that evidence was put forward.
>
> The significant shift in the thrust of the applicants' case was properly taken into account by the judge.[99]

The Tlowitsis-Mumtagila repeated their argument when they, again unsuccessfully, applied to the Court of Appeal to review MacDonald J.A.'s refusal to grant leave to appeal the chambers judge's dismissal. There they attempted to buttress their argument, claiming that "the fact that the spiritual nature of the site had not been mentioned in discussions with MacMillan Bloedel prior to bringing the action could not have any relevance unless it was used to assess the strength of the claim to the injunction."[100] Legg J.A., speaking for the Court, agreed with MacDonald J.A. that the evidence fully supported the chambers judge's observations regarding the late date at which Tlowitsis-Mumtagila decided to make the Lower Tsitika Valley's sacredness public.

As for the chambers judge's suspicions regarding the timing, he had this to say:

> The applicants filed the affidavit of Daisy Smith in support of their application before the Chambers judge and filed affidavits of May Smith and Simon Dick in this Court to support the position that the Watershed contained sacred ground which would be damaged if the injunction was not granted. May Smith and Simon Dick deposed that they attended residential Anglican schools many years ago and were punished if they spoke Kwakwala. For this and other reasons they had been afraid in the past to speak out about their religious beliefs and cultures.
>
> In my opinion, those affidavits do not offer an explanation for the lateness of the applicants' raising a claim that their right to engage in spiritual practices in the Lower Tsitika Valley Watershed was endangered.[101]

Legg J.A.'s final remark was revealing. It showed that the Court of Appeal – or at least three of its members – had next to no appreciation for the lasting ill effects of the decades of legislated (and other) suppression of Native cultural/religious practice[102] combined with residential schooling.

Roughly three months after the Tlowitsis-Mumtagila asked for and were denied an interlocutory order restraining logging operations in a sacred area, another First Nation, the Lil'wat, made a similar request. On its face, the Lil'wat advanced a stronger claim for the uniqueness of their sacred area than the Tlowitsis-Mumtagila. Nevertheless, their request to preserve the area pending the outcome of a trial of their rights was not merely denied, it was tersely denied. The difference in the court's treatment was wholly attributable to one thing, namely, the fact that the *Delgamuukw* trial judgment had finally been delivered.

Ure Creek and its surrounding area lies due east of Whistler and southeast of Pemberton, British Columbia. If one imagines Whistler and Pemberton as two points connected by a straight line and the line as the base of an equilateral triangle, the third point would roughly indicate the upper portions of the Ure Creek area. The creek itself flows eastward, emptying into Lillooet Lake's midsection. The Ure Creek area lies within the ancestral territory of the Lil'wat, an Interior Salish people. It is among the most sacred of Lil'wat sacred sites. By Lil'wat traditional law, it is a place where, other than for the training of medicine people, few Lil'wat are permitted to go.

In 1982, Interfor was granted a fifteen-year licence to log in a timber supply area that included the Ure Creek area. To access the Ure Creek area, Interfor hired Howe Sound Timber Company to construct a haul road south from the Pemberton–Duffy Lake road (Highway 99), along the west side of Lillooet Lake, to Ure Creek. Construction of the road began in January 1990. Interfor's goal was to complete the road and begin harvesting the Ure Creek area in 1992.

After several months of construction, work on the road came to a halt when workers found a pictograph. The pictograph, it turned out, was associated with an archaeologically significant cache site. Construction resumed briefly in December 1990 after the route was changed to protect the site. Over the Christmas holidays, some of Howe Sound's equipment was vandalized and so work on the road did not start again until 21 January 1991. The next day, when Howe Sound's workers returned to work, they met a blockade manned by Lil'wat people and sympathizers. On 23 January, Interfor and Howe Sound launched an action against the blockaders. On 1 February, they were granted an injunction restraining the protesters from interfering with the road's construction. A number of blockaders chose to ignore the injunction. And so, on 9 February, about a dozen, mostly Lil'wat people were arrested.

Among the Lil'wat arrested (and subsequently found guilty of criminal contempt[103]) was Harold Pascal. Mr. Pascal was entrusted with special responsibilities within Lil'wat society. He was a hereditary watchman of Lil'wat burial and sacred sites. The Ure Creek area was among the sacred sites under his care.[104] The arrest of Mr. Pascal and the others proved to be the last in a long series of events that finally impelled the Lil'wat people to launch their own action on 21 February 1991 seeking a declaration of Aboriginal title and other rights. In conjunction with their action, they applied for an interlocutory injunction calling a halt to the construction of Interfor's Ure Creek haul road.

From 27 February through 6 March 1991, Mr. Justice Macdonell heard arguments. On 26 March he delivered a terse judgment dismissing the Lil'wat's application.

Among the chambers judge's conclusions was one that the Lil'wat could not have predicted, namely, that their case did not raise a serious question for trial. In their action, the Lil'wat claimed Aboriginal title to their traditional territory, including the Ure Creek area. They also claimed Aboriginal rights, "including exclusive use of the territory in question, not only for sustenance activities ... but also for spiritual purposes and the protection of sacred areas, such as burial sites."[105] In light of the *Meares Island* case, the Lil'wat must have assumed that getting their petition for interlocutory relief over the serious question threshold would be a mere formality. The crucial test would be whether the balance of convenience favoured preserving the Ure Creek area or completing the road and then logging the area. On this issue, again in light of the *Meares Island* case, they must have thought that they had a reasonable prospect of success, especially given the strength of their claim for the Ure Creek area's sacredness. When argument ended on 6 March 1991, the Lil'wat must have been hopeful. Two days later, however, Chief Justice McEachern delivered his decision in the *Delgamuukw* case. According to the Chief Justice of British Columbia, Aboriginal title had been extinguished[106] and all surviving Aboriginal rights regarding unoccupied Crown land were merely usufructuary and non-exclusive.[107] The implications for the Lil'wat's petition were plain. They had failed to establish that they had a serious question to be tried with regard to their claims of Aboriginal title or exclusive Aboriginal rights. Macdonell J. summed up the situation bluntly, saying, "[a]s I view this case, all the efforts of counsel are in vain with respect to the principal legal issues of aboriginal title and aboriginal rights."[108]

Although McEachern C.J. held that all Aboriginal rights to and on the land that might otherwise have been constitutionally protected by s. 35(1) of the *Constitution Act, 1982* had been extinguished,[109] he did allow that a range of usufructuary rights still existed. That is, although First Nations peoples no longer owned the land or possessed exclusive rights to use it as they saw fit, they still enjoyed existing legally enforceable rights, "as against the Crown but subject to the general law, to use unoccupied, vacant Crown lands within the [First Nation's] territory for aboriginal sustenance activities until it is required for an adverse purpose."[110] The origin of these usufructuary rights was a long-standing promise by the Crown dating back to colonial days that they could continue to use vacant Crown land on the conditions mentioned above. The promise was given by the Crown in its capacity as fiduciary. Thus, the Crown – and here, more specifically, the provincial Crown – owed, the Chief Justice held, a fiduciary duty to the province's First Nations not to arbitrarily or unduly limit their usufructuary rights.

Interestingly, the Lil'wat had argued that the Crown owed them a fiduciary duty, that as a fiduciary, the Crown was legally obliged to respect their rights to and on their traditional territory (including the right to protect and preserve the Ure Creek area as sacred), and that the Crown was in breach of its fiduciary duty by allowing the Ure Creek road to be built and Interfor's logging operations to go forward. Furthermore, they argued, their claim that the Crown had breached its fiduciary duty towards them raised a serious question for trial. Macdonell J. disagreed, however. Given the Chief Justice's finding in *Delgamuukw* that First Nations people possessed only non-exclusive usufructuary rights in relation to vacant Crown land, he explained, "again a fair question does not exist to be tried or decided as there is no suggestion in the evidence that the plaintiff is precluded from entering upon the territories to pursue its rights to sustenance and, no doubt, to roam the area and absorb the spiritual surroundings."[111] The chambers judge's final remark that the Lil'wat remained free, as he put it, "to roam the area and absorb the spiritual surroundings," indicated a surprising lack of appreciation of the significance of the Ure Creek area – or indeed of any of their other sacred areas – to the Lil'wat. Few Lil'wat were permitted to venture into the Ure Creek area, and then only for serious purposes. It was an insult to say simply that they could still, like some coterie of eighteenth-century romantics on an excursion into the country, "roam the area and absorb the spiritual surroundings."

The Lil'wat, in Macdonell J.'s view, had one remaining argument supporting the idea that their case raised a serious question for trial. They had argued that the road construction would damage or destroy burial grounds and other sites of heritage or historical importance. To this he responded: "Examination of the evidence before me leads me to the conclusion that there are no demonstrated burial grounds, pictographs or other matters of heritage or historical significance within the road allowance."[112] Then, reminiscent of the chambers judge's decision in the *Meares Island* case,[113] he added: "The evidence advanced by the plaintiff is of a very general nature, lacking any specificity which would make it possible to determine affirmatively or otherwise the existence of any area or site within the road allowance which should be protected."[114] In any case, he continued, should any heritage site come to light during the road's construction, it would be protected under the province's *Heritage Conservation Act.*[115]

Having concluded that the Lil'wat's case did not raise a serious question for trial, Macdonell J. had no need to go to the next stage of the inquiry. Nonetheless, he did go on to make a summary assessment of the balance of convenience. What he found was that, given the protection afforded by the *Heritage Conservation Act,* other provincial legislation, government policy, and Interfor's and Howe Sound's commitments, construction of the Ure Creek road would not result in damage rising to the level of irreparable harm. "On the other side of the coin," he went on, "the companies stand to suffer irreparable harm if they are not allowed to proceed with the construction of the road and harvest the timber within the area that Interfor is entitled to log with approval by the Forest Minister."[116] Public interest, including that of the Lil'wat people, also, he added, weighed heavily in favour of Interfor's road: "The harm is manifold to all those in the area who depend on the woods, industry, and of course that includes a great number of the members of the Lil'wat Band who work in the woods."[117] Thus, he concluded, even if it turned out that he was wrong in his application of the serious question test, the balance of convenience did not favour halting the road's construction pending the outcome of a trial. Accordingly, he dismissed the Lil'wat's application for an interlocutory injunction.

The failure of the Meares strategy in *Mount Currie Indian Band v. International Forest Products (Ure Creek* case) marked the beginning of a long hiatus in British Columbia. Similar attempts to protect sacred sites would not be made until after the Supreme Court of Canada handed down its own decision in the *Delgamuukw* case on 11 December 1997. Outside British Columbia, the same situation prevailed, with one exception. In Ontario, six months after the Lil'wat's application was dismissed, the Poplar Point Ojibway Nation applied – in conjunction with an (intended) action seeking a declaration of Aboriginal rights – for an interlocutory injunction to protect a sacred site. The threat in *McCrady v. Ontario,*[118] or the *High Falls* case, was not logging or logging-related operations but the construction of a hydroelectric dam.

The Namewaminikan (Sturgeon) River empties into Lake Nipigon near Beardmore, in northeastern Ontario. Located within the Ojibway people's traditional territory, the river possesses certain natural features of great significance to the Ojibway: a long stretch of rapids (Long Rapids) followed by a dramatic falls (High Falls); for convenience, I shall occasionally refer to the whole as the High Falls area. Within Ojibway culture, rushing water facilitates communication between the living and the dead. Thus, places where their ancestors are buried in proximity to rushing water are sacred to the Ojibway. The High Falls area not only is such a place, it is paradigmatic. It is, then, an area especially sacred to the local Ojibway, who include the Poplar Point Ojibway Nation.[119]

The Poplar Point Ojibway were forced to abandon their village in the 1940s due to cyanide pollution from mine tailings. They have never been compensated for their loss.[120] They decided to form their own band in April 1988. In spite of the fact that the individual members of the band were federally recognized or Status Indians, they were not granted the federally recognized status of *band* as defined by the *Indian Act*.[121] The band is still unrecognized. Although the Poplar Point Ojibway's traditional territory is within the area of the Robinson-Superior Treaty of 1850 (a pre-Confederation treaty negotiated with the Ojibway), they remain an unaffiliated band. Consequently, in spite of their efforts to press their land claim, a claim including the High Falls area, they are still without their own reserve lands.

In the late 1980s, Nipigon Power, an Ontario corporation, approached the Ontario Ministry of Natural Resources and other provincial and federal agencies about the possibility of building a small hydroelectric dam on the Namewaminikan River. Although an alternate site was available, the Ministry decided that from an environmental point of view, if a dam was to be built, the better site was just downriver from the High Falls. One of the consequences of building the dam there would be that the dam's reservoir would, when filled, cover the falls. After inquiries were made to the Minister of Culture and Communications, Nipigon was told that there were no known archaeological or burial sites in the proposed project area.[122] By the spring of 1991, Nipigon's High Falls hydroelectric project had obtained both the provincial and the federal go-ahead. In early August, Nipigon began moving equipment into the area, its first task being improvements to an existing road leading to the river. The company's goal was to have the High Falls project completed and to be selling power to Ontario Hydro by early December 1992.

On 7 August 1991, the day after Nipigon commenced work on the road to the project site, workers were met by a peaceful blockade. Among those manning the blockade were Chief Theron McCrady and other members of the Poplar Point Ojibway Nation, representatives of six Aboriginal communities affiliated with the Northern Lake Superior Aboriginal Association (NLSAA, of which Chief McCrady was then president),[123] and a number of non-Aboriginal residents of Beardmore who opposed the dam.

The blockade could not have been entirely unexpected. For starters, the dam site fell within the Poplar Point Ojibway's traditional territory and their claim to the area was being ignored. As a consequence, they were not consulted about the proposed project. After the project was approved, they had few remaining options. In a last-ditch effort to get their concerns before the provincial authorities, Chief McCrady wrote to the Minister of Environment on 6 June 1991 expressing his people's concerns about "the potential impacts of the project on our Aboriginal food and medicine harvesting rights and on *our sacred sites*" [emphasis added].[124] He asked the minister to order an environmental assessment before allowing the project to proceed. What Chief McCrady, along with many others, did not know was that the Ministry of Natural Resources had previously decided (fall 1998) that there would be no public environmental assessment. Thus, the Minister of Environment's negative response to Chief McCrady's request was preordained. In a letter signed on 9 July 1991, he listed his reasons for denying the request:

> [T]here are not significant environmental concerns; mitigative and compensation measures, as specified by the Federal Department of Fisheries and Oceans, should ensure that the adverse environmental impacts on the fisheries habitat are of a temporary nature;
>
> all the necessary requirements have been met by the proponent in order to obtain the necessary approvals and permits under all the relevant legislation;
>
> the concerns you raise centre around the broader issue of aboriginal rights and treaty rights, and not environmental assessment issues; and the MNR [Ministry of Natural Resources] has stated that, in the future, it will ensure that the Poplar Point Ojibway Nation will be consulted on all proposed waterpower developments in the Nipigon District.[125]

The minister was, of course, correct to point out that the concerns raised by Chief McCrady involved the broader issues of Aboriginal and treaty rights. What the minister may not have fully appreciated was that the chief had made his request out of necessity. Because the broader issues of their Aboriginal and treaty rights – including their rights to their sacred places – had been shut out of the official process, the Poplar Point Ojibway had nothing left but the narrower issues of environmental impact to argue.

The Ontario government responded quickly to the blockade. The Minister of Natural Resources agreed to postpone work on the High Falls project for an initial period of two weeks pending discussions with the protestors. On 9 August 1991, after being in place only two days, the blockade was removed.

On 22 August 1991, Chief McCrady, on behalf of an alliance of the protestors, and Ron Running, District Manager, on behalf of the Minister of Natural Resources, reached an agreement.[126] The agreement contained fourteen numbered paragraphs setting forth the steps that would be taken in connection with pre- and post-construction environmental impacts and monitoring of the High Falls project. The first four paragraphs, for instance, set forth certain soil, water, and fish sampling procedures to be carried out, in some cases before the flooding of the reservoir. The fifth paragraph provided for the establishment of a monitoring committee, whose terms of reference and members were to be negotiated by the district manager and Chief McCrady or their representatives. The tenth paragraph – in retrospect an especially significant paragraph – stated that "Ron Running [the District Manager] will request the Deputy Minister [of Natural Resources] that no construction activities will take place prior to Saturday, 31 Aug 91 within sight or sound of the High Falls to permit a traditional aboriginal gathering."[127] With the agreement in place, Nipigon was allowed to resume improving the road to its project site. On Monday, 26 August 1991, the day work resumed, the road's reconstruction was underway at a distance of about three kilometres from the High Falls. The Ministry of Natural Resources had given Nipigon permission to work up to but not within a one-kilometre buffer zone and had posted signs accordingly. The depth of the buffer zone was premised on the assumption that the falls would effectively muffle the noise of the construction equipment.

Although not mentioned in the 22 August agreement, the purpose of the traditional gathering at High Falls was connected to the area's sacredness. As Chief McCrady later explained, its purpose was to allow the area's Ojibway people to pay their "last respects to the River which would soon be raped and desecrated by the Dam."[128] The gathering, therefore, was to be a most sombre one. Thus, from the Ojibway point of view, to carry on construction within sight or sound of High Falls during the gathering would have been the height of disrespect.

On the morning of 27 August 1991, Chief McCrady and an elder who accompanied him attempted to drive to the gathering site. All was not as they had expected. The previous day's construction had made the road impassable to ordinary vehicles. Additionally, they were surprised to find the construction taking place only three kilometres from the gathering site and to learn that the workers had permission to operate their heavy equipment up to one kilometre from the site. The distances were, they felt, far from adequate. Angered by what they found, the pair immediately notified the Minister of Natural Resources that they considered the 22 August agreement void because of Nipigon's "flagrant, deliberate breach of the most important term in it," and that the Poplar Point Ojibway would not permit further work on the project until they received "satisfactory guarantees that ... [their] Aboriginal rights with respect to the River will not be violated."[129] Although the district manager wrote to Chief McCrady the next day, 28 August, assuring him of both Nipigon's commitment to ensure that the road would be passable throughout the week and the Ministry's willingness to expand the buffer zone if necessary, the blockade was re-established on 31 August.

On 3 September 1991, the Attorney General of Ontario obtained an injunction restraining Chief McCrady and the other protesters from interfering with Nipigon's construction. On that same day, the Poplar Point Ojibway launched an application for judicial review and sought an order quashing all land-use permits concerning the High Falls hydroelectric project. Two weeks later they also served a notice of motion in an intended action seeking an interlocutory injunction calling a halt to the project.

On 26-27 September, Mr. Justice Kurisko heard both the application for judicial review and the motion in an intended action for an interlocutory injunction shutting down the project. He adjourned the application for judicial review[130] and reserved his judgment concerning the injunction.

On 1 October 1991, Kurisko J. delivered his judgment dismissing the Poplar Point Ojibway's application. The (intended) case[131] on which the application was based did not, he concluded, raise a serious question for trial. Thus, the application failed to satisfy the first criterion for obtaining an interlocutory injunction.

It may be recalled that only six months earlier in British Columbia, the Lil'wat's application for interlocutory injunction in the *Ure Creek* case was similarly rejected because it had, the chambers judge concluded, failed to pose a serious question. It may also be recalled that the chambers judge felt constrained to conclude as he did because of the then recently delivered *Delgamuukw* trial decision. Although Kurisko J. arrived at the same conclusion as his British Columbia counterpart, he reasoned from very different legal premises, none of which were informed by the *Delgamuukw* decision.

The Poplar Point Ojibway were, however, prepared to address *Delgamuukw*. The action they intended to launch involved a claim of Aboriginal rights. In their submissions before Kurisko J., they claimed first that "the Poplar Point Ojibway Nation ... [is] a body of Indians within the meaning of section 91(24) of the *Constitution Act 1867* that has occupied and used the River and the area around the River since time immemorial."[132] They then claimed "that the [Namewaminikan] River and surrounding territory is within the area governed by the *Royal Proclamation of 1763* which guarantees that Aboriginal rights continue to exist until they have been extinguished by voluntary surrender or by conquest."[133] This claim's significance becomes fully apparent when it is noted that the Chief Justice of British Columbia, in his *Delgamuukw* decision, had concluded that "the *Royal Proclamation, 1763* has never had any application or operation in British Columbia."[134]

Having given the court a good reason to think that their general claim of Aboriginal rights posed a serious question for trial, the Poplar Point Ojibway then went on to articulate the specific rights that would, they said, be jeopardized by the construction of the High Falls dam. They included:

(1) the right to protect the fish and the fish spawning beds in the River; (2) *the right to prevent damage to sacred and cultural sites including, (i) burial grounds which will be inundated, (ii) the falls of the river which will be silenced by the dam, (iii) the River valley itself;* (3) the right to harvest food and medicinal plants which will be significantly damaged by flooding." [emphasis added][135]

Their basic argument, then, was that these Aboriginal rights – none of which, they said, had ever been extinguished – would be irreparably harmed if construction of the High Falls dam were allowed to continue.

As it turned out, Kurisko J. was able to bypass the issue of Aboriginal rights – and therefore the issues of the balance of convenience and irreparable harm – altogether. As he put it, "[t]he application falls to be determined on the undisputed fact that the applicants entered into a contract with [District Manager] Running and the Minister [of Natural Resources] on August 22, 1991, under which the applicants permitted construction of the hydro project to proceed."[136] The fact that the 22 August agreement set forth a number of steps to be taken in connection with what it termed "pre- and post-construction impacts" itself sufficed to prove that the parties to the agreement envisioned the project going forward. In short, then, when Chief McCrady "signed the [22 August] agreement on behalf of the Poplar Point Ojibway Nation, McCrady and the Poplar Point Ojibway Nation must be taken to have conceded they were forego- ing [sic] any claim for Aboriginal rights in return for concessions made by the Minister."[137]

As for the applicants' argument that Nipigon's road construction within three kilometres of the gathering site at High Falls violated a crucial term of the agreement and therefore rendered the agreement void, Kurisko J. had this to say: "I am satisfied that any breach of paragraph [ten] ... that may have occurred was the result of an error in judgment and was not motivated [by] the lack of respect for the traditions, rights or ceremonial customs of the Poplar Point Ojibway Nation. I am also satisfied the acts complained of do not constitute sufficient reason for terminating the entire agreement."[138] The agreement, then, remained in effect. And because it remained in effect, the High Falls project could "continue unimpeded by claims for Aboriginal rights."[139]

After dismissing the Poplar Point Ojibway's application for an interlocutory injunction, Kurisko J. added a final, curious comment. He said:

The willingness of the Minister [of Natural Resources] to abide by the terms of the agreement is a great advance over the deaf ears that were turned to the earlier entreaties by McCrady for an environmental assessment. As a result of the pressure and insistence of the applicants, the Minister has acknowledged that the people closest to the environment affected by the hydro project will have a say in the management of that environment. This is as it should be and as it should have been from the very outset of this project. The peaceful and non-violent conduct of the applicants in protecting their legitimate interests in their environment stands in enviable contrast to many of the protests conducted in this day and age by White Society. The Poplar Point Ojibway Nation has achieved a victory not only for itself but for all of the people of Northwestern Ontario. And the environment will be better and more secure as a result of this victory.[140]

It is not surprising that Kurisko J. should have praised Chief McCrady and the Poplar Point Ojibway for pressing the minister to give the local people a say in the High Falls hydroelectric project and for conducting a peaceful protest. It is curious, however, that he chose to refashion what was primarily a fight to protect a sacred site into a fight to protect the environment. While the comment may have been intended as little more than a piece of consolatory rhetoric, it nonetheless raises a doubt that the Poplar Point Ojibway's concerns over the sacredness of the High Falls area were properly appreciated.

Before turning to the next case, let me add a brief postscript. On 9 September 1992, almost a year after Kurisko J. dismissed the Poplar Point Ojibway's application for an interlocutory injunction, a construction worker found human skeletal remains on a knoll overlooking the High Falls. The remains, a brief examination later revealed, were those of an adult Amerindian male whose body had been ritually prepared for burial and buried at least 200 years ago. On 14 September, the Ontario Provincial Police notified the Registrar of Cemeteries of the worker's discovery. That same day, the Poplar Point Ojibway set up a new blockade, which once again brought Nipigon's project to a halt.

The next day, the Deputy Registrar of Cemeteries ordered the Ministry of Natural Resources to have an archaeological investigation made. The key questions to be answered were: (1) where the burial site was, (2) whether the burial was part of an unapproved Aboriginal peoples cemetery,[141] and, if so, (3) what the cemetery's boundaries were. The investigation promptly revealed that the burial site was on the upper slopes of the knoll overlooking the High Falls. There was little doubt also, based on the cultural information gathered by the archaeologist, that the burial was one of many[142] and therefore part of an unapproved Aboriginal peoples cemetery.[143] A designation of *unapproved Aboriginal peoples cemetery* meant that the provincial Crown would be required to negotiate with the Poplar Point Ojibway with a view to entering into a site disposition agreement.[144] The only difficult question, then, was the third: what were the cemetery's boundaries?

The investigating archaeologist, Professor Scott Hamilton, completed his final report on 19 October 1992. In it, he took up the question of the cemetery's boundaries. He prefaced his remarks by noting that from the Ojibway perspective, the burial places were merely parts, albeit integral parts, of a larger whole. He wrote: "According to the Elders, the actual burial places do not necessarily represent limits of the sacred area. The sacred character of the falls is what is important. The burials are an incidental part of that larger spiritual complex. Some Elders speak of the sacred place as being the entire High Falls locality, while others speak of the falls as they integrate into the larger spiritual value of the river between High Falls and Long Rapids."[145] He went on to explain that the damage to the area caused by construction together with the limitations the band had imposed on subsurface testing made it difficult to ascertain the present physical boundaries of the burial locality. In a follow-up letter to the Registrar, Professor Hamilton reiterated his point that from the Ojibway perspective the attempt to isolate the burial sites from the larger sacred system was misguided: "In order for you to proceed with decision-making you require a boundary around the extent of the burial site. I understand this necessity, and would like to oblige. However, it reflects a notion of the bounded 'sacred precinct' of a cemetery. This is a Judeo-Christian concept that has little relevance to Native spirituality. The burial(s) is an important secondary element of a much larger sacred system that involves the whole falls area. The current regulatory process is addressing the secondary element, but is ignoring the larger sacred issue."[146]

Relying on Professor Hamilton's final report, the Poplar Point Ojibway decided to apply for an order compelling the Registrar of Cemeteries "to declare the watershed of the Namewaminikan River, from the base of High Falls to the Twin Rapids, an 'unapproved Aboriginal Peoples Cemetery'," and for an injunction against any further construction pending the Registrar's decision.[147]

As before, Kurisko J. heard arguments. On 26 October 1992, he delivered his judgment, dismissing the application for an order compelling the Registrar to make the aforesaid declaration but granting the injunction pending the Registrar's decision.[148]

The injunction was short-lived, however. The following week, on 3 November 1992, the Registrar announced his decision. He declared "the site more particularly described as the upper slopes of the knoll overlooking the east bank of High Falls, and facing southwest toward the falls and downstream portion of the Namewaminikan River to be an unapproved aboriginal peoples' cemetery."[149] Since the knoll's upper slopes would be well above the dam reservoir's water line, what this meant was that Nipigon's construction could continue virtually unaffected and that the High Falls could be flooded as planned.

A fortnight later, dissatisfied with the Registrar's narrow determination of cemetery boundaries, the Poplar Point Ojibway applied for judicial review. Their application was unanimously dismissed.[150]

In the final analysis, the dispute over High Falls was a lose-lose battle. The local Ojibway people lost an especially sacred site – an inestimable and irreplaceable part of their culture. Nipigon Power finished its project but, due to financial and technical difficulties, its High Falls dam has never operated.[151]

The failure of the Meares strategy to protect sacred sites in the *Lower Tsitika Valley* case in late 1990 and the *Ure Creek* and *High Falls* cases in 1991 marked the beginning of a hiatus. It would be roughly eight years before the strategy would be re-employed. Although many things had changed (thanks largely to the Supreme Court of Canada's *Delgamuukw* decision), the results did not.

One case stands out: *Siska Indian Band v. British Columbia,*[152] or the *Siska Creek* case.

The Siska watershed, taking its name from Siska Creek, which flows into the Fraser River, is located east of the Fraser River and north of Boston Bar. Much of the watershed's timber was ravaged by a forest fire in the late 1950s. Thus, because it contained little marketable old-growth timber, it, unlike neighbouring watersheds, remained untouched by commercial logging at the start of the 1990s.

The Siska watershed falls within the traditional territory of the Siska Indian Band specifically and the Nlah7kápmx (Thompson) First Nation (to which they belong) more generally. The Nlah7kápmx are an Interior Salish people. The Siska people value the watershed for a number of reasons. It provides sustenance through fishing, hunting, and gathering. It contains the only stand of old-growth cedar within Siska territory, the cedar serving a variety of cultural purposes. Most important, however, the Siska watershed is a sacred area. The people still use the area for spiritual/religious ceremonies and activities, including vision quests. To the Siska, any significant human alteration of the watershed goes against the ethic of the place. Accordingly, they have long been public about their opposition to logging in the watershed.[153]

In the early 1990s, J.S. Jones Holdings, a relatively small logging company, began developing its plans for harvesting timber in the Siska watershed. Aware of the Siska Band's opposition, the company, with the provincial Crown's concurrence, attempted to identify specific conflicts and to modify its plans accordingly.

For example, an archaeological study of the area commissioned by the company, in which the Band participated, identified seventeen post-1846 culturally modified trees. As a result, the company and the Crown amended the company's forest development plan to exclude those trees from the relevant cutblock and to provide a buffer zone to protect them. As well, they modified the plan further to provide a riparian zone along Siska Creek to protect old-growth cedar trees and to preserve the habitat of certain species of wildlife about which the Band had expressed concern.[154]

In addition, the company "stated its intention to avoid interfering with other objects of importance as heritage to the Band, if any should be encountered."[155]

By the beginning of summer 1998, J.S. Jones was poised to begin road building from an adjacent forest licence area into the Siska Valley. Its immediate goal was to log the area during the summers of 1999 and 2000, with further logging to take place in later years. Although the company's short-term plan was to harvest only 2 percent of the Siska watershed's timber, that meant taking all of the watershed's available mature timber.

Shortly before J.S. Jones's road building was to commence, the Siska Band brought an application for judicial review to quash certain decisions of the district managers of the Lillooet and Chilliwack Forest Districts concerning the proposed logging and road building. In their application, the band sought two orders pending judicial review: (1) an injunction restraining the company's operations in the Siska watershed, and (2) an injunction restraining the Minister of Forests, the Minister of Small Business, Tourism and Culture, and the district managers from authorizing any logging or logging-related activities in the watershed. Since I will be presenting the details in the next chapter, it will suffice to note here simply that Mr. Justice Smith, in a decision delivered on 9 July 1998, dismissed the band's application for interlocutory relief.

In the middle of July 1998, J.S. Jones commenced constructing the access roads. The following year, shortly after being issued a cutting permit at the end of July 1999, the company was logging in the Siska Valley. On 6 October 1999, however, logging operations were brought to a halt. That morning a group of about forty Siska Band members blocked the road accessing the cutting area.[156] The next day, J.S. Jones applied for and was granted an interim injunction. The injunction was subsequently amended to continue until judgment had been given on its application for an interlocutory injunction. On 12 October 1999, the Siska Band launched an action seeking a declaration regarding its Aboriginal title and other Aboriginal rights in the Siska watershed. It also applied for an interlocutory injunction restraining J.S. Jones from interfering with its rights by its logging in the Siska watershed. On 19-20 October 1999, Mr. Justice Sigurdson heard both applications. And on 25 October, he delivered his judgment, dismissing the Siska Band's application and granting the logging company's.

Since both parties agreed that the other had raised a serious question for trial, the only issue Sigurdson J. had to determine was the balance of convenience. Both parties had, he was satisfied, established irreparable harm. J.S. Jones had shown that it would require the balance of the 1999 harvest of Siska Valley to keep its Boston Bar mill operating during the coming winter and that it had only a few weeks left to finish the harvest before weather would prevent further logging. An injunction halting the harvest would, the company argued, jeopardize not only a mill already at risk but also the company itself. The Siska Band, for their part, had shown that they were still able to enjoy the Siska Valley in its natural state. An injunction against them would, they urged, threaten their long-standing and ongoing economic, cultural, and spiritual connection to the valley.

Since both parties had established irreparable harm, Sigurdson J. decided, following Esson J.A.'s analysis of the *Meares Island* case,[157] that it fell to the Siska Band to establish that the Siska watershed was sufficiently unique to warrant the inference that the harm they would suffer outweighed not only the harm that J.S. Jones would suffer but also the larger (mainly economic) public interest factors that would otherwise tilt the balance of convenience in favour of the logging company. In support of the Siska Valley's uniqueness, the band argued that the area had never before been logged, that it contained very little mature timber, and that it was their preferred – in some cases, their only – area for pursuing their traditional sustenance, cultural, and spiritual pursuits.

In the *Lower Tsitika Valley* case, the chambers judge had found that the circumstances in which the Tlowitsis-Mumtagila had adduced their evidence undercut their claim for the area's uniqueness and suggested that the harm that they would suffer if the logging went forward was not sufficient to tilt the balance of convenience in their favour. Similarly, Sigurdson J. found that the facts that the band did not forthwith take steps to establish their Aboriginal title and rights after Smith J. refused their request for interlocutory relief at the end of October 1998, and that they delayed seeking an injunction until almost two and a half months after J.S. Jones was issued the cutting permit at the close of July 1999, called into question the band's claim for the uniqueness of the Siska watershed and suggested, therefore, that the harm they would suffer if the logging went forward was not sufficient to tilt the balance of convenience in their favour.

Another factor also, in Sigurdson J.'s estimation, diminished the Siska Band's claim of uniqueness. The band had given very little evidence showing specifically how J.S. Jones's logging would interfere with their asserted Aboriginal rights. Due to its lack of specificity, then, the evidence failed to single out the Siska Valley as unique compared with many other relatively pristine areas in British Columbia. Once again, what this implied was that the evidence did not support the conclusion that the harm the band would suffer if the logging went forward outweighed the overall harm that would accrue to the logging company and the public interest if it did not. Having concluded that the balance of convenience favoured J.S. Jones, Sigurdson J. granted the company's application and dismissed the Siska Band's.[158]

What Went Wrong?

It is a paradox that the Meares strategy succeeded in affording at least temporary protection to First Nations sacred sites in the earliest cases, where sacredness was either not explicitly mentioned or not emphasized, while it failed in subsequent cases, where sacredness was both explicitly mentioned and emphasized. The paradox is not of an insoluble sort, however. The change from early success to subsequent failure can be explained. In this section, I offer an explanation for the change.

As a starting point, it is best to set the *Ure Creek* and *High Falls* cases to one side. They are anomalies. The *Delgamuukw* trial decision rendered the Meares strategy temporarily nonviable in British Columbia. No claim of Aboriginal title or Aboriginal rights (other than non-exclusive usufructuary rights) could pose a serious question for trial. To speak accurately, then, the Meares strategy did not fail in the *Ure Creek* case for the simple reason that it could not have succeeded no matter the facts of the case. In the *High Falls* case, the First Nation entered into an agreement with the Crown that precluded seeking interlocutory relief based on an Aboriginal rights claim. Similarly, then, the Meares strategy cannot be said to have been tried and to have failed in the *High Falls* case for the reason that, given the agreement, it could not have succeeded.

This leaves only the bookend cases, the *Lower Tsitika Valley* and *Siska Creek* cases. Why did the Meares strategy fail in these cases?

A general answer is ready to hand: the Meares strategy failed because in both instances the cases foundered on the uniqueness requirement.

Albeit legally correct, the aforementioned general answer is only minimally illuminating, for it in turn raises the question of why those cases foundered on the uniqueness requirement. With this question, things become complicated. Sacredness and uniqueness are both relative and matters of degree. Sacred things are sacred relative to things that are not. Hence, we distinguish between what is sacred and what is, say, profane. Similarly, unique things are unique relative to things that are not. And so we distinguish between what is unique and what is, say, common. Among sacred things, some are more and some less sacred than others. Likewise, among unique things, some are more and some less unique than others. Now, since sacred things serve other than ordinary purposes or functions, sacred things are unique things. Consequently, sacred sites are unique sites and, moreover, more or less unique relative to other unique sites.

One of the propositions that the Lower Tsitika Valley and Siska Creek cases establish, then, is that the uniqueness that accompanies a site's sacredness need not qualify the site as sufficiently unique to warrant inter-locutory protection. In both cases, the petitioners established to the court's satisfaction that the site in question was sacred. What they failed to establish was that this fact – whether taken alone or in conjunction with other supported facts – implied a sufficient level of uniqueness.

The *Lower Tsitika Valley* and *Siska Creek* cases, it should be noted, sug-gest answers to two key subsidiary questions: (1) Does the level of a site's sacredness affect the level of a site's uniqueness? (2) May the level of a site's sacredness qualify it as sufficiently unique to warrant interlocutory protection? Both cases suggest that the answer to both questions is yes. In the *Lower Tsitika Valley* case, the chambers judge's analysis relied on the following counterfactual proposition: if the Lower Tsitika Valley were sufficiently unique, the Tlowitsis-Mumtagila would have asserted its sacred-ness sooner. What this proposition presupposes is that had the Tlowitsis-Mumtagila asserted the valley's sacredness sooner, the valley might have qualified as sufficiently unique. But what, one might ask, does the time at which the valley's sacredness was asserted have to do with the valley's sacredness? The time of assertion was, the chambers judge assumed, an indicator not of the valley's sacredness but of the degree of sacredness the Tlowitsis-Mumtagila attached to it. The chambers judge was suggesting, then, that if the Tlowitsis-Mumtagila had asserted the valley's sacredness sooner, he might have found, other things being equal, that it was sacred enough to qualify as sufficiently unique to tilt the balance of convenience in the Tlowitsis-Mumtagila's favour. In the *Siska Creek* case, the chambers judge similarly assumed that the Siska Band's delay in pursuing litigation was an indicator of the level of sacredness the band attached to the Siska Valley. Had the band acted with greater dispatch, he was suggesting, he might have found, again other things being equal, that the valley was sacred enough to qualify as sufficiently unique to tilt the balance of conve-nience in the band's favour. Both cases suggest that the level of a site's sacredness affects the level of its uniqueness, and that the level of a site's sacredness may, other things being equal, qualify it as sufficiently unique to warrant interlocutory protection.

The *Lower Tsitika Valley* and *Siska Creek* cases show that for the Meares strategy to succeed in obtaining at least temporary protection for their sacred sites, First Nations must do more than establish that the site in question is sacred. They must prove that it is highly sacred and that, as highly sacred, its integrity is crucial to their cultural identity and well-being. They must also, as the aforementioned pair of cases show, take care that they do nothing by their actions (leading up to and during litigation) that would suggest that the site is less than highly sacred to them.

These remarks do not, however, help to resolve the paradox stated in the opening paragraph. To reiterate, the paradox is that the Meares strategy succeeded in affording protection to First Nations sacred sites in the earliest cases, where sacredness was either not explicitly mentioned or not emphasized, while it failed in subsequent cases, such as in the *Lower Tsitika Valley* and *Siska Creek* cases, where sacredness was both explicitly mentioned and emphasized. The previous remarks would help to resolve the paradox only if it were true that the Nuu-chah-nulth, Kwakwak'wakw, and Gitksan and Wet'suwet'en had established the uniqueness of Meares Island, Deer Island, and the Shedin, respectively, on the basis of not only sacredness but also a high degree of sacredness. The paradox cannot be resolved by pointing to the failure of the Tlowitsis-Mumtagila and the Siska Band to prove that their sacred areas were highly sacred.

Perhaps some headway can be made by examining something the paradox presupposes. It presupposes, among other things, that the mere addition of sacredness (as an explicit and emphasized feature) in the subsequent cases should have added significant weight to the First Nations' side in the balance of convenience test. Relying on this assumption, one might take the failure of the subsequent cases to indicate that the addition of sacredness added little or no weight to the First Nations' side. One might conclude that the courts have a "tin ear" when it comes to talk of sacredness. While the conclusion undoubtedly applies to some judges, it does not apply to all. More important, however, one might draw a rather different, more useful conclusion relying on the same assumption. For one might hold both that the mere addition of sacredness in the subsequent cases should have added significant weight to the First Nations' side in the balance of convenience test and, what is more, that the addition of sacredness did add significant weight to the First Nations' side. One might then take the failure of the subsequent cases to indicate that the bar had been raised.

Had the bar been raised? If it had, we can say with a high degree of certainty when and by whom. Esson J.A., in his judgment in the *Westar* case, proposed as a general rule derived from the British Columbia Court of Appeal's decision in the *Meares Island* case that "the court should not grant an injunction if the economic consequences of doing so would have a serious impact upon the economic health of the province, the region or the logging company."[159] He further proposed as an exception, also derived from the Court of Appeal's decision, that the court could, nonetheless, grant an injunction with regard to "particular sites which have unique qualities."[160] (For the sake of convenience, I shall sometimes refer to these two propositions as "Esson's Rule.") One might reasonably argue that because of Esson J.A.'s interpretation of the Court of Appeal's decision in the *Meares Island* case, the Court of Appeal in the *Westar* case placed greater emphasis on the public interest in the balance of convenience test than the earlier Court had placed on it and that subsequent court decisions simply followed suit.[161] Accordingly, one might reasonably conclude that the greater weight given to public interest resulted in the subsequent failures of the Meares strategy to protect sacred sites.

It is interesting to note here that the aforementioned pair of propositions that Esson J.A. claimed were derived from the Court of Appeal's decision in the *Meares Island* case do not state the rule followed by the majority of the Court in that case. The majority in the *Meares* case argued that the case was unique in an effort to counter the charge that an injunction granted there would cascade into a rash of similar injunctions across the province. The majority did not decide, as both Esson J.A. (writing for the majority) and Locke J.A. (in dissent) suggested in *Westar,* that in spite of the serious economic consequences that would befall the company, the region, or the province if an injunction were granted, it would make an exception in the case of Meares Island because of its "unique qualities." Indeed, the majority granted the injunction with the belief that the amount of timber on the island was insignificant to MacMillan Bloedel's local and regional operations, and therefore to the local, regional, and provincial economies.

Thus, the uniqueness mentioned in Esson's Rule does not correspond to the uniqueness mentioned by the majority in the *Meares Island* case. Esson's Rule posits uniqueness as a requirement for granting an injunction as an exception to a general rule against granting injunctions in Aboriginal rights cases where serious economic consequences would follow. The majority of the Court of Appeal in the *Meares Island* case argued that the case was unique and that as such it could not cause a cascade of similar injunctions across the province, shutting down the province's forest and other resource-related industries. One of the features that made the *Meares* case unique, the majority insisted, was that an injunction would have no serious economic consequences for MacMillan Bloedel, the region, or the province.[162] In short, the uniqueness of Esson's Rule takes serious economic consequences as a given, while the uniqueness advanced by the majority of the Court of Appeal in the *Meares Island* case excludes them.

Esson's Rule does not faithfully represent the majority of the Court of Appeal in the *Meares Island* case but neither does it contradict it. It is always open to a court to grant an injunction in spite of serious economic consequences provided that the circumstances justify it. The working assumption is that circumstances will seldom justify it. Esson's Rule merely states that this is so for interlocutory applications based on claims of Aboriginal rights. Nothing in the majority's decision in the *Meares Island* case suggested otherwise.

To return to the main thread, what does this have to do with the argument that the Court of Appeal's decision in the *Westar* case marked a shift in the weight given to public interest in interlocutory proceedings based on claims of Aboriginal rights and that the greater weight accorded to public interest was responsible for the subsequent failures of the Meares strategy to protect sacred sites? Just this. If we believe that Meares Island, Deer Island, and the Shedin met the uniqueness requirement articulated in Esson's Rule, then we will need to explain why the Lower Tsitika Valley and the Siska Valley did not. The need will seem especially pressing given that neither the Lower Tsitika Valley nor the Siska Valley seem any less unique than the Shedin. One fairly obvious explanation suggests itself, that is, that greater weight was given to public interest. The problem with the explanation is that it assumes (falsely) that Meares Island and the Shedin met the uniqueness requirement articulated in Esson's Rule.[163] The injunctions granted in the *Meares Island* and *Westar* cases were not perceived as a serious economic threat to the logging companies, the regions, or the province. They were not, as the aforementioned assumption would have it, treated as exceptions to the general rule against granting interlocutory injunctions in cases where such serious economic consequences will follow. Since it is a thesis based on a false assumption, it is probably better to look elsewhere than to a purported shift in the weight given to public interest to explain why the Meares strategy failed to protect sacred sites in subsequent cases.

A more satisfying explanation is, I think, to be found by observing that the courts that granted the injunctions in the *Meares Island* and *Westar* cases restraining road building and logging operations concluded that the injunctions did not give rise to serious negative public interest concerns. Thus, there were no such public interest considerations weighing against granting them. On the other hand, the courts that refused the injunctions in the *Lower Tsitika Valley* and *Siska Creek* cases concluded that injunctions in those cases would engage serious negative public interest concerns. Those concerns, in the form of serious economic consequences for the logging companies, the local communities, the regions, and perhaps the province, weighed heavily against granting the injunctions. With serious negative public interest concerns engaged, the courts in the *Lower Tsitika Valley* and *Siska Creek* cases would have granted injunctions only if, following Esson's Rule, the petitioners had established a sufficient degree of uniqueness to justify it.

The explanation for the failure of the Meares strategy in the subsequent cases is thus twofold: it failed, first, because, unlike in the earlier cases, serious negative public interest concerns were engaged and, second, because uniqueness sufficient to override those concerns was not established.[164]

The paradox is resolved in this way. The Meares strategy failed to protect sacred sites in subsequent cases where sacredness was both explicitly mentioned and emphasized, first, because, unlike in the earlier cases, serious negative public interest concerns were engaged and, second, because uniqueness sufficient to override those concerns was not established. Basically, while sacredness might have weighed heavily in favour of granting the injunctions in other circumstances, in the *Lower Tsitika Valley* and *Siska Creek* cases, with serious negative public interest concerns engaged, it seems unlikely that sacredness alone, even of the highest degree, could have tilted the balance of convenience in favour of the First Nations.

4
In Canada's Courts: The Haida Strategy

The Meares strategy is a litigation strategy available to First Nations whose off-reserve sacred sites are under threat. Adopting the Meares strategy, First Nations try to leverage their claims of Aboriginal or treaty rights into at least temporary protection of their sacred sites. The Haida strategy is an alternative litigation strategy whereby First Nations may also try to leverage their claims of Aboriginal or treaty rights into at least temporary protection of their sacred sites. Although the Meares strategy relies on interlocutory proceedings and the Haida strategy on judicial review, both involve attempts to protect sacred sites by asking a court to give a measure of legal effect to asserted but unestablished Aboriginal or treaty rights. There is, however, an important difference in relation to the origins of the legal effect. What, if any, legal effect the Meares strategy gives to a First Nation's asserted Aboriginal or treaty rights depends entirely on the court considering the petition for interlocutory relief. The First Nation's claimed rights acquire no legal effect unless the court finds sufficient prospective warrant to give them legal effect, usually in the form of an interlocutory injunction protecting them against certain proscribed interference pending their establishment or rejection at trial. The Haida strategy rests on the proposition that a First Nation's asserted but unestablished Aboriginal (or disputed treaty) rights may have a measure of legal effect prior to the litigation process. More specifically, it rests on the proposition that such asserted but unestablished rights may trigger legally enforceable constitutional duties on the part of the Crown. Thus, First Nations who employ the Haida strategy are not asking courts to give their asserted but unestablished Aboriginal rights over their sacred sites legal effect in view of their prospects for future confirmation at trial, but rather to agree that those asserted rights already possess legal effect.

The Haida strategy has only recently taken clear shape. That it has is due largely to the recent decisions of the British Columbia Court of Appeal in the *Taku River* and *Haida* cases. Not surprisingly, no First Nation has yet employed the Haida strategy (in any strict sense of the term[1]) in an attempt to protect the use or integrity of a sacred site. Nonetheless, there are a few earlier cases in which First Nations have tried to employ what may be termed a *proto-Haida* strategy. Three cases stand out: *Halfway River First Nation v. British Columbia (Ministry of Forests)*, the earlier *Siska Creek* case, and *Kelly Lake Cree Nation v. Canada (Ministry of Energy and Mines)*, or the *Twin Sisters* cases.

The *Taku River* and *Haida* Cases

I shall discuss all three cases presently. First, however, I want to summarize the *Taku River* and *Haida* cases. With some understanding of these two cases in hand, readers will be better able to navigate the factual, legal, and other complexities of the second and third sections of this chapter.

The *Taku River* case was prompted by the joint decision of the Minister of Energy, Mines and Petroleum Resources and the Minister of Environment, Lands and Parks in March 1998 to issue a Project Approval Certificate authorizing Redfern Resources Limited to proceed with its proposal to reopen the Tulsequah Chief Mine, a multi-metal (copper, lead, zinc, gold, and silver) mine in northwestern British Columbia. The Tulsequah Chief Mine, whose earlier operation began and ended in the 1950s, is located on the Tulsequah River and therefore within both the Taku River watershed and the Taku River Tlingit First Nation's traditional territory. As a crucial element of its proposal, Redfern's plans included the construction of a road 160 kilometres long for the purposes of providing access to the mine and transporting ore north to Atlin, British Columbia. During the mine's previous life, the ore was barged down the Taku River to Juneau, Alaska. The planned road would, it so happened, "open up the heartland of the Tlingit territory for the first time,"[2] the area "where their traditional land use activities are most concentrated."[3]

Redfern initiated the process of having its proposal to reopen the Tulsequah Chief Mine considered in September 1994. Two months later, the Tulsequah Chief Project Committee was created. The committee's functions included coordinating the overall review of the project proposal and, at the end of the review process, providing its recommendations to the ministers responsible for making the final decision. The Taku River Tlingit First Nation was invited and accepted the invitation to join the committee. In November 1996, Redfern, after tailoring its proposal to meet the project committee's final project report specifications, submitted its Tulsequah Chief Project Report to the Environmental Assessment Office for review. In August 1997, the Environmental Assessment Office accepted Redfern's revised project report for public review. In March 1998, the Tulsequah Chief Project Committee submitted its Recommendations Report to the provincial ministers for their final decision.[4] The majority of the committee recommended the project's approval. Dissatisfied with the project committee's Recommendations Report, the Taku River Tlingit First Nation decided to submit its own.[5] Both the committee's and the Tlingits' reports were provided to the ministers on 12 March 1998. The following day, the Minister of Energy, Mines and Petroleum Resources signed the reasons for the decision to approve Redfern's project. A day shy of a week later, the Minister of Environment, Lands and Parks added her signature. That same day, 19 March 1998, Redfern was issued the Project Approval Certificate.

At every stage of the environmental review process leading up to the ministers' decision, the Taku River Tlingit First Nation expressed its concerns about Redfern's proposal to reopen the mine generally and its plan to construct the access road particularly. The Tlingits' chief concern was that the project would threaten their sustainability as a people. Their economic, social, and cultural system is, they explained, rooted in the land and their uses of the land and its natural resources.[6] The proposed project, particularly the road, would, they argued, disrupt their traditional patterns of use, loosen their connection to the land, and thus threaten their sustainability as a people. Were the road built, it would, they insisted, constitute both an immediate and a long-term disruption to their traditional patterns of use. It would constitute an immediate disruption through its adverse effects on habitat, fish and wildlife, and the Tlingits' harvesting needs and practices. It would constitute a long-term disruption by making the heart of Tlingit territory easily accessible to outsiders and inviting further Crown-sanctioned resource exploitation.

The Taku River Tlingits also articulated several related concerns, including concerns that the proposed project would compromise their treaty negotiations and interfere with their Aboriginal rights. The First Nation had been involved in treaty negotiations since 1984, initially with the federal government in its Comprehensive Claims process and later with both the federal and provincial governments in the British Columbia Treaty Process.[7] Permitting Redfern's project to go forward prior to the conclusion of their treaty negotiations would, they explained, "prejudice and limit the options available [to them as to their future power to decide for themselves how to use their land and resources] ... in ... treaty negotiations."[8] Such advance diminishment of their future decision-making power would, they suggested, threaten their future viability as a people. The proposed project would also, they asserted, impact negatively on the exercise of their Aboriginal rights, including Aboriginal title and Aboriginal rights connected with their harvest of the area's natural resources. As these rights serve to protect their relationship with the land, upon which their sustainability as a people depends, the project's effect on the exercise of their Aboriginal rights would, the Tlingits implied, pose an added threat to their sustainability as a people.

Shortly after the provincial ministers' decision to issue the Project

Approval Certificate in March 1998, the Taku River Tlingit First Nation applied for judicial review, asking the British Columbia Supreme Court to, among other things, quash the decision and set aside the certificate. Originally, the Tlingits advanced nine grounds in support of their application, three of which involved issues requiring a determination of Aboriginal rights and title.[9] But before their application was to be heard, the respondents, including the aforementioned ministers, applied "for an order that those issues raised in the petition for judicial review which require proof of aboriginal rights or aboriginal title be severed from the petition and referred to the trial list."[10] The respondents argued "that questions of aboriginal rights and title are not suitable for summary determination because such questions raise complex issues of fact and law."[11] Siding with the respondents, Madam Justice Kirkpatrick, the chambers judge, referred "the issues concerning the determination of the Tlingits' claims of aboriginal right and title ... to the trial list."[12]

Most of the issues remaining to be determined when Kirkpatrick J. heard the Tlingits' petition in March 2000 were standard administrative law fare, such as whether the ministers had breached rules of procedural fairness in arriving at their decision to give the go-ahead to Redfern's project. To the vexation of the provincial Crown, however, there remained also – despite the prior severance of issues requiring a determination of the Tlingits' claims of Aboriginal title and rights – issues as to whether the Crown owed constitutional and fiduciary duties to the Tlingits and, if so, whether it breached the duties it owed during the project review process leading up to the ministers' decision to approve the project.

Stated most generally, the main constitutional issue was whether s. 35(1) of the *Constitution Act, 1982* obliged the Crown to effectively address the substance of the Tlingits' concerns – insofar as they were frameable in terms of Aboriginal rights – prior to its decision to approve Redfern's project. The Tlingits, citing several court judgments, including the British Columbia Court of Appeal's majority decision in the *Halfway River* case (to be discussed presently), argued basically that s. 35(1) obliged the Crown to safeguard their sustainability as a people throughout its decision-making process. Moreover, they added, the Crown failed to fulfill its constitutional obligation by failing to address a number of their central concerns bearing on their sustainability. The respondents, citing several Supreme Court of Canada judgments, including *Sparrow,* countered that "s. 35 of the *Constitution Act, 1982* is not engaged until such time as the Tlingits have established [in a court of law] the aboriginal rights and title they say would be unjustifiably infringed by the Project."[13]

As for the issue of the Crown's fiduciary obligations, the Tlingits argued that the Crown owed them fiduciary obligations arising "from the Crown's general fiduciary relationship to aboriginal peoples, the Crown's unilateral powers [as expressed in its discretionary power regarding Redfern's project], and the Tlingits' corresponding vulnerability."[14] Specifically, the Crown had, the Tlingits said, duties to meaningfully consult with them about, and to effectively address, their concerns – duties, they added, the Crown had failed to fulfill. The respondents relied on their previous argument, that is, that the Crown's fiduciary duty to the Tlingits would not be engaged until the Tlingits had established their Aboriginal rights and title in a court of law.

In her judgment delivered on 28 June 2000, Kirkpatrick J. allowed the Taku River Tlingit First Nation's application. She found the ministers' decision to approve the Tulsequah Chief Mine Project invalid on administrative law, constitutional, and fiduciary grounds. As for the administrative law grounds, she concluded that the final stages of the decision-making process were tainted by substantive and procedural errors. Basically, she found that the decision to approve the project was made without either prior determination of the effects that the road would have on the Tlingits' sustainability as a people or adequate consideration of information detailing and confirming their concerns.

As for the constitutional law grounds, Kirkpatrick J. found generally that, contrary to what the respondents had argued, "the weight of authority, particularly emanating from the Supreme Court of Canada, [supports the proposition] that the existence of aboriginal interests [not yet established as Aboriginal rights in a court of law] should inform governments who make decisions which are likely to affect those interests."[15] It would, of course, have been unfair to hold the provincial Crown accountable for Aboriginal interests of which it was not or could not have been aware. The Tlingits' interests were well known, however. As Kirkpatrick J. observed:

> The federal government agreed to negotiate land claims with the Tlingits in 1984 on the basis of a preliminary determination that they had aboriginal rights in their territory flowing from their pre-existing use and occupation of the land and resources of the area. This, together with the fact that the federal government accepted the Tlingits' claim under the Comprehensive Land Claims Policy, was known to the provincial government when it entered into a framework agreement to negotiate with the Tlingits under the B.C. treaty process. Furthermore, the Tlingits have asserted their aboriginal rights at all stages of the environmental review.[16]

Given the Crown's knowledge not only of the Tlingits' claims but also of the apparent strength of their claims, "the Ministers should have been mindful," the chambers judge found, "of the possibility that their decision might infringe aboriginal rights." In the circumstances, they had a constitutional duty "to ensure that they had effectively addressed the substance of the

Tlingits' concerns with respect to when, and on what terms and conditions, the mineral rights to be exploited by Redfern should be developed."[17] Because they made their decision without having effectively addressed the substance of the Tlingits' concerns, especially those bearing on their sustainability as a people, the ministers violated their constitutional duty to recognize and affirm the Taku River Tlingit First Nation's Aboriginal rights.

As for the fiduciary grounds for finding the ministers' decision invalid, Kirkpatrick J. agreed with the Tlingits that the Crown had fiduciary obligations to fulfill in the review process. The Crown's obligations included, she held, duties to meaningfully consult with the Tlingits and to consider solutions to disputes involving their concerns.[18] Although the Crown had fulfilled its fiduciary obligations during the early and middle stages of the review process, in its rush to complete the last stages of the process, it failed to fully inform itself of the Tlingits' final concerns (expressed mainly in their Recommendations Report). Because it had failed to fully inform itself of their final concerns, and therefore failed to consider ways of addressing them, it failed to satisfy its fiduciary obligations to the Tlingits.

Having decided to quash the ministers' decision to approve the Tulsequah Chief Mine Project, Kirkpatrick J. ordered the matter referred back to them "for reconsideration after a revised project committee report, which meaningfully addresses the Tlingits' concerns, has been delivered to the Ministers."[19]

The Attorney General of British Columbia, the Minister of Energy, Mines and Petroleum Resources, the Minister of Environment, Lands and Parks, and the other respondents in the earlier proceedings (henceforth, the appellants) immediately appealed the chambers judge's decision.[20] The appellants sought mainly to have the British Columbia Court of Appeal set aside Kirkpatrick J.'s orders quashing the ministers' decision to approve Redfern's project and referring the matter back for reconsideration. They argued that the chambers judge erred chiefly in finding, first, that the Crown had failed to satisfy its administrative law duties and, second, that it had constitutional and fiduciary duties to consult with the Taku River Tlingits about the project. Regarding the second alleged error, the appellants' main submission was that "the constitutional or fiduciary obligation to consult with First Nations, as distinct from any administrative law duty of procedural fairness, only arises after there has been a determination that the First Nation has existing aboriginal or treaty rights under s. 35 of the *Constitution Act, 1982*, and that those rights may be infringed by Crown sanctioned activities."[21] The appellants also made the subsidiary submission that because a judicial consideration of the issues concerning the Crown's constitutional and fiduciary duties presupposes a prior determination of the Tlingits' Aboriginal rights and title, and because the chambers judge had previously severed the issues requiring a determination of their Aboriginal rights and title, the chambers judge erred by considering constitutional and fiduciary issues not properly before her.[22]

The British Columbia Court of Appeal delivered its judgment on 31 January 2002, dismissing the appeal of the chambers judge's order quashing the Project Approval Certificate. The Court appeared to agree that the Crown had, contrary to the chambers judge's findings, satisfied its administrative duties during its review of the Tulsequah Chief Mine Project.[23] But it also, more significantly, appeared to agree that the Crown had, contrary to the appellants' submission, constitutional and/or fiduciary duties to consult with the Taku River Tlingits about their asserted but unestablished Aboriginal rights prior to its decision to approve the project.[24] The Court split two to one, however, on whether the Crown had fulfilled those duties. Madam Justice Rowles, with Madam Justice Huddart's concurrence, held that the Crown had failed to satisfy its constitutional and fiduciary duties. Madam Justice Southin, finding it "plain that the Tlingit have some sort of rights in northwestern British Columbia" and thus rejecting the appellants' claim that the Crown had "no duty at all,"[25] concluded that its consultation efforts had satisfied whatever duties it owed.

Because of her highly enthymemic approach to the issue of whether the chambers judge had erred about the Crown's constitutional and fiduciary duties, the full force of Rowles J.A.'s reasoning does not reveal itself on initial reading. To appreciate its full force, it is crucial, when trying to follow her reasoning,[26] to keep in mind the main question under consideration: did the chambers judge err in finding that the Crown had constitutional and fiduciary duties to consult with the Taku River Tlingits about the effects of the proposed project on their asserted but unestablished Aboriginal rights and title prior to the final decision to approve the project? The appellants argued, of course, that the chambers judge erred because the Crown, they insisted, has no constitutional or fiduciary duty to consult with First Nations about the effects of contemplated activities on their Aboriginal rights until such rights have been established in court proceedings. (For the sake of convenience, I shall henceforth refer to the appellants' position that the Crown's constitutional and fiduciary duties of consultation are contingent upon the establishment of aboriginal rights in a court of law as the *Crown's Fundamental Position*. Also, since it was the Attorney General of British Columbia specifically who advanced the position, I shall henceforth speak more often of the Crown and its position, its argument, and so on than of the appellants generally.) As authority for its Fundamental Position, the Crown cited several Supreme Court of Canada decisions, including most importantly *Sparrow* and *Delgamuukw*. Rowles J.A., as I have already noted, answered the main question in the negative.

Her supporting reasoning proceeded in two stages. In the first, she refuted the Crown's Fundamental Position by showing that the Supreme

Court of Canada's decisions do not support it. In the second, she showed that the Supreme Court's decisions do support the chambers judge's finding that the Crown had constitutional and fiduciary duties to consult with the Tlingits about their asserted but unestablished Aboriginal rights and title prior to making the decision to approve the mine project.

Through her patient assembly and analysis of the passages cited by the Crown, Rowles J.A. demonstrated that the Supreme Court of Canada's decisions neither state nor imply the Crown's Fundamental Position that it has no constitutional or fiduciary duties to consult about the effects of a contemplated activity on a First Nation's Aboriginal rights prior to the establishment of those rights in a court of law. Accordingly, she drew the conclusion that the Court's decisions do not, contrary to the Crown's assertion, support the Crown's Fundamental Position.

Rowles J.A. pushed her reasoning further, however. She also demonstrated that the Crown's Fundamental Position is inconsistent with the Supreme Court of Canada's decisions in at least three ways. First, the Crown's Fundamental Position is, she observed, inconsistent with what the Court has said about the Crown's historical fiduciary role vis-à-vis Aboriginal peoples. For, she explained, "[t]o accept the Crown's proposition that the obligation to consult is only triggered when an aboriginal right has been established in court proceedings would ignore the substance of what the Supreme Court has said, not only in *Sparrow* but in earlier decisions which have emphasized the responsibility of government to protect the rights of Indians arising from the special trust relationship created by history, treaties and legislation."[27] Second, the Crown's Fundamental Position is also, she noted, inconsistent with the Supreme Court's insistence that s. 35(1) "provides a solid constitutional base upon which subsequent [treaty] negotiations can take place."[28] Were the Crown correct in saying "that establishment of the aboriginal rights or title in court proceedings is required before consultation is required," Rowles J.A. reasoned, it "would effectively end any prospect of meaningful negotiation or settlement of Aboriginal land claims."[29]

Third and finally, the Crown's Fundamental Position is, Rowles J.A. found, inconsistent with what the Supreme Court has identified as the purpose of s. 35(1) relative to Aboriginal rights. Because some sense of the reasoning underlying this conclusion is crucial to appreciating the full force of her larger analysis, a closer investigation is warranted. I begin, then, with the purpose of s. 35(1). In *Van der Peet*, the Court stated that "what s. 35(1) does [by recognizing and affirming the existing Aboriginal rights of Aboriginal peoples] is provide the constitutional framework through which the fact that aboriginals lived on the land in distinctive societies, with their own practices, traditions and cultures, is acknowledged and reconciled with the sovereignty of the Crown."[30] Although the

Court associated two basic purposes with s. 35(1), acknowledgment and reconciliation, clearly, since the acknowledgment of the pre-existence of aboriginal societies is ordered to their reconciliation with Crown sovereignty, reconciliation is its ultimate, and therefore its more basic, purpose.

According to the Supreme Court of Canada's jurisprudence on s. 35(1), the constitutionalization of Aboriginal rights in 1982 yielded a framework for reconciliation fashioned, like a primary supporting arch, from two complementary halves. On one side, the constitutionalization of Aboriginal rights placed restraints on the Canadian state's claimed sovereignty over Aboriginal peoples and their lands. Henceforth, it could neither extinguish Aboriginal rights unilaterally nor interfere with the exercise of those rights as it pleased.[31] On the other side, the constitutionalization of Aboriginal rights not only constitutionally secured rights that had previously enjoyed only common law protection[32] but also – corresponding to the restraints placed on the state's power to interfere with the exercise of those rights – cleared the way for Aboriginal peoples to exercise their rights more freely and thus more fully within broader Canadian society.

But if the hoped-for reconciliation is to be effected, and thus if s. 35(1) is to work its purpose, the basic framework must be wholly in place. Had the constitutionalization of Aboriginal rights yielded a framework consisting only of the restraint on the Canadian state's extinguishment power coupled with the increased security for Aboriginal rights, the result would not have altered the pre-1982 social and political dynamics and thus would not have set the reconciliation process in motion. The further restraint on the state's power to interfere with the exercise of Aboriginal rights, together with the corresponding increase in the freedom to exercise those rights, was necessary. The latter pair of complementary factors is what, in the final analysis, motivates the parties to seek reconciliation.

The Crown has, then, a twofold constitutional duty to limit its interference with the exercise of Aboriginal rights and to ensure their free and full exercise (that is, to ensure that Aboriginal peoples are able to sustain those practices, customs, and traditions central to their distinctive cultures[33]). Following the Supreme Court of Canada's jurisprudence, the twofold duty flows from the fundamental constitutional duty to recognize and affirm Aboriginal rights set forth in s. 35(1). But the Crown cannot properly discharge its constitutional duty to limit its interference with the exercise of Aboriginal rights and to ensure their free and full exercise unless it consults with Aboriginal peoples about their rights in an effort either to avoid their infringement or, when there are "compelling and substantial" legislative objectives counselling otherwise,[34] to proceed with "sensitivity to and respect for the rights of aboriginal peoples."[35] As a necessary condition for the Crown's satisfaction of its twofold constitutional duty, such consultation is itself a constitutional duty.

The Crown's Fundamental Position would, were it correct, undermine the constitutional foundations of the reconciliation process and thus "would," as Rowles J.A. stated, "largely negate the purpose of the constitutional protection provided by s. 35(1)."[36] Now I can explain how. Given that the Crown has a constitutional duty to consult when making a decision involving a potentially infringing activity – the duty being itself an integral part of its twofold constitutional duty to limit its interference with the exercise of Aboriginal rights and to ensure their free and full exercise – were the Crown's Fundamental Position correct, the Crown would not be burdened by the aforesaid twofold duty until the rights in question have been established in a court of law. But if the Crown is not so burdened, this means that the basic framework – said by the Supreme Court of Canada to undergird the reconciliation process – not only was not wholly in place when Aboriginal rights were constitutionalized in 1982 but also will never be wholly in place. Because its twofold constitutional duty to limit its interference with the exercise of Aboriginal rights and to ensure their free and full exercise must, according to the Crown's Fundamental Position, await the establishment of Aboriginal rights, and because their establishment involves an often prohibitively expensive, time-consuming, case-by-case process, the basic framework undergirding the reconciliation process will only ever be in place to the extent necessary to ensure the free and full exercise of *established* Aboriginal rights. Moreover, it will only ever be in place to the extent necessary to ensure the free and full exercise of established Aboriginal rights in those places where those established rights subsist. Hence, the basic framework undergirding the reconciliation process will never be wholly in place and, to the extent that it is in place, it will only ever be present in Canada in patchwork fashion. But if, as the Crown' Fundamental Position implies, the basic framework's purchase in Canadian society depends upon the establishment of Aboriginal rights, the reconciliation process it undergirds will only ever have a very partial effect. The reconciliation of Aboriginal peoples with the Crown's assertion of sovereignty envisioned by the Supreme Court of Canada will thus be largely and indefinitely postponed. The Crown's Fundamental Position is therefore, as Rowles J.A. rightly noted, at odds with s. 35(1)'s purpose.

Besides showing that the Supreme Court of Canada's decisions do not support the Crown's Fundamental Position considered in its own right, Rowles J.A. also showed that the Court's decisions fail to support a key proposition presupposed by the Crown's Fundamental Position.

The Crown's Fundamental Position is purportedly derived from the Supreme Court of Canada's jurisprudence on s. 35(1). It is not, as Rowles J.A. proved, derived directly therefrom. Therefore, if it is derived, it must be derived indirectly from other things the Court more or less plainly holds. The most obvious and promising candidate for the Crown's first premise is the unassailable claim that a constitutional or fiduciary duty to consult with Aboriginal peoples about their Aboriginal rights extends only to their *existing* Aboriginal rights. Section 35(1) protects only existing Aboriginal rights. Extinguished rights cannot trigger legal duties.

It is not logically possible, however, to derive the Crown's Fundamental Position from the aforementioned premise alone. A further premise is required. That premise is this: Aboriginal rights do not exist until they have been established in a court of law. The resulting syllogism is this: (1) only existing Aboriginal rights can trigger the Crown's constitutional and fiduciary duties to consult; (2) only Aboriginal rights established in a court of law exist; therefore, (3) only established Aboriginal rights can trigger the Crown's constitutional and fiduciary duties to consult. The syllogism's conclusion is, of course, a version of the Crown's Fundamental Position. If the Crown wishes to claim that its Fundamental Position is derived from the first premise, it must accept the second or middle premise as what is needed to close the logical gap between its starting premise and its desired conclusion. It was the second premise that I referred to earlier when I spoke of a key proposition presupposed by the Crown's Fundamental Position.

As she did with the Crown's Fundamental Position considered by itself, Rowles J.A. showed that the key proposition is neither stated nor implied in the Court's decisions[37] and that it is inconsistent with those decisions. As to its inconsistency, after setting forth the relevant passages, she noted that the Court's decisions in *Sparrow* and *Van der Peet* "make clear that aboriginal rights and title were not created by the *Constitution Act, 1982* but pre-dated the constitutionalization of those rights."[38]

Appreciating that the Crown's submission – that the Supreme Court of Canada's decisions support its Fundamental Position – possessed surface plausibility, Rowles J.A. went on to identify its source. The submission's surface plausibility rested, she found, on a misreading of the Court's remarks, most notably its remarks in *Sparrow*, on what is required for an Aboriginal rights defence to succeed in cases involving a prosecution for a regulatory offence.

A successful Aboriginal rights defence requires, to reduce it to its essentials, the establishment of two things: (1) that the act that gave rise to the charge was an exercise of an existing Aboriginal right, and (2) that the Crown's interference with the right's exercise was inconsistent with its constitutional obligation under s. 35(1) to recognize and affirm existing Aboriginal rights. If it is established that the Crown's interference was inconsistent with its s. 35(1) obligations, it follows, by virtue of s. 52(1) of the *Constitution Act, 1982,* that the legislation and/or regulation pursuant to which the Crown was acting in laying the charge is, "to the extent of the inconsistency, of no force or effect."[39]

Not all interference with the exercise of Aboriginal rights is inconsistent with s. 35(1), however. As I noted earlier, although the constitutionalization of Aboriginal rights placed restraints on the state's power to interfere with their exercise, its power still has application. Thus, as the Supreme Court of Canada determined in *Sparrow,* the Crown's interference with the exercise of Aboriginal rights is inconsistent with s. 35(1) if and only if it constitutes an unjustified infringement.[40]

Consequently, a successful Aboriginal rights defence requires the establishment of the Crown's unjustified infringement of an existing Aboriginal right in order to establish that its interference with the right's exercise was inconsistent with its constitutional obligation to recognize and affirm the right.

Analytically speaking, establishment of the Crown's unjustified infringement of an existing Aboriginal right presupposes prior establishment of its infringement of the right. And that in turn presupposes a yet prior establishment of an existing Aboriginal right.

Corresponding to these analytic relations, the Supreme Court of Canada introduced in its *Sparrow* decision a short series of three questions – a basic analytical framework,[41] if you will – to guide trial courts in their assessment of Aboriginal rights defences in cases involving prosecutions for regulatory offences. The questions and their order were as follows: (1) Was the defendant exercising an existing Aboriginal right? (2) Did the Crown infringe the defendant's Aboriginal right? (3) Was the infringement justified?

Although the overall burden of proving that the law authorizing the Crown's interference with the Aboriginal defendant's actions is inconsistent with its s. 35(1) obligations and therefore invalid (at least in part) rests on the defendant's shoulders, there are specific stages in the analysis at which, if they are reached, the burden of proof shifts from the defendant to the Crown. Let me clarify. At the first stage, the court asks whether the defendant was exercising an existing Aboriginal right. The defendant bears the onus of proving that the act that drew the charge was an exercise of an Aboriginal right.[42] If the defendant satisfies this initial onus, the court will presume that the act was an exercise of an *existing* Aboriginal right *unless* the Crown can prove that the right was extinguished prior to the constitutionalization of Aboriginal rights in 1982. The Crown bears the burden of proving extinguishment.[43] Provided that the Crown has not rebutted the presumption of existence, the analysis proceeds to the second stage. There the court asks whether the Crown infringed the defendant's existing Aboriginal right. The defendant bears the onus of proving *prima facie* infringement.[44] Proof of *prima facie* infringement suffices as proof of infringement. The analysis then proceeds to the third stage. There the court asks whether the infringement was justified. At the third stage, the burden falls upon the Crown to prove that it justifiably infringed the defendant's existing Aboriginal right.[45] Should the Crown fail to discharge its onus, the infringement is accounted unjustified and the Aboriginal rights defence entitled to succeed.

It is clear, based on the analytical framework introduced by the Supreme Court of Canada in *Sparrow,* that the onus of proving justified infringement does not fall upon the Crown unless the Aboriginal defendant has discharged the onus of proving *prima facie* infringement of an existing Aboriginal right. It is also clear, given that the onus to prove *prima facie* infringement does not accrue to the defendant otherwise, that the onus of proving justified infringement does not fall upon the Crown unless the Aboriginal right (its existence, nature, and scope) has been established. Finally, it is further clear, since proof of justification requires proof of fulfillment of the duty to consult,[46] that the subsidiary onus of proving that it fulfilled its constitutional duty to consult about the Aboriginal right does not fall upon the Crown unless the right has been established.

The surface plausibility of the Crown's submission that the Supreme Court of Canada's decision in *Sparrow* supports its Fundamental Position rests, then, on slipping, logically speaking, from the Court's insistence that the Crown does not bear the burden of proving that it satisfied its duty to consult about an Aboriginal right unless the right has been previously established to the Crown's Fundamental Position that it does not have a duty to consult unless the right has been previously established. Clearly, however, what the Court had to say about what must be established before the burden shifts to the Crown to prove justification neither presupposes nor implies the Crown's Fundamental Position. The Crown's submission's surface plausibility rests, then, on reading a false parallelism into the Court's remarks. Hence, as Rowles J.A. simply observed, "the justificatory analysis set out in *Sparrow* ... provides no foundation for the position the Crown has taken in this case."

I mentioned earlier that Rowles J.A.'s reasoning in support of her conclusion that the chambers judge did not err in finding that the Crown had constitutional and fiduciary duties to consult with the Taku River Tlingits prior to its final decision to approve the Tulsequah Chief Mine Project proceeded in two stages. She devoted the first stage to refuting the Crown's contention that the Supreme Court of Canada's jurisprudence on s. 35(1) supports its Fundamental Position. But by her refutation she also – at what I loosely spoke of as the second stage of her supporting reasoning – impliedly confirmed the chambers judge's general conclusion that the Crown may have constitutional and fiduciary duties to consult about Aboriginal rights prior to the establishment of those rights in a court of law. The step from her refutation of the Crown's contention to her confirmation of the chambers judge's general conclusion is a matter of simple logic. The Crown's Fundamental Position is, as Rowles J.A. amply demonstrated, inconsistent with the Supreme Court of Canada's jurisprudence on s. 35(1).

The chambers judge's general conclusion – that the Crown may have constitutional and fiduciary duties to consult prior to the establishment of Aboriginal rights – contradicts the Crown's Fundamental Position. As the contradictory of the Crown's Fundamental Position, the chambers judge's general conclusion is therefore consistent with the Court's jurisprudence on s. 35(1). Thus, Rowles J.A. further supported her conclusion that the chambers judge did not err by impliedly confirming the previous judge's general conclusion.

It does not follow merely from Rowles J.A.'s finding that the chambers judge's general conclusion is consistent with the Supreme Court's jurisprudence on s. 35(1) that the chambers judge was correct in holding that the Crown owed the Tlingits constitutional and fiduciary duties of consultation. It still remained for Rowles J.A. to settle whether the chambers judge was correct in holding that the circumstances in the case sufficed to trigger those duties.

Addressing the issue, Rowles J.A. drew attention to two sets of salient facts identified in the chambers judge's decision that, taken together, sufficed to trigger the Crown's duties to consult. The first set included the facts that the Tlingits had for a long time credibly asserted Aboriginal rights and title, "that the federal government had agreed to negotiate land claims with the Tlingits in 1984 on the basis of a preliminary determination that they had aboriginal rights in their territory," and that these facts were "known to the provincial government when it entered into a framework agreement to negotiate with the Tlingits under the B.C. treaty process."[47] The second set of salient facts included the facts that the Tlingits had, throughout the environmental review process, credibly asserted "[t]hat approval of the project would have a profound impact on ... [their] way of life and their ability to sustain themselves" and that the province had not disputed their assertion.[48] In Rowles J.A.'s estimation, these two sets of facts, backed by the Supreme Court of Canada's jurisprudence, fully warranted the chambers judge's finding "that, prior to the issuance of the Project Approval Certificate, the Ministers of the Crown had to be 'mindful of the possibility that their decision might infringe aboriginal rights' and, accordingly, to be careful to ensure that the substance of the Tlingits' concerns had been addressed."[49] Thus, she concluded that the chambers judge did not err in finding that the Crown had constitutional and fiduciary duties to consult with the Tlingits prior to its decision to approve the mine project.

Nor did the chambers judge err, Rowles J.A. further concluded, in finding that the Crown had failed to fulfill its duties, for "[t]he Crown did not argue, either before the chambers judge or before this Court, that the substance of the Tlingits' concerns had been met or accommodated prior to or through the issuance of the Project Approval Certificate."[50]

It should be noted in passing what, according to Rowles J.A., the Crown's consultation duty encompassed. Summarizing a point made by Lamer C.J.C. in *Delgamuukw,* she observed that "there is always a duty to consult, but what is required by way of consultation will vary with the circumstances."[51] In the passage from his judgment referred to and quoted by Rowles J.A., the then Chief Justice of Canada elaborated his point, saying:

> In occasional cases, when the breach is less serious or relatively minor, it [the duty of consultation] will be no more than a duty to discuss important decisions that will be taken with respect to lands held pursuant to Aboriginal title. Of course, even in those rare cases when the minimum acceptable standard is consultation, this consultation must be in good faith, and with the intention of substantially addressing the concerns of the Aboriginal peoples whose lands are at issue. In most cases, it will be significantly deeper than mere consultation.[52]

In the circumstances of the case, the Crown's consultation duty, Rowles J.A. found, agreeing with the chambers judge's earlier finding, required it not merely to identify and listen to those concerns that, according to the Tlingits, implicated their Aboriginal rights but also, in order to meet what Lamer C.J.C. spoke of as the minimum acceptable standard, to effectively address "the substance of the Tlingits' concerns with respect to when, and on what terms and conditions, the mineral rights to be exploited by Redfern should be developed."[53]

Rowles J.A.'s rejection of the Crown's submission that the chambers judge had erred in finding that it had constitutional and fiduciary duties to consult with the Tlingits grounded her rejection of the Crown's subsidiary submission that the chambers judge had erred by considering issues that were not properly before her. The Crown's subsidiary submission, it may be recalled, rested on its claim that until the existence, nature, and scope of an Aboriginal claimant's asserted Aboriginal rights are determined by a court of law, it cannot be determined whether it owes any constitutional or fiduciary duty to consult about those rights. Because the chambers judge had previously severed those issues requiring a determination of the Tlingits' Aboriginal rights claims, the issues concerning its constitutional and fiduciary duties were not, the Crown argued, properly before her. Since, however, Rowles J.A. held that the chambers judge was able to decide, first, whether the Crown had constitutional and fiduciary duties to consult with the Tlingits and, second, whether the Crown had breached its duties without having to make any specific determinations about the Tlingits' rights, she rejected the Crown's subsidiary submission.

Having rejected the Crown's main arguments, Rowles J.A. dismissed the appeal of the chambers judge's order quashing the decision to approve the mine project. She did, however, make one concession to the Crown. The chambers judge had also ordered the matter remitted to the Tulsequah Chief Project Committee and then to the ministers for reconsideration. Rowles J.A. set aside the order, which would have required reconvening the committee, and directed "instead that the matter simply be remitted to the Ministers."[54] Although she left her reasons unstated, Rowles J.A. altered the order because the Crown's failure was not, in her view, so much a failure to consult with the Tlingits about their concerns as it was a failure to try to accommodate them. Therefore, since the ministers – thanks largely to the committee's efforts – now had the Tlingits' concerns before them, and since it was ultimately the ministers' responsibility to see to their accommodation, an order limited to remitting the matter to the ministers would suffice to achieve the desired remedial effect.

Within slightly less than a month, another division of the British Columbia Court of Appeal, this time unanimously, reached a similar conclusion regarding the Crown's constitutional and fiduciary obligations to a First Nation. Like the *Taku River* case, the *Haida* case involved the Crown's sanctioning of corporate exploitation of a First Nation's traditional lands and resources. The prize, however, was timber rather than metals.

The islands and surrounding waters of Haida Gwaii (the Queen Charlotte Islands) form the core of the ancestral home of the Haida Nation. The northern islands, including Graham Island, fall within the sixth of seven supply blocks comprising Tree Farm Licence 39 (TFL 39).[55] (TFLs are designed to, among other things, give security of timber access to forest companies with substantial processing operations.) TFL 39 is the largest of the province's thirty-odd tree farm licences, alone covering 801,393 hectares (2,083,622 acres). Block 6 covers almost a fourth of Haida Gwaii's total area.

The history of logging within what later became Block 6 of TFL 39 began with the First World War. The reason: Sitka spruce. Old-growth Sitka spruce, possessing a near-optimum combination of strength, flexibility, and lightness, and being in abundance along the northwest Pacific coast, quickly became the wood of choice in early airplane construction. As military orders for airplanes increased during the First World War, so did the demand for old-growth Sitka spruce. Sitka spruce, it so happens, thrives – alongside red and yellow cedar – on the northern islands of Haida Gwaii. Quite naturally, Canada and its allies looked to these islands to supply their military needs, as they would also do in the buildup to and during the Second World War.

Extensive commercial logging did not begin, however, until MacMillan Bloedel was issued TFL 39 (or more accurately its predecessor, Forest Management Licence No. 39) in 1961. Under TFL 39, MacMillan Bloedel acquired the exclusive right to harvest timber within the area covered. Although the term for TFLs is twenty-five years, the province's Minister of

Forests may offer a licencee a replacement licence prior to the expiration of a TFL's term. And so, although MacMillan Bloedel's initial licence was not due to expire until 1986, the Minister of Forests issued the company a replacement in 1981 (TFL 39 proper). The minister again issued a replacement on 1 March 1995, extending TFL 39's life to 2020.

Near the close of February 1995, with the minister's signing of the replacement licence impending, the Council of the Haida Nation petitioned the British Columbia Supreme Court for judicial review of the minister's decisions to issue replacement licences in 1981 and 1995. Although the Haida were prepared to argue that they still possessed Aboriginal title over, and other aboriginal rights in, Haida Gwaii, that the Crown has "a fiduciary duty to consider and protect the[ir] legitimate title and rights,"[56] that the Crown, as fiduciary, had a duty to consult with the Haida about the effects of the replacement licences on their title and other rights prior to issuing the replacements,[57] and therefore that the Crown breached its duty by failing to consult,[58] in short order their litigation was sidetracked over an issue of statutory interpretation.[59]

With the release of the Supreme Court of Canada's decision in *Delgamuukw* on 11 December 1997 and the province's subsequent rethinking of its consultation policy, the Haida Nation decided to forgo further litigation, to re-enter the treaty negotiations process, and to strive therein to have its Aboriginal rights and title, especially as they related to the land and timber of Block 6 of TFL 39, accommodated through the negotiation of an interim measures agreement.

The Haida's hopes were soon dashed. When asked "to consider the [future] replacement of T.F.L. 39 as a subject for Interim Measures negotiations," the provincial Crown refused.[60] Then, with Weyerhaeuser poised to acquire MacMillan Bloedel at the millennium's close, the Minister of Forests, rejecting the Haida's demands for consultation as legally baseless,[61] offered MacMillan Bloedel a replacement licence, extending TFL 39's life yet further to 2025.

With TFL 39's transfer to Weyerhaeuser approved and its replacement set to take effect on 1 March 2000, the Haida Nation petitioned anew on 13 January 2000 for judicial review of the Minister of Forest's decisions to issue replacement licences in 1981, 1995, and 2000.

The Haida advanced three independent grounds for claiming that the minister had committed an error warranting judicial review. As their first, the Haida argued that their asserted Aboriginal title gave rise to a legal presumption of its existence and thus, unless the Crown rebutted the presumption, it constituted a legal encumbrance (that is, an encumbrance within the meaning of the term in s. 35 of the *Forest Act*[62]) on the Crown's title to the timber in Block 6. With the Crown's title so encumbered, the minister was statutorily barred from replacing TFL 39. As their second ground, the Haida argued that their asserted Aboriginal title constituted "an equitable encumbrance on the timber by reason of the fiduciary relationship existing between the Crown and all Aboriginal peoples."[63] The Crown, they continued, had a fiduciary duty to protect and accommodate the Haida's asserted title as long as it had not disproved the Haida's claim. Thus, they submitted, "[i]n replacing T.F.L. 39 in 1981, 1995, and 2000, without disproving the Haida claim, and without incorporating conditions in T.F.L. 39 that would adequately accommodate and protect the asserted Aboriginal title of the Haida Nation in relation to the timber on Block 6, the Minister acted in breach of the Crown's fiduciary duty, and without jurisdiction."[64] Finally, as their third ground for claiming that the minister had erred, the Haida argued as follows:

> [I]f there was no legal or equitable encumbrance on the timber within Block 6, then in 1995 and 2000, the Minister acted in breach of a fiduciary duty owed by the provincial Crown to the Haida Nation, not to replace T.F.L. 39 without first consulting with the Haida Nation in good faith, and with the intention of substantially addressing their concerns with respect to their asserted Aboriginal title to the lands comprising Block 6. In replacing T.F.L. 39 in 1995 and 2000, without first consulting with the Haida Nation in good faith, the Minister acted unlawfully and in violation of the Crown's fiduciary obligation.[65]

Based on these three grounds for claiming that the Minister of Forests had committed an error warranting judicial review of his decisions to replace TFL 39, the Haida Nation asked the BC Supreme Court for a declaration that the replacements of TFL 39 in 1981, 1995, and 2000 were, at least as they related to Block 6, invalid or, alternatively, an order quashing the 1995 and 2000 replacements.

The Crown argued, as it had barely four months earlier at the hearing of the Taku River Tlingits' petition, that asserted Aboriginal rights and title are wholly lacking in legal effect until established in a court of law.

Halfyard J. heard the Haida's petition from 31 July through 4 August 2000 in Masset. He delivered his reasons for judgment on 21 November 2000. Rejecting all three of the Haida's grounds, he dismissed their petition.

As the issues of whether the Haida's asserted Aboriginal rights and title exist and whether their asserted rights and title had been unjustifiably infringed had been previously severed from their petition,[66] the Haida were asking Halfyard J. to decide on an application for judicial review based on the issues of whether their asserted rights and title constituted an encumbrance and whether they triggered fiduciary duties of consultation and accommodation without benefit of a full and conclusive determination of their rights at trial. Specifically, they were asking him to decide those issues on the basis of their assertion of their Aboriginal rights and title.

Halfyard J.'s chief difficulty with the Haida's request was that granting it would have required him to accept it as a legal presumption that asserted Aboriginal rights and title, provided they had not been surrendered or extinguished, must be taken to exist. The problem, as he stated it, is that "the law does not," contrary to the Haida's submission, "presume the existence of Aboriginal rights, merely from proof that such rights have been asserted, and that there has been no surrender or extinguishment of the rights."[67] The law, he implied, requires proof of their existence, not merely their assertion.

For what counts as proof of an Aboriginal right's existence, Halfyard J. looked to the Supreme Court of Canada's decisions in *Sparrow, Van der Peet,* and *Delgamuukw*. Such proof, according to the Court, is cumulative. Proof of an Aboriginal right's existence requires, for instance, proof of its connections to a specific place. Proof of the existence of Aboriginal title similarly requires proof of exclusive occupation of the land at the time of the Crown's assertion of sovereignty. The simple assertion of the existence of Aboriginal rights and title could not, even in regions where those rights and title had never been surrendered or extinguished, count as proof of their existence.

But even if the Haida could surmount that problem, they would, Halfyard J. thought, face a deeper one. In *Sparrow,* the Supreme Court of Canada outlined the basic analytical framework that courts are to use to determine whether an asserted Aboriginal right exists, whether it was infringed, and whether it was unjustifiably infringed. Although the Court subsequently added and subtracted details in cases such as *Van der Peet* and *Delgamuukw,* the basic analytical framework survived. It is crucial to that framework, first, that the burden of proof is distributed variously between the claimant of the Aboriginal right and the Crown at different stages in the analysis; second, that the initial burden of proof is the claimant's, not the Crown's; and finally, that the burden shifts to the Crown only after the claimant's prior burden has been met. The Aboriginal claimant's initial burden is to prove the claimed right's existence, nature, and scope. Only if the Aboriginal claimant meets the initial burden does it fall to the Crown to try, if it so wishes, to prove the right's extinguishment. In light of these considerations, Halfyard J. concluded that were he to presume the existence of the Haida's asserted Aboriginal rights and title, as they had urged him to do, he would be, contrary to the rules set forth in *Sparrow,* placing the onus on the Crown to prove extinguishment without the Haida having first discharged their prior onus.

Halfyard J. similarly found difficulty with the Haida's request that he decide whether their asserted Aboriginal rights and title triggered fiduciary duties of consultation and accommodation and, if so, whether the Crown fulfilled them. As before, he concluded that complying with their request would require him to presume that the asserted rights and title existed. It would require him also to presume, he noted, that the nature and extent of those rights and title are just as the Haida asserted them to be.[68] As before, he concluded that were he to presume what they wished, he would be shifting the burden to the Crown to prove justified infringement without the Haida having met their burden of proving the nature and extent of the rights. It would be, moreover, without the Haida having met their further burden of proving the *prima facie* infringement of their rights and title.[69]

Halfyard J.'s latter conclusion calls for brief comment. By raising the issues of the Crown's fiduciary duties, the Haida had, the chambers judge was convinced, raised the issue of the Crown's justification for infringement. But, as *Sparrow* had made clear, a decision on the fiduciary issues *as part of a conclusive decision on the justification issue* requires the full and conclusive determination of the nature and extent of the Aboriginal rights in question. This is because the scope of the Crown's fiduciary duty reflects the nature and extent of the Aboriginal rights in question. A conclusive determination of the scope of the Crown's fiduciary duty therefore presupposes a full and conclusive determination of the nature and extent of the Aboriginal rights in question. Until such time as the Haida's asserted Aboriginal rights and title are conclusively determined at trial, the fiduciary issues would remain, Halfyard J. was convinced, outside a reviewing court's purview.

The British Columbia Court of Appeal heard the Haida Nation's appeal on 8 January 2002. For the Haida, the timing could not have been better. Just over a week earlier, Rowles J.A. had released her reasons for judgment in the *Taku River* case.

In its deliberations, the Court of Appeal set itself to address two issues. "The principal issue" was "whether there is an obligation on the Crown and on third parties to consult with an aboriginal people who have specifically claimed aboriginal title or aboriginal rights, about potential infringements, before the aboriginal title or rights have been determined by a Court of competent jurisdiction."[70] The second issue was "whether the Crown title to land and timber over which a claim to aboriginal title extends must be regarded as subject to a legal or equitable encumbrance which should have prevented the Crown from dealing with the land and timber."[71] In the judgment delivered on 27 February 2002, Lambert J.A., writing on behalf of the Court, sided against the Haida on the second issue but with them on the first.

Regarding the second issue, Lambert J.A. held that it was not open to the Court to decide it. Another division of the British Columbia Court of Appeal had already decided, as a question of law preliminary to hearing the Haida's original petition for judicial review, that "the Aboriginal title claimed by the Haida Nation, *if it exists,* constitutes an encumbrance of the Crown's title to timber"[72] [emphasis added]. The way in which the other division of the Court had construed the second issue – that is, as requiring the Haida to prove the existence of their asserted title at trial – prevented his division of the Court, Lambert J.A. held, from revisiting the previous decision of the Court.[73]

As for the principal issue, Lambert had this to say:

> Having regard to the way the issue ... [of whether the Crown owed the Taku River Tlingits a constitutional or fiduciary duty to consult about their asserted but unestablished Aboriginal rights and title prior to its decision to approve the Tulsequah Chief Mine Project] was addressed by Madam Justice Rowles, by reference to the fundamental authorities in the Supreme Court of Canada, particularly *R. v. Sparrow, R. v. Van der Peet, Guerin v. The Queen,* and *Delgamuukw v. British Columbia* [citations omitted], and by elucidating the general principles and then applying them to the facts, makes those general principles as stated by Madam Justice Rowles and as concurred in by Madam Justice Huddart binding on this Court and determinative of the outcome of this appeal.[74]

Accordingly, the Crown, Lambert J.A. found, had constitutional and fiduciary duties to consult with the Haida and to seek to accommodate their cultural and economic interests.[75] Specifically, the Crown "had an obligation to consult with the Haida people in 1999 and 2000 about accommodating the aboriginal title and aboriginal rights of the Haida people when consideration was being given to the renewal of Tree Farm Licence 39 and Block 6."[76] But since it had, as the chambers judge had found, neither consulted with the Haida about the replacements of TFL 39 and the transfer to Weyerhaeuser nor sought to accommodate their interests, the Crown was in breach of its obligations.[77]

The chambers judge's mistake, Lambert J.A. explained, was based in part on his confusion of the order of analysis followed by courts in proceedings in which Aboriginal claimants are seeking to establish Aboriginal rights and their *prima facie* infringement – the order of analysis introduced by the Supreme Court of Canada in *Sparrow* – with the social/political order in which the Crown and Aboriginal peoples are to strive to reconcile Aboriginal rights and Crown sovereignty. Lambert J.A. described the distinction this way: "[I]n factual terms the consultation ought to precede the infringement, and both are likely to precede the court determination of the existence of aboriginal title and aboriginal rights, but as a matter of logical progression in court then, first the title is proved, then the infringement is proved, and then the onus shifts to the Crown to establish that there was justification for the infringement at and before the time when the infringement occurred."[78] Put simply, the chambers judge confused the *Sparrow* analysis (*analysans*) with what it is an analysis of (*analysandum*). Thus, the chambers judge committed what Lambert J.A. called the "Timing Fallacy" by inferring that the conditions that must be met before such time as a court will consider the consultation issue as part of its consideration of the justification issue are recited by the conditions that must be met before such time as the Crown has a duty to consult.

Lambert J.A. found that the following circumstances jointly sufficed to trigger the Crown's obligation to consult and seek an accommodation:

1. The Provincial Crown had fiduciary obligations of utmost good faith to the Haida people with respect to the Haida claims to aboriginal title and aboriginal rights;
2. The Provincial Crown ... [was] aware of the Haida claims to aboriginal title and aboriginal rights over all or at least some significant part of the area covered by T.F.L. 39 and Block 6, through evidence supplied ... by the Haida people and through further evidence available ... on reasonable inquiry, an inquiry which ... [it was] obliged to make; and
3. The claims of the Haida people to aboriginal title and aboriginal rights were supported by a good *prima facie* case in relation to all or some significant part of the area covered by T.F.L. 39 and Block 6.[79]

Generalizing his point, Lambert J.A. was saying that the Crown's consultation and accommodation duties arose from the combination of its fiduciary obligations to the Haida, its awareness of the Haida's claims to Aboriginal rights and title, and the strength of the case supporting their claims.

To address the problem that had stymied the chambers judge of how the scope of the Crown's fiduciary duties to consult and to seek an accommodation can be sufficiently determined – not only by a court on an application for judicial review but also by the Crown when making a decision involving a potentially infringing activity – in the absence of a court's prior conclusive determination of the nature and extent of the Aboriginal rights or title, Lambert J.A. looked to the third of the aforementioned factors. He began by saying that "the strength of the Haida case gives content to the obligation to consult and the obligation to seek an accommodation."[80] By this he was "not saying," he cautioned, "that if there is something less than a good *prima facie* case ... there is no obligation to consult," but rather that "the scope of the consultation and the strength of the obligation to seek an accommodation will be proportional to the potential soundness of the claim for aboriginal title and aboriginal rights."[81] The fact, then, that the Haida had a good *prima facie* case suggesting that the nature and extent of their rights and title within Block 6 were much as they said they were gave content to the Crown's duties of consultation and accommodation. Moreover, the content it gave was, Lambert J.A. implied, sufficient to provide both the Crown with a decent working sense of what its fiduciary obligations to the Haida were in regard to Block 6 and a court with what it needed to decide – in the interim before their rights and title are finally determined at trial or by treaty – whether the Crown had satisfied its duties.

Throughout the greater part of his discussion, Lambert J.A. simply assumed, logically speaking, that the Crown's overall fiduciary obligation to the Haida includes obligations to consult and to seek accommodation. This was deliberate on his part. Given the assumption, he could direct most of his attention to more pressing legal/practical issues, such as what had triggered those duties and what their scope was.

He did not, however, quit his discussion without elaborating on the assumption. As he presented it, the connection between the Crown's over-all fiduciary obligation to the Haida and its obligations to consult and to seek accommodation is immediate. The latter obligations stand, he stated, on the "fiduciary footing of the Crown's relationship with the Indian peoples who are under its protection."[82] He might have added – since it was, as will be seen presently, his view – that those obligations stand immediately on the aforementioned fiduciary footing.

The *Sparrow* analysis had inadvertently, he thought, obscured the truth. In *Sparrow* (and in subsequent Supreme Court of Canada decisions such as *Delgamuukw*), the obligations to consult and to seek accommodation were introduced as being what the Crown's fiduciary relationship with Aboriginal peoples demands if it is going to infringe Aboriginal rights and title justifiably. *Sparrow* might be taken to suggest that the requirements for justifiable infringement are what connect the obligations to consult and to seek accommodation to the Crown's fiduciary relationship with Aboriginal peoples. It might also be taken, as Halfyard J. had taken it, to suggest that apart from the issue of justifiable infringement, the Crown's overall fiduciary duty is not sufficient to ground duties of consultation and accommodation. Lambert J.A. saw the matter differently, however: "The duty to consult and seek an accommodation does not arise simply from a *Sparrow* analysis of s. 35. It stands on the *broader* fiduciary footing of the Crown's relationship with the Indian peoples who are under its protection"[83] [emphasis added]. Accordingly, he concluded, "where there are fiduciary duties of the Crown to Indian peoples it is my opinion that the obligation to consult is a free standing enforceable legal and equitable duty."[84]

Lambert J.A.'s conclusion impliedly spoke to the relevance of the *Sparrow* analysis to judicial review proceedings such as the Haida's. Let me explain. Because the Crown's consultation and accommodation duties are free-standing enforceable legal and equitable duties, courts do not need, when faced with applications for judicial review, to invoke the entire *Sparrow* apparatus in order to determine whether the Crown breached its duties. For just as the Crown's consultation and accommodation duties are not wholly circumscribed by its duty to infringe Aboriginal rights justifiably or not at all, so too the judiciary's approach to deciding, on applications for judicial review, whether the Crown breached its duties is not rigidly dictated by the *Sparrow* analysis.

Having found the Crown in breach of its constitutional and fiduciary duties to consult with the Haida Nation about its claims to Aboriginal rights and title and to seek to accommodate them, the British Columbia Court of Appeal was faced with crafting an appropriate remedy. The Haida were seeking primarily a declaration that the 1995 and 2000 replacements of TFL 39 were invalid, at least as they related to Block 6. The Court, however, decided against such a declaration. A declaration of invalidity "would have terminated all of Weyerhaeuser's rights under the licence, with serious economic consequences to it, its employees and others."[85]

As a matter of justice, however, the Haida were entitled to a remedy of some sort. As a start, the Court decided to grant a declaration stating that the Crown had in 1999, 2000, and earlier, and continued to have, a legally enforceable duty to consult with the Haida in good faith and to seek a workable accommodation of their interests. To this declaration, the Court decided to add an order allowing the parties to apply to the British Columbia Supreme Court "for whatever orders they be instructed to seek, pending the conclusion of the proceedings with respect to the determination of aboriginal title and aboriginal rights, infringement and justification."[86] Hence, the order left the Haida free to seek, as part of the same interim proceedings, a final declaration of invalidity should the Crown further compound its failures of consultation and accommodation.

Although a step in the direction of justice, a declaration stating merely that the Crown had and continues to have duties to consult and seek accommodation would not be, the Court reasoned, sufficient. The problem was that it was Weyerhaeuser, not the Crown, who had day-to-day control of activities and operations. As Lambert J.A. observed, "when it comes to management decisions in relation to activities and operations in the forests, the Crown provincial no longer has day to day control of activities which may be carried out in such a way as to increase or lessen the impact of the acts of infringement. The choice of how to carry out those activities and operations is Weyerhaeuser's alone."[87] Clearly, then, if "Weyerhaeuser had no duty to consult, the Crown would lack effective power to address any of the Haida's concerns, or to accommodate their legitimate economic objectives."[88] And so, in order that justice be done, the Court decided to issue a declaration stating that both the Crown and Weyerhaeuser had and continued to have legally enforceable duties to consult with the Haida in good faith and to seek a workable accommodation of their interests.[89]

Assuming their basic thrust survives the Supreme Court of Canada's scrutiny (see "Postscript," page 152), the British Columbia Court of Appeal's decisions in the *Taku River* and *Haida* cases settled and/or brought needed clarity to the following three questions:

1   May an Aboriginal people's asserted but unestablished Aboriginal rights and title trigger the Crown's constitutional duties to consult and to seek an accommodation prior to forming a decision to undertake or sanction a potentially infringing activity?
2   May the Crown's prior efforts to consult about and to accommodate an Aboriginal people's asserted but unestablished Aboriginal rights and title be subject matter for an application for judicial review?
3   What is the relevance of the *Sparrow* analysis to judicial review proceedings in which issues involving asserted but unestablished Aboriginal rights and title arise?

The British Columbia Court of Appeal has given an affirmative answer to the first two questions. As for the third, it has made it clear that the *Sparrow* analysis does not cover the full ambit of the Crown's legally enforceable obligations to consult and to seek accommodation.

Although the British Columbia Court of Appeal's decisions in the *Taku River* and *Haida* cases answered and/or brought needed clarity to the aforementioned questions, they were not – directly, at any rate – concerned with sacred sites.[90] The three cases discussed next were. Moreover, in all three, First Nations employed or attempted to employ judicial review in an effort to protect the use or integrity of their sacred sites. They also argued, with mixed success, that their asserted but unestablished rights over their sacred sites triggered constitutional and/or fiduciary duties on the part of the Crown to consult with them and to seek to accommodate their concerns prior to forming a decision to sanction resource exploitation activities that, they claimed, threatened their sites. Because these cases were decided before the *Taku River* and *Haida* cases, the courts were still struggling with the aforementioned questions. For the sake of comprehension as well as charity, it is important to keep their struggle in mind when reflecting on their decisions.

To reiterate, the three cases discussed in the next section are the *Halfway River*, the earlier *Siska Creek*, and the *Twin Sisters* cases. I shall begin as I shall end, with the *Halfway River* case.

First Forays

The territory of the Beaver people (Dunne-Za), an Athabascan-speaking people, encompasses much of the upper Peace River country, extending from northwestern Alberta into northeastern British Columbia. In 1900, one year after the federal government had completed negotiations, those Beaver people who lived within the boundaries of British Columbia adhered to Treaty 8.[91] Almost a decade and a half later, two reserves were created for them, one about half an hour's drive south of Hudson's Hope and the other a drive of about an hour and a half northwest of Fort St. John. The latter reserve, which borders the Halfway River on its north bank, is home to the Halfway River First Nation.

Like their ancestors, members of the Halfway River First Nation depend upon their environment for sustenance. Hunting, fishing, trapping, and gathering remain important activities. As their reserve is far too small to answer their sustenance needs, the Halfway River people must do most of their hunting, fishing, and so on off-reserve. Indeed, having foreseen this problem generally, Treaty 8 guaranteed First Nations signatories

> the right to pursue their usual vocations of hunting, trapping and fishing throughout the tract surrendered ... subject to such regulations as may from time to time be made by the Government of the country ... and excepting such tracts as may be required or taken up from time to time for settlement, mining, lumbering, trading or other purposes.[92]

Of the off-reserve areas they depend on for sustenance purposes, the Halfway River people depend most on the area immediately south of their reserve, an area they call the Tusdzuh.

They also, it should be noted, use the Tusdzuh for a number of other purposes, including religious and spiritual ones. Thus, the area is sacred to the Halfway River people on practical religious grounds at least.

In the mid-1980s, the Halfway River First Nation began discussions with the provincial and federal governments about the expansion of its reserve lands. As one justification, they argued that when their reserve was created in 1914, there was a shortfall of over 800 hectares (2,000 acres). In 1995, they advanced a Treaty Land Entitlement Claim under the Federal Specific Claims process for over 14,000 hectares (35,000 acres) of additional land. Their hope was that whatever the total area of their entitlement turned out to be, it would include the Tusdzuh in whole or in part. Their claim is yet to be resolved.

Also in the 1980s, Canadian Forest Products Limited (Canfor) obtained two forest licences in northeastern British Columbia that were later amalgamated into one, namely, forest licence A18154. Forest licence A18154 covered a substantial area of northeastern British Columbia, including the provincial Crown land in the vicinity of the Halfway River reserve. Canfor first proposed harvesting the area near the reserve, including the Tusdzuh, as part of its Forest Development Plan for 1991-96. Canfor later revised its proposal for the Tusdzuh area, deciding to delay its harvest until the 1995-96 and 1996-97 seasons. In October 1995, the company applied for the requisite cutting permit. Nearly a year later, on 13 September 1996, the district manager for the Ministry of Forests at Fort St. John approved Cutting Permit 212 (CP212), allowing Canfor to harvest the Tusdzuh's timber.

On 27 November 1996, the day Canfor decided to begin road building, workers travelling to the worksite were met by a blockade. As early as June 1995 and as late as November 1996, Chief Metecheah of the Halfway River First Nation had threatened a blockade. The earliest threat came only after almost three and a half years of communications and meetings between the Halfway River First Nation, Ministry of Forests officials, and Canfor representatives had proved to Chief Metecheah's satisfaction that the province was intent on logging the Tusdzuh in spite of the Halfway River people's Treaty Land Entitlement Claim and wishes to the contrary, and that their Aboriginal and treaty rights associated with the area were not being respected. And so, in December 1996, shortly after Canfor had applied for an interlocutory injunction to end the blockade, the Halfway River First Nation applied for judicial review of the district manager's decision of 13 September approving CP212.

Madam Justice Dorgan heard arguments during the first and second weeks of January 1997 and delivered her reasons for judgment on 24 June 1997. Having found that the district manager's decision was faulty on administrative and Aboriginal (constitutional and fiduciary) law grounds, she ordered his decision quashed. In her consideration of the administrative law issues, Dorgan J. found that the district manager had violated the principles of administrative law in four ways: (1) by fettering his discretion, (2) by acting so as to raise a reasonable apprehension of bias, (3) by making a patently unreasonable error of fact, and (4) by violating principles of procedural fairness with regard to giving notice and providing an opportunity to be heard. Since the administrative law issues are largely tangential to my discussion, I will touch on each of these only briefly.

Dorgan J. found that the district manager had failed to make the decision to approve CP212 on its own merits and had therefore fettered his discretion. In March 1995, the Halfway River First Nation asked the Ministry of Forests to set aside and protect the Tusdzuh from logging pending the resolution of their soon-to-be-submitted Treaty Land Entitlement Claim. Government policy, however, was not to halt resource development pending the resolution of such claims. A decision maker who simply applies policy without regard to the specific circumstances of the case before him or her fetters his or her discretion. Fettering one's discretion is a violation of the principles of administrative law. Dorgan J. found that the district manager had fettered his discretion "by treating the government policy of not halting development as a given and by simply following the direction of the Minister of Forests not to halt development."[93]

Dorgan J. also found that the district manager had conducted himself in such a way as to give rise to a reasonable apprehension of bias. That is, it was reasonable to infer from how he acted in advance of his formal decision that he had closed his mind to any further information the Halfway River First Nation might have wished to bring forward. The main basis for the inference, Dorgan J. decided, was a letter from the district manager to Chief Metecheah, dated 29 August 1996, in which he wrote: "I must inform you that if the application is in order and abides by all Ministry regulations and the Forest Practices Code *I have no compelling reasons not to approve their application*"[94] [emphasis added]. Dorgan J. took this statement as grounds for reasonably concluding that the district manager had closed his mind to the possible legitimacy of the Halfway River First Nation's claims that logging the Tusdzuh would infringe their Aboriginal and treaty rights.

Dorgan J. also found that by concluding that the logging of the Tusdzuh would not infringe any Aboriginal or treaty rights, the district manager had made an error of fact. Although some evidence was available to the district manager to support his conclusion, he had nonetheless failed to obtain any of his information from the Halfway River people themselves as to the nature and scope of their rights. And so, "in the absence of significant information and in the face of assertions by Halfway as to their uses of CP212," Dorgan J. concluded, "it was patently unreasonable for [District Manager] Lawson to conclude that there was no infringement."[95]

Finally, Dorgan J. found that the district manager had breached his duty of procedural fairness in two respects. First, the duty of procedural fairness obliged him to give notice to the Halfway River First Nation of, among other things, the specifics of Canfor's logging plans and the date on which he would be making his decision. The notice he gave was, the chambers judge concluded, inadequate. Second, the duty of procedural fairness obliged him to ensure that the Halfway River First Nation had an effective opportunity to be heard. In the circumstances, his duty to ensure that the opportunity was effective implied, Dorgan J. reasoned, a duty to consult the Halfway River people to ascertain their position. As he failed to consult them, he failed to ensure them an effective opportunity to be heard and thus again breached his duty of procedural fairness.

Besides the administrative law issues, Dorgan J. considered two Aboriginal law issues:

1. Does the approval of CP212 infringe [and, if so, unjustifiably infringe] the Aboriginal or Treaty Rights of Halfway, as guaranteed by s. 35(1) of the Constitution Act, 1982?
2. Does the provincial Crown owe a fiduciary duty to Halfway? If so, what is the scope of this duty, and has the MOF [Ministry of Forests] breached it?[96]

Since it will make the Court of Appeal's subsequent split decision more comprehensible, I will present Dorgan J.'s discussion of each of these issues in detail.

In her discussion of the first issue, Dorgan J. first set forth the *Sparrow* test for justifiable infringement[97] and then applied it. There are two basic stages to the test. At the first stage, the onus is on the First Nation to establish *prima facie* infringement of its constitutionally protected rights. At the second stage, the onus in on the government to show that the infringement was justified.

To establish *prima facie* infringement of a right, it is necessary to establish first the nature and scope of the right and then interference with its exercise rising to the level of *prima facie* infringement. In requiring the First Nation, as part of its onus of establishing *prima facie* infringement, to establish the nature and scope of the right purportedly infringed, the court must, Dorgan J. noted, "be sensitive to the aboriginal perspective on the meaning of the rights at stake."[98] As for proving that the interference with the right's exercise constitutes *prima facie* infringement, the First Nation must show, for instance, either that the interference is unreasonable or that it causes undue hardship or that it denies its people's preferred means of exercising the right.

If the First Nation establishes *prima facie* infringement, the onus shifts to the Crown to show that the infringement was justified. Establishing justification requires proving two things: (1) that there is a valid legislative objective underlying the infringement, and (2) that the infringement upholds the honour of the Crown in its fiduciary capacity. The court may ask a number of questions in its effort to determine whether the honour of the Crown was upheld, including whether priority was given to Native rights, whether there was as little infringement as possible, and whether there was consultation. If the Crown fails to prove that there is a valid legislative objective or that the infringement upholds the honour of the Crown, the infringement is unjustified.

What, then, were the Halfway River First Nation's rights that would be purportedly infringed by Canfor's road building and logging? To answer the question, Dorgan J. looked to Treaty 8. In return for their surrender of the land, the Halfway River people, like the other signatories of the treaty, were guaranteed "the right to pursue their usual vocations of hunting, trapping and fishing throughout the tract surrendered."

Since Canfor's road building and logging operations would clearly interfere directly and indirectly with the Halfway River people's exercise of these treaty rights, especially with the right to hunt, the question became, did the interference constitute *prima facie* infringement?

Canfor urged that the geographical limitation placed on Treaty 8 rights implied that their operations in the Tusdzuh could not be considered a *prima facie* infringement. The treaty stipulated, they observed, that the rights to hunt, trap, and fish were limited not merely to "the tract surrendered" but, more specifically, to those portions of the surrendered tract that have not been "required or taken up ... for settlement, mining, *lumbering,* trading or others purposes" [emphasis added]. Their operations in the Tusdzuh were, they argued, in accord with the geographical limitation inherent in Treaty 8 rights and therefore could not be considered a *prima facie* infringement of those rights.

Dorgan J. responded to Canfor's argument by drawing attention to Cory J.'s detailed analysis of Treaty 8 in *R. v. Badger.*[99] There, Cory J. held that the treaty recognized a distinction between geographical limitation of the treaty rights and limitation by regulation for the sake of conservation.[100] But, although finding that there was a geographical limitation to the rights, Cory J.'s analysis, according to Dorgan J., assumed, nonetheless, "that any interference with the right to hunt, fish or trap constitutes a *prima facie* infringement of Treaty 8 rights."[101] Therefore, Dorgan J. concluded, the admitted geographical limitation of the Halfway River First Nation's Treaty 8 rights did not imply that timber harvesting and other such activities on surrendered tracts could not amount to *prima facie* infringement.

In arriving at the conclusion that the interference with the Halfway River First Nation's treaty rights permitted by CP212 constituted a *prima facie* infringement of those rights, Dorgan J. found: (1) that it was doubtful that CP212 represented a reasonable limit on those rights, (2) that it would pose an undue hardship, and (3) that it was a denial of their preferred means of exercising those rights. Both the Ministry of Forests and Canfor argued that since only a small portion of the Tusdzuh would be logged, leaving a vast area for the Halfway River people to exercise their rights, the cutting permit was a reasonable limit on those rights. Dorgan J. responded that the argument ignored the Halfway River people's perspective on the meaning of their rights. To them, she observed, "the Tusdzuh region is one of the last unspoiled areas of wilderness where they can exercise their traditional way of life."[102] In their view, she went on, "[l]ogging [together with the attendant road construction] even in a limited area of the Tusdzuh would irrevocably change its character."[103] It was doubtful, the chambers judge concluded, that CP212 represented a reasonable limit on the Halfway River First Nation's treaty rights.

Chief Metecheah had deposed that his people "depend on hunting to feed their families and the proximity of the Tusdzuh area to the reserve allows Halfway members easy access to quality hunting areas where they can harvest game to feed their families."[104] Since the evidence suggested that previous encroachments on their traditional territory had forced the Halfway River people to go ever further distances to hunt game to feed their families, Dorgan J. held that "[t]he reasonable inference to be drawn ... is that logging in CP212 will be another 'further encroachment' which will cause the petitioners [undue] hardship."[105]

Finally, both the Ministry of Forests and Canfor argued that the logging operations would not constitute a denial of the Halfway River people's preferred means of exercising their treaty rights since they would still have the rest of the Tusdzuh area to enjoy their preferred means of exercise. To this, Dorgan J. responded, that "this again ignores the holistic perspective of Halfway. Their preferred means are to exercise their rights to hunt, trap and fish in an unspoiled wilderness in close proximity to their reserve lands."[106] Thus, she concluded, CP212 represented a denial of the Halfway River First Nation's preferred means of exercising its treaty rights.

The Ministry of Forests had, Dorgan J. noted, one final argument meant to block the otherwise immediate inference that the interference permitted by CP212 amounted to *prima facie* infringement. The argument, borrowed from the *Lower Tsitika Valley* case, is a now familiar one. Here is how Dorgan J. described it:

> The MOF poses a final argument respecting *prima facie* infringement: that the evidence contained in the [Chief] Metecheah Affidavit as to how Halfway uses CP212 (in particular evidence respecting cultural sites) was not put before [District Manager] Lawson. The MOF further submits that 'Where such assertions are made at the last minute in the course of court proceedings, the court is entitled to take that circumstance into account in assessing that evidence and is entitled to expect some explanation for the lateness of that claim,' citing *Tlowitsis-Mumtagila Band v. MacMillan Bloedel Ltd.*[107]

In the *Lower Tsitika Valley* case, the argument had served to undercut the Tlowitsis-Mumtagila's claim of uniqueness and thus fatally undermined their petition for interlocutory relief. Here, however, it did not succeed. Dorgan J., referring to more than a half-dozen exhibits, simply stated that "there is substantial evidence to refute this argument."[108]

Given that the Halfway River First Nation had established that the interference with their treaty rights constituted *prima facie* infringement, the onus then shifted from them to the provincial Crown to prove that the infringement was justified.

As Dorgan J. had no hesitation in finding that the objective in approving CP212 – "to enhance the economy of northern British Columbia through the harvesting of its forest resources"[109] – was valid, the only issue to be decided was whether approval of CP212 upheld the honour of the Crown.

In deciding the issue, Dorgan J., following *Sparrow*, asked three questions: (1) Was priority given to the Halfway River people's rights? (2) Was there minimal infringement? (3) Was there consultation?

Regarding the first question, she observed that the approval of CP212 appeared to give priority to Canfor's rights. She also observed, however, that both the Ministry of Forests and Canfor claimed that the appearance was deceiving, arguing that "had evidence of traditional use [of the Tusdzuh] been provided by Halfway, logging would not have been approved for the areas to which this evidence related."[110] Regarding the second question, she noted: (1) that Canfor likely had alternative areas available where the Halfway River people did not exercise their traditional rights, (2) that Canfor, in its response, had stated that its proposed logging would affect only a small percentage of the Tusdzuh, and (3) that the doctrine of minimal infringement did not imply that there could be no other, less infringing avenues available. Thus, based on the first two questions, although the chambers judge's analysis found little support for the Crown's claim that the infringement was justified, it, all the same, did not suggest that it was unjustified. Regarding the third question, however, Dorgan J. concluded that the Ministry of Forests failed to adequately consult with the Halfway River First Nation prior to approving CP212, and therefore that the cutting permit unjustifiably infringed their treaty rights to hunt, fish, and trap in the Tusdzuh area.

Since Dorgan J. incorporated her reasons for concluding that the ministry had failed in its duty to consult into her discussion of the second main issue – whether the provincial Crown owes a fiduciary duty – I now turn to it.

In 1984 in *Guerin v. the Queen*,[111] the Supreme Court of Canada held that the federal Crown owed a fiduciary duty to Aboriginal peoples. For a number of years following *Guerin*, it was debated whether or not the provincial Crown also owed them a fiduciary duty. Finally, in 1996 in *Badger*, the Supreme Court brought the debate to a close by applying fiduciary principles to the provincial Crown.[112] And so, following *Badger*, Dorgan J. found that the provincial Crown owed a fiduciary duty to the Halfway River First Nation.

As for the scope of the provincial Crown's fiduciary duty, Dorgan J. held that it clearly included a duty to consult. Halfway River had argued that it also included a duty to provide funding to enable them to gather information so as to have meaningful input, but Dorgan J. expressed her doubt that it extended so far. The province's duty to consult meant, she noted, a duty to consult prior to taking any actions that might affect Aboriginal or treaty rights. More particularly, in the circumstances, the province's duty meant that the Ministry of Forests had a duty to consult with the Halfway River First Nation prior to making any decisions that might affect their Aboriginal or treaty rights. Yet more particularly, the ministry had a duty to inform itself of the Halfway River people's traditional uses of the Tusdzuh and to share its relevant information (such as information on the impact on wildlife) with them.

In its submissions, the Ministry of Forests argued that the duty to consult was not engaged until the First Nation established *prima facie* infringement. In support of its argument, the ministry pointed to the *Sparrow* test for justifiable infringement. The fact that, according to the test, the onus of justifying its infringement falls upon the Crown only after the First Nation has discharged its onus of establishing *prima facie* infringement presupposes, the ministry suggested, that the Crown's duty to consult is not engaged until the First Nation has established *prima facie* infringement. This is because on the *Sparrow* analysis, questions about consultation arise only at the second stage of the test, the justification stage, and thus presuppose that *prima facie* infringement has been established.

In response to this argument, Dorgan J. stated that she considered the ministry's suggested approach to consultation both "inconsistent with the cases referred to and ... inappropriate given the relationship between the Crown and native people."[113] She then summarized the aforementioned cases on the issue as follows: "Based on the *Jack, Noel,* and *Delgamuukw* cases, the Crown has an obligation to undertake reasonable consultation with a First Nation which may be affected by its decision. In order for the Crown to consult reasonably, it must fully inform itself of the practices and of the views of the Nation affected. In so doing, it must ensure that the group affected is provided with full information with respect to the proposed legislation or decision and its potential impact on aboriginal rights."[114] The Crown's duty to consult was not, Dorgan J. implied, contingent upon the First Nation supplying proof to the Crown of *prima facie* infringement.

In considering whether the Crown had fulfilled its consultation duty, Dorgan J. found that the Ministry of Forests' efforts were inadequate. While it had, she acknowledged, made some efforts to inform itself, it nonetheless failed to take the steps needed to adequately inform itself about the Halfway River First Nation's Aboriginal and treaty rights and potential infringements thereof. Moreover, she added, the ministry "failed to ensure that Halfway was provided with full information with respect to the proposed decision," including making a wildlife impact study available in a reasonably timely fashion.[115]

Taking aim at the claim that it had failed to fulfill its duty to consult, the Ministry of Forests submitted that the Halfway River First Nation had made fulfillment of its duty impossible by its lack of cooperation. In response, Dorgan J. agreed that the Crown's duty to consult implied a reciprocal duty on Halfway River's part to make reasonable efforts to facilitate consultation. She also conceded that the First Nation might "not have been entirely reasonable" in the process.[116] That did not, however, change the fact that the Ministry of Forests had "failed to make all reasonable efforts to consult."[117] As a consequence of having failed on that score, the provincial Crown failed to satisfy its fiduciary obligations towards the Halfway River First Nation.

Having concluded that the district manager's decision to approve Canfor's application to log the Tusdzuh was defective on both administrative and Aboriginal (constitutional and fiduciary) law grounds, Dorgan J. then had to decide what, if any, sort of order to give. The Halfway River First Nation, in its amended petition, had requested an order doing the following:

(1) Quashing the approval of CP212.
(2) Declaring that the MOF owes a fiduciary and constitutional duty to adequately consult with Halfway and that the level of consultation to date is insufficient.
(3) Compelling the MOF to consult with Halfway on the effects of harvesting on Aboriginal and Treaty Rights and to provide Halfway with funding to support this consultation process.
(4) Remitting the matter back to the MOF to complete the consultation process and then reconsider the application for CP212.
(5) Prohibiting any decision regarding CP212 until consultation is complete.
(6) Retaining jurisdiction so that the parties may return for further directions.[118]

In the end, Dorgan J. opted to grant only the first part of the six-part request. She gave an order quashing the district manager's decision of 13 September 1996, then closed her remarks with the hope "that no further decision will be made without meaningful consultation with, and inclusion of, the petitioners, which is an integral component of the Crown's fiduciary obligation as well as being vital to the requirement of procedural fairness."[119]

The district manager, the Ministry of Forests, and Canfor subsequently appealed Dorgan J.'s decision. I will present the Court of Appeal's decision shortly. First, however, I want to return to the *Siska Creek* case and then turn to the *Twin Sisters* case. Besides the fact that it makes chronological and therefore historical sense to deal with both cases before the Court of Appeal's decision, dealing with them first will also add intelligibility to the subsequent judicial attempts to articulate and settle the crucial legal issues.

I discussed the *Siska Creek* case earlier in the previous chapter (see the section "Failure"). There, I mentioned that the Siska Band, in the summer of 1998, in an effort to prevent the construction of a logging road into the Siska Valley, which they hold sacred, brought an application for judicial review to quash certain decisions of the district managers of the Lillooet and Chilliwack Forest Districts concerning the proposed logging of and road building in the Siska watershed. I also mentioned that the band, on their application, sought two orders pending judicial review: (1) an injunction restraining the logging company's operations in the watershed and (2) an injunction restraining government officials from authorizing any logging or logging-related activities in the watershed. Finally, I stated that I would be presenting the specifics in this chapter. I then moved on to discuss in detail the Siska Band's later unsuccessful attempt, in October 1999, to obtain – based on an action seeking a declaration of Aboriginal title and other Aboriginal rights associated with the Siska Valley – an interlocutory injunction to bring the already-commenced logging to a halt.

As the primary ground of their petition for judicial review of the Lillooet and Chilliwack district managers' decisions regarding the Siska Valley, the Siska Band asserted that the road building into and logging of the valley constituted infringements of their Aboriginal title and other Aboriginal rights, that the Crown had not fulfilled its duty of consultation, and therefore that the infringements were unjustified. Their goal was to obtain an order quashing the district managers' decisions.[120]

Because road construction was imminent, the band decided to seek the following pair of orders pending judicial review:

1. An injunction restraining the [logging] company "from any logging or road building activities or alterations of culturally modified trees or other cultural heritage resources in ... or to access [the Siska watershed]"; and
2. an injunction restraining the respondent Ministers and District Managers "from authorizing any logging or road building activities or alterations of culturally modified trees or other cultural heritage resources in ... or to access [the Siska watershed]."[121]

Despite the mention of culturally modified trees in their petition, Mr. Justice Smith – rightly, I think – inferred that

[t]he real issue dividing the parties arises out of their different perspectives. The respondents want the Band to identify what are described as site-specific infringements so that they may take steps to prevent them. The Band insists that it does not rely on site-specific infringements but on intangible values that involve all things in the watershed. As the petitioner's counsel put it, the Band takes a holistic approach to the watershed and asserts that any timber harvesting activity whatsoever will permanently damage the cultural and spiritual practices of its members.[122]

Among other things, then, what the band was (by implication) claiming was that the whole Siska Valley, not merely one or more of its parts, was sacred, and furthermore that the proposed road building and logging would seriously violate the ethic of the place.

Smith J. decided against granting the requested injunction against the respondent ministers (of Forests and of Small Business, Tourism and Culture) and forest district managers on procedural grounds. The *Crown Proceedings Act*,[123] he held, barred issuing an injunction against officers of the Crown so long as they are acting lawfully in the performance of their duties. The Siska Band had argued that approvals for harvesting timber in the Siska Valley could "not be granted lawfully without the Crown first taking adequate notice of the Band's aboriginal rights and title."[124] The flaw in the argument was that if the court were to grant the requested injunction – which could enjoin only future approvals – it would have to presume that the Crown officers "will act unlawfully when they come to deal with the [logging] company's applications in future."[125] It was a presumption Smith J. could not make.[126]

In deciding whether the logging company should be enjoined from road building and timber harvesting in the Siska watershed, Smith J. applied the standard analysis. The Siska Band had articulated a number of questions that, it said, constituted serious questions to be tried, including the following:

1. whether the Aboriginal rights and title of the band may be infringed by the road building and logging in the Siska Creek watershed;
2. whether the officers of the Crown have breached their fiduciary duty to consult "as laid down by the Supreme Court of Canada in *Delgamuukw*."[127]

Regarding the questions, Smith J. noted, "these questions are all grounded in the assertions that the Band had aboriginal title to the area and that the Crown has failed to consult fully with the Band before approving the company's operational plans and roadbuilding permit."[128] In reply, the respondents had argued, first, that the evidence of Aboriginal title was weak and, second, that "the duty to consult that was identified in *Delgamuukw* arises only after Aboriginal title had been established and that there is no duty at this stage. In any event ... they have consulted fully with the Band over the past several years."[129] The second argument was basically a reiteration of the argument advanced by the Ministry of Forests in *Halfway River*.[130] All that had changed was that the disputed authority was now the Supreme Court of Canada's decision in *Delgamuukw* rather than its decision in *Sparrow*.[131] Smith J., although finding some force in the respondents' arguments with respect to both the weight of the Siska Band's evidence and the assertion that there had been full consultation, decided that the band had raised a triable issue with regard to its rights. "Moreover," he added (alluding to the dispute over how to construe *Delgamuukw* on the Crown's duty to consult), "the assertion of a duty to consult raises a serious legal question as to the Crown's obligations."[132]

In assessing the balance of convenience, Smith J. found that the Siska Band had not established that irreparable harm would follow if their requested injunction against the logging company were refused. With regard to the impending road construction, it would not, he observed, interfere with "any site-specific interests of the Band" other than a seldom used hunting trail that it would cross.[133] There was no suggestion that the road would interfere with hunting but even if it did, he concluded, damages would be an adequate remedy. Smith J. acknowledged that the Siska Band's approach to the Siska Valley was holistic rather than site-specific and that, like Dorgan J. in *Halfway River,* he was obliged to be sensitive to the Aboriginal perspective in determining the meaning of their rights and therefore of what constituted harm in relation to those rights. He found, however, that the band's evidence proved at most that the proposed logging of the Siska watershed, not the road, would irreparably harm the band's intangible interests therein.[134] But since logging in the watershed would not begin for another year, there would be "ample time for the pending judicial review to be completed before the Band will suffer any significant harm."[135]

Smith J. found, on the other hand, that the logging company would suffer significant harm should the injunction be granted. By the middle of the following year, 1999, the company's mill at Boston Bar would begin requiring timber harvested in the Siska watershed to continue operating. The company's plans to begin harvesting the area's timber in the summer of 1999 were contingent upon having road access completed by the end of summer 1998. Thus, an injunction halting road construction would jeopardize the company's Boston Bar operations. Moreover, Smith J. noted, by jeopardizing its Boston Bar operations, the injunction would threaten the company's financial viability. There were also larger public interest concerns at stake. The company, through its road building, logging, and Boston

Bar milling operations, was the largest employer in the Fraser Canyon area, so its proposed logging of the Siska watershed was critical to the well-being of the local and regional economies. All in all, the balance of convenience was, Smith J. concluded, heavily tilted against granting the Siska Band's request to issue an injunction against the company.

Almost two and a half months after Smith J. delivered his decision in the earlier *Siska Creek* case, two more British Columbia First Nations petitioned for judicial review of a decision to approve resource development in a sacred area. This time, however, the threat was not logging but oil and gas exploration.

The heart of the aforementioned sacred area, a twin-peaked mountain, is known by several names. First Nations peoples have long referred to it as the Twin Sisters. The settlers, naming it after one of their own ranks who settled early in the vicinity, came to call it Beattie Peaks. For the sake of uniformity and convenience, I will speak of the mountain itself as the Twin Sisters and the entire sacred area surrounding and including the mountain as the Twin Sisters area.

The Twin Sisters is situated at the headwaters of several drainages to the Peace River system. Among others, it is at the headwaters of the Moberly River watershed. To its south is Mount Montieth. The two mountains face each other across a forest valley of fir (at the higher valley elevation) and spruce (at the lower). The Twin Sisters area is located about fifty kilometres east of Moberly Lake. The lake is roughly halfway between the towns of Hudson's Hope to the north and Chetwynd to the south.

The Twin Sisters area is sacred to several of the region's First Nations. The Beaver people (Dunne-Za), most of whom belong to the West Moberly and Halfway River First Nations, consider it sacred. The West Moberly First Nation, as its name suggests, makes its home on the west side of Moberly Lake, where its reserve is located. The Halfway River First Nation, as we have already seen, occupies a reserve along the Halfway River about an hour and a half drive northwest of Fort St. John. The Saulteau First Nation also considers the Twin Sisters area sacred. Sometime around the 1870s, Saulteau people began migrating from the Great Lakes area to the region. Their migration's terminus was chosen in accordance with a Saulteau prophecy concerning the Twin Sisters area. The Saulteau First Nation occupies a reserve on the eastern shore of Moberly Lake. Finally, the Kelly Lake Cree Nation also considers the Twin Sisters area sacred. Kelly Lake is located eighty kilometres southeast of Dawson Creek, near the British Columbia–Alberta Border. Three Aboriginal groups are identified with Kelly Lake: the Kelly Lake First Nation, the Kelly Lake Cree Nation, and the Kelly Lake Métis Settlement Society. The Kelly Lake Cree Nation split from the Kelly Lake First Nation in 1996. Members of the Kelly Lake Cree Nation descend from Beaver (Dunne-Za), Iroquois, and Cree peoples. The West Moberly,

Halfway River, and Saulteau First Nations are signatories of Treaty 8 and have federally recognized status as Indian Bands. The Halfway River and Saulteau First Nations are members of the Treaty 8 Tribal Association. The West Moberly First Nation, a former member, has officially withdrawn. The Kelly Lake Cree Nation, like the Kelly Lake First Nation from which it split, is not a signatory to Treaty 8, does not have federally recognized status, and is not a member of the Treaty 8 Tribal Association.[136]

One of the features that makes the Twin Sisters area unique as a First Nations sacred site is that it is recognized as sacred by at least four First Nations communities, although not for precisely the same reasons in each case. One would expect that, being descended from the same Beaver people (Dunne-Za), if either the West Moberly or the Halfway River First Nation held the area as sacred, the other would as well. One might also expect that since many members of the Saulteau First Nation and Kelly Lake Cree Nation claim at least some Beaver (Dunne-Za) ancestry, they too would hold the area sacred. Finally, one would expect that the Twin Sisters area would symbolize similar things to all four communities.

Indeed, there is much commonality. All four agree that the area's sacredness is grounded primarily in its theological/cosmological significance and only secondarily, if at all, in its practical/religious use.[137] All four treat the Twin Sisters area as a sanctuary and refuge and see themselves as its stewards. Although the area is used for sustenance purposes, all four agree that the area's function as a sacred place is uppermost. The commonality of symbolism is not identity, however. For example, the West Moberly and Saulteau First Nations adhere to somewhat different theological/cosmological grounds for counting the Twin Sisters area as sacred. Hence, they associate somewhat different ethics with the sacred site. For instance, while the West Moberly First Nation holds that hunting is forbidden in the area, the Saulteau hold that it is permitted.[138]

In spite of decades of intense resource development in the Peace River country on both sides of the Alberta–British Columbia border, the Twin Sisters area entered the 1990s with its resource development potential untapped. In 1991, however, Amoco, which had acquired the oil and gas drilling licence for the general area and which had evidence of a substantial gas deposit in the Twin Sisters area, applied to the Ministry of Energy and Mines (MEM) for permission to drill an exploratory sour gas well on the slopes of the Twin Sisters.

Following Amoco's application, MEM and the Treaty 8 Tribal Association came to an agreement that an ethno-historical study of the proposed drilling area would be undertaken prior to any consideration of the application. The study involved elders and other members of the West Moberly, Halfway River, and Saulteau First Nations. A report based on the study was completed by December 1992. It made no reference to the Aboriginal people of Kelly Lake. The report recommended, among other things, a "moratorium in further industrial activity in the Upper Moberly/Carbon [Creek] watersheds."[139] The moratorium's purpose was "to help to minimize the potential for serious conflict and provide an opportunity to develop a mechanism for upholding the obligations assumed by the government and First Nations of Treaty 8."[140]

The next year, on 17 December 1993, a meeting was convened to discuss this report. Representatives of MEM and the West Moberly, Halfway River, and Saulteau First Nations attended. Discussions led to the formation of the Co-Management Advisory Committee (CMAC). CMAC membership consisted of officials from MEM, an Amoco representative, and two representatives from each of the West Moberly, Halfway River, and Saulteau First Nations. The CMAC met at various times over the following year. On 4 November 1994, it issued its report, which MEM subsequently accepted. The report described the Twin Sisters area as unique in terms of First Nations history, culture, and spirituality. "The immediate result of ... [the] CMAC report and its acceptance by the Ministry was," as was later noted, "that Amoco would not be permitted to drill [as it had proposed] in the slopes of the Twin Sisters. Instead, Amoco would have to meet and conduct further meetings with the SFN [Saulteau First Nation] and the other two First Nations."[141] Again, there was no reference to the Aboriginal people at Kelly Lake.

On 13 March 1995, the first trilateral discussions took place between representatives of a number of First Nations under the umbrella of the Treaty 8 Tribal Association, including the Saulteau First Nation, provincial government officials, and Amoco representatives. The trilateral format did not work, however. Some First Nations, including the Saulteau First Nation, were not in accord with the objectives of the Tribal Association. When the Saulteau First Nation representative did not attend the 20 July meeting, it became clear that the trilateral approach would have to be abandoned. Within a week, the Treaty 8 Tribal Association notified MEM of a suspension of discussions.

From October 1995 to May 1996, MEM officials and Amoco representatives met with Saulteau First Nations representatives a number of times. One of the things to emerge from the discussions was an agreement to undertake a government-funded traditional use study (TUS) of the Twin Sisters area. The study was to have four phases. Phase I began in early 1996. Although phase II was later completed, phases III and IV were never undertaken. They were never undertaken because the Saulteau First Nation and MEM were unable to conclude a sub-agreement regarding information sharing.[142] As an alternative, the government later entered into an agreement with the Treaty 8 Tribal Association to undertake a broader TUS designed to include what would have been covered in the narrower uncompleted study. The broader study commenced in the fall of 1997. Before the close of the year, the Saulteau First Nation informed the Treaty 8 Tribal Association of its interest in participating in the broader study.

Earlier, in April 1997, the Twin Sisters Special Management Committee (TSSMC) was established. As a starting point, the TSSMC accepted both the earlier CMAC report's characterization of the Twin Sisters area as a place with "unique cultural, heritage, spiritual and traditional values of significance to local First Nations"[143] and its definition of the area's boundary. The TSSMC's formal purpose was to formulate a comprehensive set of recommendations for the Twin Sisters area to be later incorporated into the Dawson Creek Land and Resource Management Plan. But its "greatest purpose," as the TSSMC itself put it, was to help "First Nations, resource agencies and resource tenure holders to work cooperatively to resolve resource management issues in a small, but very unique land area called Twin Sisters."[144] Accordingly, those invited to participate included various government ministries, the West Moberly, Halfway River, and Saulteau First Nations, two forest companies with interests in the area (including Canfor), and Amoco. All of these invitees accepted.

Within weeks, the TSSMC produced an initial draft report. The report divided the whole Twin Sisters area as originally defined by the CMAC into three distinct zones. Basically, the CMAC defined the Twin Sisters area by drawing a boundary around an area that included the Twin Sisters and the valley stretching from the Twin Sisters to Mount Montieth to the south. Although a geometrical oversimplification, I shall, for the sake of convenience, speak of the boundaries of the TSSMC's three zones as forming concentric circles. The boundary of the first and smallest zone immediately encircled the peaks of the Twin Sisters. The boundary of the second zone encircled the mountain. Thus, the second zone included the rest of the mountain. Finally, the boundary of the third zone corresponded to the original boundary defined by the CMAC report. The third zone, then, consisted of the remaining portion of the Twin Sisters area, including the area stretching across the valley to Mount Montieth.

The TSSMC's initial and final report recommended that the first zone be designated the Klin-se-za Protected Area.[145] Such protection meant, for instance, no surface drilling in the area. As for the other two zones, the report recommended, among other things, that opportunities for oil and gas exploration and development and timber harvesting be maintained subject to various conditions, including detailed consultation with First Nations.

On 21 April 1997, the TSSMC participants met by teleconference to discuss the initial draft report. Subject to minor amendments, all the participants, including Chief Napolean of the Saulteau First Nation, approved the draft report.

After the teleconference, Chief Napolean informed the Amoco representative that he would have to ask the band council and the rest of his people for their views on the TSSMC's draft recommendations. Clearly, their
views were unfavourable, because the Saulteau First Nation ceased to participate in the TSSMC discussions thereafter.[146] Although it became clear
only later, what upset the Saulteau First Nation most was the fact that only
the innermost portion of the Twin Sisters area would be fully protected. As
far as they were concerned, the whole area was sacred and deserving of
the same protection. Adding to their concern was the fact that although
Amoco had abandoned its original proposal to drill in the slopes of the
Twin Sisters, it was now proposing to drill its exploratory well in the valley between the Twin Sisters and Mount Monteith.

On 19 February 1997, Amoco informed the West Moberly, Halfway
River, and Saulteau First Nations that it was preparing to apply for a permit to drill in the valley near Mount Monteith. On 3 March, MEM wrote
to each of the three First Nations telling them "that Amoco was preparing
an application that would trigger a review process in which the issue of
the spirituality and environment of the Twin Sisters would be of major
concern."[147] On 9 April, Amoco provided the three First Nations with
copies of a draft of its application. Finally, on 4 June 1997, Amoco filed its
application. Copies were subsequently delivered to MEM and all three First
Nations. As required by the government, Amoco asked each of the three
First Nations for comments on its application.

For the rest of 1997 and the first half of 1998, MEM officials and Amoco
representatives continued to meet or otherwise communicate with the
leaders and members of the West Moberly, Halfway River, and Saulteau
First Nations. Finally, on 23 July 1998, Gerald German, an acting assistant
deputy minister of the Energy Resource Division of MEM, approved
Amoco's Mount Montieth application.

Apparently, neither the West Moberly nor the Halfway River First Nation
were dissatisfied with the consultation process. Indeed, more than ten
months prior to the approval of Amoco's Mount Montieth project, Chief
Desjarlais of the West Moberly First Nation wrote to Amoco thanking it
for its efforts to address his people's concerns regarding the Twin Sisters
area and acknowledging that the company had successfully completed its
consultations with the First Nation.[148] The Saulteau First Nation was of
a different view, however. Since at least 1995, it had repeatedly and con-
sistently expressed its opposition to any resource development in the overall Twin Sisters area. At the close of 1997, it began complaining that the
consultation process was faulty. Not surprisingly, as the time to decide
Amoco's application drew nearer, the First Nation grew increasingly less
interested in participating in the process.

From 1991 through 1995, neither MEM nor Amoco approached the

Aboriginal people of Kelly Lake about the company's proposed drilling in the Twin Sisters area. After learning that the newly formed Kelly Lake Cree Nation had commenced an action in federal court involving the claim that its traditional lands included the Twin Sisters area,[149] MEM sent an official to meet with its members. The meeting took place on 5 December 1996. Later, in June 1997, an Amoco representative met with Chief Calliou of the Kelly Lake Cree Nation. Immediately following that meeting, on 9 June 1997, Amoco mailed a copy of its Mount Montieth application to Chief Calliou along with an invitation to forward comments back to the company before 30 June. Amoco received no response. There were no further discussions or communications between either MEM or Amoco and the Kelly Lake Cree Nation regarding the Mount Montieth project.

By the middle of August 1998, Amoco was set to begin an upgrade on an existing road as the first stage of the road construction that would be required to access their Mount Montieth project. On the morning of 17 August, arriving workers were turned back by a peaceful blockade of First Nations people, most of them members of the Saulteau First Nation. Amoco applied for an injunction. On 26 August, it was granted an injunction enjoining the blockaders from interfering with the first stage of the road work. The protest camp remained in place but allowed workers to pass through. Near the middle of September, the Saulteau First Nation applied for a judicial review of MEM's decision to approve the Mount Montieth project. The Kelly Lake Cree Nation also applied for a judicial review of the same decision. Both sought orders setting aside the decision and requiring further consultation before any new decision could be made regarding the project. Because of their common ground, both First Nations applied to join their separate applications. By the consent of all parties, Mr. Justice Taylor ordered as asked. And so, over eight days at the end of September, he heard both applications together.

Although both the Saulteau First Nation and the Kelly Lake Cree Nation raised administrative law and *Canadian Charter of Rights and Freedoms* issues, their core issues concerned Aboriginal and treaty rights. Their basic shared position was this. The exploratory well authorized by the MEM decision would affect their Aboriginal and treaty rights in the Twin Sisters area. In the circumstances, the provincial Crown had, as part of its fiduciary obligations, a duty to meaningfully consult with them prior to making a decision. The Crown did not fulfill its duty.

The respondents' (MEM's, the Ministry of Forests',[150] and Amoco's) counterclaim was equally straightforward. They stated that the Crown did meaningfully consult with the Saulteau First Nation prior to making the decision and thus that it had fulfilled its duty. As for the Kelly Lake Cree Nation, the respondents' claimed simply that the Crown had no duty to consult with it regarding Amoco's proposed project.

On 21 September 1998, the first day of the judicial review proceedings, counsel for MEM "raised an objection to [the] admissibility of certain evidence that he viewed as going to the establishment of aboriginal rights, as distinct from an assertion of those rights."[151] Counsel's argument was "that an application for judicial review is a form of summary hearing, as opposed to a trial with all its attendant discovery procedures and thus is not an appropriate forum for a determination of aboriginal rights other than those affirmed by the state or confirmed by the Courts."[152] He suggested that if either of the petitioners was seeking a determination of its Aboriginal rights, the matter "should either be adjourned in its entirety, or the aspect of the establishment of such aboriginal rights should be referred to the trial list."[153]

In his consideration of the objection, Taylor J. found that both the Saulteau First Nation and the Kelly Lake Cree Nation had, in their petitions, raised issues whose resolution would require the court to rule on the existence of certain Aboriginal rights. He summarized and stated the rationale behind the relevant law on the establishment of such rights: "[F]or some time the law has been clear in this province that the establishment of such rights is not a matter for summary disposition. The rationale for this is simply that the existence of such rights can have implications of wide ramifications and therefore should not ... be determined on a summary basis without the benefit of a discovery process in which those rights and those who may be affected by those rights can be determined and heard respectively."[154] The assertion of Aboriginal rights was, however, another matter. MEM's counsel had conceded, he observed, "that in the context of administrative decisions that may be affected by asserted rights, that is, where there is an assertion of an aboriginal right, there then may arise a duty to consult with those who assert the rights."[155] MEM's counsel had, it should be noted, conceded only that there was an issue to be settled as to whether the assertion of such rights was sufficient to trigger a duty to consult. It was not a concession that such assertions did in fact trigger the duty on the part of the Crown. The concession did, however, imply that evidence put forth to prove the assertion of Aboriginal rights was admissible. "Accordingly," Taylor ruled, "the evidence of assertion of aboriginal rights is admissible; the evidence tendered to establish the existence of the aboriginal rights is not."[156]

Although he failed to make it clear in his ruling, he intended it to extend to the determination of treaty as well as Aboriginal rights. As he later stated in his main judgment, "I ruled [early in these proceedings] that this judicial review was not the place to determine the existence, limitation or extinguishment of any of the following rights: those existing under the treaty either in its written form or any oral form that it may have taken, aboriginal rights existing independent of treaty rights."[157]

The extension of the ruling to treaty rights meant that the Saulteau First Nation could not enter evidence of the existence of any of its treaty rights, only evidence of its assertion of treaty rights. Although the evidentiary limitation was partly overcome by the Crown's willingness to acknowledge rights to hunt, fish, and trap under Treaty 8, it left the Saulteau First Nation to rely entirely on asserted rights with regard to the sacred character of the Twin Sisters area.

Taylor J. then summed up what he took to be the core issue as follows: "The simple issue to be determined in this review is where asserted rights may be affected by the [administrative] decision, was there a duty to consult with either or both of the applicants before the decisions were made, and if so, whether there [was] fulfillment of that duty."[158] Next he summed up the Crown's position:

> The position of the Crown is that the [legal] duty to consult arises only in respect of aboriginal or treaty rights that have been established either through determination by the courts or by the acknowledgment of the Crown as to their existence. With respect to the SFN [Saulteau First Nation], the Crown accepts the SFN has treaty rights [to hunt, fish, and trap] under Treaty No. 8, and that being so there is a [legal] duty on the Crown to engage in consultation with First Nations who may be affected by the decisions sought by Amoco.[159]

Unstated but implied was the Crown's further position that asserted but unestablished or unaffirmed Aboriginal and treaty rights did not give rise to a legal duty to consult.

Taylor J. split his discussion of the issues between complaints specific to the Kelly Lake Cree Nation and complaints specific to the Saulteau First Nation. He divided both sets of complaints into administrative law, *Charter*, and Aboriginal law issues. In what follows, I will, with regard to the Kelly Lake Cree Nation and the Saulteau First Nation, respectively, briefly summarize Taylor J.'s findings on the administrative law issues and then detail his analysis of the Aboriginal law issues. Finally, I will, taking both First Nations together, touch upon his treatment of the *Charter* issues.

The Kelly Lake Cree Nation complained that the decision makers had breached their administrative duty of procedural fairness in a number of respects, namely, by failing to give the First Nation a fair hearing, by acting so as to raise a reasonable apprehension of bias, by fettering their discretion, and by taking irrelevant considerations into account.

Taylor J. decided that although the Kelly Lake Cree Nation was entitled to procedural fairness, the procedural fairness it was entitled to did not include a right to a hearing. The chambers judge's decision was based mainly on two findings: (1) that the nature of MEM's decision was not that of a tribunal deciding on evidence put before it but rather that of "a statutory authority charged with the responsibility of issuing permits for forms of economic activity,"[160] and (2) that the Kelly Lake Cree Nation's standing in the process was not that of a party, strictly speaking, but was at most akin to that of an interested person. Given these findings, Taylor J. decided that procedural fairness did not entitle the Kelly Lake Cree Nation to a hearing before the statutory decision maker. He concluded, therefore, that MEM did not breach its duty of procedural fairness by not giving the First Nation a hearing.

He also decided that the duty of procedural fairness did entitle the Kelly Lake Cree Nation to the opportunity to make representations. Since both MEM and Amoco had given the First Nation opportunities to comment on the Monteith project both in person and in writing, however, and since the First Nation failed to take advantage of the opportunities given, MEM did not, he held, breach its duty of procedural fairness by failing to give the opportunity to make representations.

Before moving to the next administrative law issue, it is worth pausing to note that the Kelly Lake Cree Nation appealed to Madam Justice Dorgan's decision in *Halfway River* in an attempt to persuade Taylor J. that procedural fairness entitled them to more than an opportunity to make representations. They argued that Dorgan J. had (impliedly) found that the Halfway River First Nation deserved the standing of a party in the decision-making process that led to the Ministry of Forests' approval of Canfor's cutting permit in the Tusdzuh, that the standing entailed a higher degree of procedural fairness, that the Kelly Lake Cree Nation was deserving of similar standing, and finally that they too were entitled to a higher degree of procedural fairness.

Taylor J. responded to this argument by distinguishing the *Halfway River* decision on the facts on which it was based. The evidence before Dorgan J. was, he noted, "that the area in dispute was used for traditional purposes, including hunting, gathering plants, food and medicinal purposes, and spiritual purposes." Thus, he explained, "[s]he concluded ... that logging operations 'could significantly affect Halfway's very way of life.'"[161] The evidence in the case before him was significantly different. He explained:

> The evidence in this case is that the area is of spiritual significance but not that it is used, rather that it is simply preserved by those who claim a spiritual significance. The evidence does not establish a physical use other than occasionally. Rather it is simply preserved by those who claim a spiritual significance. There is no evidence that the effect of the decision would have the same impact upon members of the KLCN [Kelly Lake Cree Nation] or indeed others included in the three First Nations who did

participate in the consultative process to the extent that the decision by the official of [the] Ministry of Forests would have in *Halfway River*.[162]

The obvious but unstated proximate conclusion was that Amoco's Mount Monteith project would have no significant impact on the Kelly Lake Cree Nation's way of life, or indeed on the West Moberly, Halfway River, and Saulteau First Nations' ways of life. The ultimate and also unstated conclusion was that the Kelly Lake Cree Nation's standing in the decision-making process did not warrant a higher level of procedural fairness.

Several assumptions undergirding Taylor J.'s proximate conclusion merit remark. They are assumptions about what counts as a *way of life* and what counts as *having a significant impact on* a way of life. It is clear that Taylor J.'s conception of a way of life put emphasis on day-to-day (including seasonal) activities. (Note his focus on the *use* of an area.) Hence, in his conception, whatever significantly affects a First Nation's day-to-day use of an area significantly affects its way of life. But there are deeper assumptions also at play. Among others, Taylor J. assumed that cultural connections to an area that do not find expression in day-to-day activities in the area are less significant to a First Nation's way of life than cultural connections to an area grounded in day-to-day activities. He also, as a consequence, assumed that areas that serve wholly or virtually wholly theological/cosmological functions within a First Nation's culture are less crucial to its way of life than areas that serve practical religious and/or other day-to-day mundane functions. These are serious extralegal assumptions. They are serious because their implications for First Nations litigants are serious. I shall have more to say on these matters in Chapter 5.

As for the Kelly Lake Cree Nation's charge that MEM's decision maker had acted so as to give rise to a reasonable apprehension of bias, Taylor J. simply observed that no evidence had been led.

The First Nation also argued that the decision maker had fettered his discretion in two ways: (1) by treating as a given the government's policy of refusing to halt resource development in the face of Native land claims, and (2) by acceding to pressures to give a quick decision arising from the fact that much of the work on the Mount Monteith project would have to be done in the winter months. Taylor J. found that not only did the evidence fail to support these assertions, it supported their opposites.

Finally, the Kelly Lake Cree Nation argued that MEM took irrelevant considerations into account in making its decision. As evidence, it pointed to the fact that the decision maker had taken into account Amoco's need to do most of its work on the project during the winter and the government's concern that further delay would cause a loss of confidence in British Columbia's oil and gas industry. Basically, Taylor J. found that the considerations were not, contrary to the First Nation's claims, irrelevant. He wrote:

Given the detailed process ... such considerations by the decision-makers were relevant in my opinion. It was not in my view a question of the quickness of the decision but rather that the time had come for the decision to be made. It is clear on the evidence that the singular and fundamental issue was the sanctity of this area to aboriginal First Nation people. The reasons for decision clearly establish it was a significant consideration undertaken by Mr. German [MEM's decision maker] and it is inconceivable that any additional studies would have varied the import of the utmost spiritual significance this area held for First Nations.[163]

The upshot was that MEM had not, Taylor J. concluded, breached its administrative duty of procedural fairness either by taking into account irrelevant considerations or by any of the other ways alleged.

In his discussion of the consultation issue, Taylor J. began by dealing with the Crown's duty of consultation, first as it relates to established or affirmed Aboriginal rights (including title) and then as it relates to asserted rights. He noted first that the respondents agreed that the Crown has a legal duty to consult with First Nations before authorizing any activity that may infringe their established or Crown-affirmed Aboriginal or treaty rights. They also agreed, he further noted, that *Sparrow* and *Delgamuukw* had made the honour of the Crown the standard for determining whether or not the Crown had fulfilled its consultation duty in any given case in which an established or affirmed Aboriginal or treaty right had been infringed. He then observed that the provincial government had adopted a policy requiring it – as a matter of ethics rather than law – to consult with First Nations asserting Aboriginal rights in certain circumstances. As he explained it,

[t]he invoking of that policy ... involves an assessment by the Crown whether the asserted right has some factual underpinning that would, if established, require fulfillment of its honour by the undertaking of meaningful consultation as to possible infringements upon the asserted right or title by the affects [sic] of a proposed activity.[164]

Thus, the Crown had determined that it had a duty to consult with the West Moberly, Halfway River, and Saulteau First Nations on both legal and policy grounds. First, all three First Nations possessed recognized treaty rights to hunt, fish, and trap in the Twin Sisters area. Second, their assertions of rights to the area in connection with its sacredness had strong factual underpinnings. As for the Kelly Lake Cree Nation, the Crown argued, on the one hand, that it lacked either established or affirmed Aboriginal or treaty rights and, on the other, that it was too removed from the Twin Sisters area to give any assertions of Aboriginal rights a strong factual underpinning and that, in any case, it had failed to assert Aboriginal rights to the area when presented with opportunities to do so within the parameters of the decision-making process.[165] The First Nation's failure to reciprocate by asserting its rights should not, the Crown urged, be charged to it as a failure to fulfill its duty to consult. Thus, lacking either a legal or an ethical duty to consult with the Kelly Lake Cree Nation regarding the Mount Monteith project, it could not have committed a breach.

Accepting the Crown's arguments, Taylor J. found that "there was no [legal or ethical] duty [triggerable by an assertion of rights] to consult with the KLCN [Kelly Lake Cree Nation] given the remoteness of the KLCN to the area in question and the claims of the SFN [Saulteau First Nation], WM [West Moberly First Nation] and the Halfway First Nation."[166] But "even if," he went on to add, "the Crown had a [legal or ethical] duty to consult on the basis of an asserted right, that obligation was fulfilled when KLCN as represented by Chief Calliou [by failing to respond to Amoco's request for comments] failed to express any interest in the proposed Monteith Mountain project."[167]

I turn now to Taylor J.'s consideration of the Saulteau First Nation's claim that the decision-making process that culminated in MEM's approval of Amoco's application violated various principles of administrative law.

The Saulteau First Nation claimed specifically that the decision maker conducted himself so as to raise a reasonable apprehension of bias, committed errors of fact and law, ignored relevant considerations, fettered his discretion, and denied their right to be heard. In each case, Taylor J. found that the Crown had fulfilled its administrative duties to the Saulteau First Nation. Since a presentation of each of these claims together with the chambers judge's responses would contribute little to my overall discussion, I shall ignore all but one of the claims, to wit, the Saulteau First Nation's claim that it had been denied its right to be heard.

The Kelly Lake Cree Nation had also argued that as a matter of procedural fairness it had a right to be heard by the decision maker and that its right had been denied. Taylor J. concluded that the procedural fairness it was due did not include a right to be heard. As for the Saulteau First Nation, he found that the same conclusion applied.

Taylor J.'s discussion of the issue did not end there, however. Underlying the Saulteau First Nation's complaint, there was, he inferred, a deeper complaint, a complaint that the decision maker had made his decision without adequate information regarding the First Nation's concerns and rights with regard to the Twin Sisters area. Accordingly, he went on to note that although the Crown did not, as part of its duty to be procedurally fair, owe the Saulteau First Nation a hearing before its decision maker, it did owe it a duty to consult in a meaningful manner. And consulting in a meaningful manner included taking into serious consideration the information provided by the First Nation. Thus, MEM's decision maker was duty-bound to give serious consideration to the information provided by the Saulteau First Nation.

It was true, Taylor J. conceded, that MEM's decision maker had not been personally engaged in consultations with any of the three First Nations involved in the consultation process. Nonetheless, he was, as Taylor J. put it, the repository of the process.[168] As for any concern on the Saulteau First Nation's part that there was a gap in the information gathered by those personally involved in consultations and the information ultimately considered by MEM's decision maker, the chambers judge found that those upon whom the decision maker relied "took steps to fully inform those who would decide of the aboriginal and treaty rights of the SFN [Saulteau First Nation]."[169] In any case, Taylor J. added, the blame for any inadequacy in the information ultimately considered by MEM's decision maker was ultimately traceable to the Saulteau First Nation itself. For, he explained, "any gap in the information was not through want of trying to obtain it. There were repeated attempts to involve the SFN in consultation but this was met by the failure of Chief Cameron on behalf of the SFN to participate in this two-way process."[170] The Saulteau First Nation could not, he went on to say, dodge the blame by arguing that as a community of limited means it could not provide the information requested. Pointing to the "sophistication and complexity" of the information provided in its Treaty Land Entitlement Claim,[171] he observed that despite the fact that it had been prepared "with the substantial assistance" of the Treaty 8 Tribal Association, it was a document illustrating "the ability of the SFN to respond to the kind of request for information made of it by both the Province and Amoco, and more importantly to participate in the process of consultation."[172] Finally, regarding the Saulteau First Nation's claims that it needed to obtain more information before it could respond adequately and that the province's refusal to fund "an impact study involving traditional and contemporary use of the 'Twin Sisters Area' and its cultural and spiritual values" made obtaining that information impossible, Taylor J. had this to say:

> What ... counsel [does not refer to] ... is the substantial body of information developed through a plethora of studies, all of which were directed at the values ascribed to this area in terms of archeological, environmental, cultural and spiritual values. There is no suggestion that the utmost spiritual significance attached to the Twin Sisters Area was any greater or less to the SFN than to any of the other First Nations people whose history also includes the prophecies. What then could the decision-maker have additionally derived from any further studies other than the sense that the project and its impact were being studied ad nauseam?[173]

Hence, Taylor J. concluded, the fact that the Saulteau First Nation was not entitled to a hearing implied neither that MEM's decision maker did not have an adequate grasp of its concerns, interests, and rights regarding the Twin Sisters area nor that it had been denied the opportunity to put its concerns, interests, and rights before him.

The Saulteau First Nation raised only one Aboriginal law issue: whether the Crown had unjustifiably infringed its rights under Treaty 8. The Crown acknowledged the First Nation's rights to hunt, fish, and trap in the Twin Sisters area and therefore accepted that Amoco's application to drill in the area triggered a duty to consult, as the Supreme Court of Canada said in *Delgamuukw*, "in good faith, and with the intention of substantially addressing the concerns of the aboriginal peoples whose lands are at issue."[174] The Crown refused to acknowledge, however, any further treaty (or Aboriginal) rights with regard to the area as sacred. Given the limitations imposed by Taylor J. at the outset of the proceedings, its refusal meant that the Saulteau First Nation had only asserted rights to plead with regard to the area's sacredness. The Crown, of course, denied that such asserted rights, however well founded, triggered a legal duty to consult. The Crown submitted that it had, nonetheless, "conducted itself in a manner consistent with the existence of the asserted spiritual or religious rights."[175] It thus implied that it had not unjustifiably infringed the Saulteau First Nation's acknowledged or (assuming they entailed a legal duty to consult) asserted rights with regard to the area.

Taylor J. stated his agreement with the Crown's submission, explaining:

> A substantial portion of the plethora of discussions, inquiries and consultations of all three First Nations was directed towards the treaty rights as they would be affected by the drilling project, in particular the sanctity of the area surrounding the Twin Sisters. That is particularly so in respect of the consultations that evolved through the TSSMC, resulting in the development of a protected area and areas of special management that were formulated and agreed upon. The SFN began as a part of that TSSMC process but because of an apparent internal disputes [sic], withdrew under the leadership of Chief Cameron. Despite that, the process continued at which a minimization of infringement was addressed of not only the recognized treaty rights but also the spiritual significance or religious rights.[176]

He concluded that the Crown had conducted itself so as to fulfill its duty to consult "in good faith, and with the intention of substantially addressing the concerns of the aboriginal peoples whose lands are at issue." In short, whatever infringements of the Saulteau First Nation's Aboriginal or treaty rights might have resulted from MEM's approval of Amoco's Mount Monteith project, they were justified infringements.

Both the Kelly Lake Cree Nation and Saulteau First Nation submitted that the project's approval violated their right to religious freedom as guaranteed by the *Charter*.[177] Basically, their argument was as follows. The *Charter* protects freedom of religion. Section 2(a) says:

> 2. Everyone has the following fundamental freedoms:
> (a) freedom of conscience and religion.

Section 7 states the extent to which such fundamental freedoms are protected:

> 7. Everyone has the right to life, liberty and security of the person and the right not to be deprived thereof except in accordance with the principles of fundamental justice.

Section 2(a), their argument continued, encompasses not only the right of the members of the Kelly Lake Cree Nation and the Saulteau First Nation to use the Twin Sisters area for certain spiritual or religious purposes but also the right to exercise stewardship over the area in accordance with their respective prophecies (theological/cosmological beliefs) concerning the area. Amoco's access trail and exploratory gas well constituted violations of those rights. Therefore, MEM's approval of the Mount Monteith project violated their fundamental rights and freedoms.

Taylor J. dealt with the alleged *Charter* right to use the Twin Sisters area for spiritual or religious purposes first. In spite of the fact that there was very little evidence of the consistent use of the area for practical religious purposes, especially on the part of the Kelly Lake Cree Nation,[178] he accepted that both the Kelly Lake Cree Nation and the Saulteau First Nation had constitutionally protected religious rights involving the use of the Twin Sisters area. He found, however, that Amoco's Mount Monteith project would not prevent the exercise of any religiously significant practices in the area. He concluded that MEM's approval of the project did not violate the right of the Kelly Lake Cree Nation and the Saulteau First Nation to use the Twin Sisters area for spiritual or religious purposes.[179]

As for the alleged right to exercise stewardship over the area, Taylor J. found that s. 2(a) did not "protect a concept of stewardship of a place of worship under the protection of religious freedom."[180] He added that "even if I were incorrect in that conclusion, the adherence of the decision-makers to the TSSMC recommendations within the protected area in fact protects an area for both alpine and sub-alpine activities upon which there can be an absolute stewardship and within area I and II a lesser form of stewardship."[181] Or, as he put it near the close of his judgment:

The intellectual aspect of a concept of stewardship for times of need in refuge is not impugned and while in a perfect world as viewed by the SFN [Saulteau First Nation], such drilling would never occur, the activity does not deny that concept. The provisions of a protected area provides a basis for that continued intellectual stewardship that is an aspect of the area's spirituality. While geographically constricted, it is not eliminated to the extent that there is limitation or coercion of the existence of the religious rights.[182]

Having held against both the Kelly Lake Cree Nation and the Saulteau First Nation in all three categories of issues – administrative law, Aboriginal law, and *Charter* issues – Taylor J. dismissed both petitions.

Before turning, finally, to the Court of Appeal's decision in *Halfway River,* it should be noted that despite the fact that he set it as "the simple issue to be determined" in the judicial review,[183] Taylor J. never pronounced on whether or not asserted Aboriginal or treaty rights triggered a duty to consult. Logically speaking, the most he committed himself to was the conditional proposition of the form, "if asserted rights trigger a duty to consult, then ..."

On 12 August 1999, over two years after Madam Justice Dorgan had delivered hers, the Court of Appeal delivered its decision in the *Halfway River* case. The Court split two to one in favour of affirming the chambers judge's order setting aside the Ministry of Forests district manager's approval of CP212, permitting Canfor to log in the Tusdzuh. Mr. Justice Finch and Madam Justice Huddart wrote separate but ultimately concurring reasons for judgment. Madam Justice Southin wrote in dissent.

Besides splitting two to one on the ultimate issue before it – whether to affirm the chambers judge's order – the Court variously split two to one on four subordinate but fundamental questions:

1   Did the chambers judge err in holding that the district manager's decision to approve Canfor's cutting permit violated certain principles of administrative law?
2   Was judicial review a proper proceeding in which to consider issues of Aboriginal or treaty rights?
3   Should the chambers judge have applied the *Sparrow* analysis?
4   What is the legal responsibility of administrative decision makers to inform themselves of and determine Aboriginal and treaty rights issues?

On the first question, Finch J.A. held that the chambers judge erred in her decisions on most but not all of the specific administrative law issues;

Huddart J.A. concurred, whereas Southin J.A. dismissed the question. On the second question, Finch and Huddart JJ.A. concurred, while Southin vigorously dissented. On the third question, Huddart J.A. parted company with Finch J.A. and claimed, with the implied agreement of Southin J.A., that the *Sparrow* analysis had no application in the case. Finally, on the fourth question, Huddart J.A., with Finch J.A.'s largely implied agreement, articulated the decision maker's responsibilities as an expression of the Crown's constitutional and fiduciary obligations, and thus as including a duty both to consult about and, if necessary, to accommodate Aboriginal or treaty rights. Southin J.A. disagreed with her articulation, arguing that it was far too burdensome. In what follows, I shall present the majority and minority positions on each of these four questions in the order in which they are listed above.

For reasons that will become apparent when I consider the second question, Southin J.A. looked upon what she termed "the so-called administrative law issues" in the case as "nothing but distractions from issues arising on the Treaty [8]."[184] That is all she said on the matter. But since she would have allowed the appeal and set aside the order below, it is clear that she thought that the chambers judge erred in holding that the district manager's decision to approve CP212 had violated various principles of administrative law.

Finch J.A., however, gave a detailed analysis of the administrative law issues and the chambers judge's handling of them.[185] The specific issues were whether the district manager had fettered his discretion, raised a reasonable apprehension of bias, failed to give adequate notice, failed to provide an effective opportunity to be heard, and committed an error of fact. On the first issue, Finch J.A. held that the chambers judge erred in holding that the district manager had fettered his discretion by slavishly adhering to the government's policy of not halting resource development pending resolution of land claims. As he explained, the government's policy did not imply that a cutting permit would be automatically issued regardless of Aboriginal or treaty rights, and it was apparent that "the District Manager gave a full consideration to the information before him concerning those ... rights."[186] On the second administrative law issue, Finch J.A. held that the chambers judge erred in holding that the district manager's statement to Chief Metecheah – that if Canfor's application was in order, he would have "no compelling reasons not to approve their application" – raised a reasonable apprehension of bias. He pointed out that it was necessary to distinguish between the district manager's investigative and adjudicative roles and then observed that forming tentative or preliminary opinions was part and parcel of the investigative role. Thus, "[a] fair reading of his statement is that he had formed a tentative view on the information then available that the permit should issue, but that the final decision had not been made, and he was prepared to refuse issuance of the permit if there was a good reason to do so."[187] On the third administrative law issue, Finch J.A. held that the chambers judge erred in holding that the district manager had failed to give adequate notice of his impending decision. He found both that the district manager was under no obligation to give notice of a fixed date on which his decision would be made and that he had, in any case, given ample notice of his impending decision. On the fourth issue, however, Finch J.A. decided that the chambers judge was correct in holding that procedural fairness entitled the Halfway River First Nation to an effective opportunity to be heard and that the district manager had, by failing to consult with them, denied them their rightful opportunity to be heard.

On the fifth administrative law issue, Finch J.A. held that the chambers judge was correct to conclude that the district manager had erred in deciding that Canfor's logging of the Tusdzuh would not infringe the Halfway River First Nation's Aboriginal or treaty rights. He disagreed, however, with her characterization of the district manager's error as an error of fact and her identification of the standard of review as patent unreasonableness:

> With respect, interpreting the treaty, deciding on the scope and interplay of the rights granted by it to both the petitioners and the Crown, and determining whether the petitioners' rights under the treaty were infringed, are all questions of law, although the last question may be one of mixed fact and law. Even though he has a fiduciary duty, the District Manager had no special expertise in deciding any of these issues, and as I understand the legislation, he has no authority to decide questions of general law such as these. To the extent that his decisions involve legal components, in the absence of any preclusive clause, they are reviewable on the standard of correctness.[188]

But in spite of the fact that Dorgan J. had, in his view, erred both by mischaracterizing questions of law (or mixed law and fact) as questions of fact and by showing too much deference to the district manager by adopting the "patently unreasonable" standard of review, Finch J.A. held that she was nonetheless correct in her general conclusion that the district manager had erred in deciding that Canfor's logging would not be infringing.

For her part, Huddart J.A. simply stated her full agreement with Finch J.A. on the administrative law issues.

On the second subordinate question, Southin J.A. urged that judicial review was not the proper proceeding for considering issues of Aboriginal or treaty rights. The proper proceeding was, she contended, an action on the treaty in which the central issue would have been whether the Crown had conducted itself so as to be in breach of its treaty obligations. The problem with judicial review in such cases, and especially in this case, was the implications:

> If this were not the first case on the implications for British Columbia of Treaty 8 and if these implications did not go far beyond whether Canfor can or cannot log these cut blocks, I would agree ... that, as the parties did not object to the mode of proceeding, it must be taken to be satisfactory. But, in my opinion, the courts do have an obligation to ensure that a case the implications of which extend beyond the parties; and the implications of this case may extend not only to all the inhabitants of the Peace River but also, because the Peace River country is not poor in resources, to all the inhabitants of British Columbia; is fully explored on proper evidence.[189]

The nature of the aforesaid implications she spelled out later: "This case has serious economic consequences. To decide the issues arising on the evidence here adduced, which, as the parties chose to proceed, was not focused on that question only, is a course fraught with danger, especially to third parties."[190] Besides the economic implications of permitting the province's resource-related decisions to be judicially reviewed with regard to Aboriginal and treaty rights, there was, she added, an element of injustice or unfairness. Since it was the fault of the Crown alone if the treaty had been breached, it was "not right that Canfor and all others, who in accordance with the Statutes of British Columbia have obtained from the Crown rights to lands in the Peace River and conducted their affairs in the not unreasonable belief that they were exercising legal rights, should find themselves under attack in a proceeding such as this."[191] In Southin J.A.'s view, the chambers judge erred by not ordering a trial of the Aboriginal and treaty rights issues.

Finch J.A. (with Huddart J.A.'s concurrence) adopted a stance opposed to Southin J.A.'s. He began by noting that "[w]here the issues raised on such an application are sufficiently complex, and are closely tied to questions of fact, a chambers judge has a discretion to order a trial of the proceedings."[192] He also noted that the court's power to convert judicial review and other proceedings into a trial can be invoked either "on the court's own motion or on an application of a party."[193] Although counsel for the Ministry of Forests claimed that he had taken the position before the chambers judge "that the issue of Treaty rights and their breach had not been properly raised in the petition, and could not properly be decided on affidavit evidence, and without pleadings," he nevertheless, Finch J.A. observed, made no motion to have the proceedings converted. Hence, counsel's failure to make the motion, although not decisive, served to weaken the Ministry of Forests' complaint against the chambers judge.

To Finch J.A.'s mind, however, two facts in particular suggested that judicial review was an appropriate proceeding in which to consider Aboriginal or treaty rights issues insofar as they had been pronounced on by the district manager: (1) that judicial review is the usual way to challenge administrative decisions, and (2) that the district manager could not avoid confronting such issues. On the second fact, Finch J.A. had this to say: "In considering whether to issue C.P.212, the District Manager must be taken to have been aware of his fiduciary duty to the petitioners, as an agent of the Crown, of the right the petitioners asserted under Treaty 8, and of the possibility that issuance of the permit might constitute an infringement of that right. *Of necessity* his decision included a ruling on legal and constitutional rights"[194] [emphasis added]. Regarding the first fact, Finch J.A. saw no reason why, generally speaking, such matters could not be disposed of on affidavit evidence on an application for judicial review. Moreover, if such matters could not be so disposed of, "the District Manager and the forest industry would be in an impossible situation if, before deciding to issue a cutting permit, the applicant was required to commence an action by writ for resolution of any dispute over treaty rights, and the District Manager was bound to wait for the disposition of such an action (and the appeals) before deciding to issue a permit."[195] All things considered, he was not persuaded that the chambers judge erred in exercising her discretion to proceed by way of judicial review.

The third fundamental question on which the Court split was whether the chambers judge should have applied the *Sparrow* test for justifiable infringement. On this question, Huddart J.A. parted company with Finch J.A. By implication, Southin J.A. – since she held that it was an error to decide such Aboriginal or treaty rights issues on judicial review – held that the *Sparrow* test should not have been applied. Huddart J.A. also held that the *Sparrow* test should not have been applied, although she adopted a more flexible approach than Southin J.A.'s concerning the circumstances in which it might be applied on judicial review. Finch J.A. alone held not only that it might be applied on judicial review but also that the chambers judge was correct in applying it. I will begin with Finch J.A.'s discussion.

Treaty 8, as Finch J.A. noted, set up a regime of competing rights over surrendered lands. First Nations signatories acquired treaty rights to continue to hunt, trap, and fish on those lands, while the Crown acquired treaty rights to regulate those activities and to take up land for various purposes including lumbering (the latter of the Crown's rights being the so-called geographical limitation). Finch J.A. went on to insist that both sets of rights had to be understood in reference to one another: The First Nations' rights were qualified by the Crown's rights and the Crown's rights could not be exercised so as to render the First Nations' rights meaningless (that is, the Crown's rights were not absolute). He added that s. 35 of the

Constitution Act, 1982 had strengthened the First Nations' treaty rights by according them constitutional status. Prior to s. 35's enactment, Parliament "had the power to vary or repeal treaty rights" as it wished.[196] Since its enactment, however, First Nations' treaty rights could not "be infringed or restricted other than in conformity with constitutional norms."[197]

Because the Crown's rights under Treaty 8 qualified the First Nations' rights, the Crown could not exercise its rights without affecting the First Nations' rights. By implication, the Crown could not exercise its right to take up land – land including the Tusdzuh – for lumbering without affecting the Halfway River First Nation's rights, especially its right to hunt in the Tusdzuh. The question, then, was how seriously CP212 would affect Halfway River's right to hunt. In Finch J.A.'s view, the interference resulting from CP212 amounted to infringement: "Given the fiduciary nature of the relationship between government and Indians, and the constitutional protection afforded by s. 35 over the treaty right to hunt, it seems to me that the interference contemplated by C.P.212 amounts to an infringement of the petitioners' right to hunt."[198] Hence, he concluded, the chambers judge did not err in holding that "any interference with the right to hunt is a *prima facie* infringement of the Indians' treaty right as protected by s. 35 of the Constitution Act, 1982."[199]

Given that he agreed with the chambers judge both that the Halfway River First Nation possessed a treaty right to hunt in the Tusdzuh and that CP212 constituted *prima facie* infringement, Finch J.A. had left to decide only whether the chambers judge erred in concluding that the Crown, by the district manager's approval of Canfor's permit, had unjustifiably infringed the right. Following the list of questions suggested in *Sparrow* as an aid to determining whether an infringement is justifiable, he inquired: (1) whether the objective of the province's forestry legislation was sufficiently important to warrant infringement, (2) whether Canfor's proposed operations would minimally impair the Halfway River people's right to hunt, (3) whether the effects of infringement outweighed the benefits of the infringing action, and (4) whether there had been adequate consultation. On the first question, Finch J.A. held that the objectives of the province's forestry legislation included not only the economic needs of all the province's peoples and communities but also cultural needs and conservation goals. Thus, he concluded, the legislative objective was sufficiently important to warrant infringement of the Halfway River people's right to hunt. On the second question, adopting the findings of the district manager, he held that CP212 would have a minimal impact on the right to hunt. On the third question, he reasoned: "Given the minimal effects on hunting that the proposed logging would have ... and in the absence of any evidence to the contrary, it is my view a fair inference that the benefits to be derived from implementation of the legislative scheme, and the issuance of cutting permits in accordance with its requirements, would outweigh any detriment to the petitioners caused by the infringement of the right to hunt."[200] Thus, with respect to the first three questions, Finch J.A. concluded that the Crown had satisfied the requirements for justifiable infringement.[201]

With regard to the fourth *Sparrow*-inspired question, however, he concluded that the Crown had failed to justify its infringement of the Halfway First Nation's treaty rights. It had failed in its duty to consult meaningfully with the First Nation. Specifically, it had failed "to provide in a timely way information the aboriginal group would need in order to inform itself on the effects of the proposed actions, and to ensure that the aboriginal group had an opportunity to express their interests and concerns."[202] Noting that the Halfway River First Nation had a reciprocal duty to participate in the consultation, he then stated his agreement with the chambers judge that a failure on the First Nation's part did not relieve the Crown of its duty: "I respectfully agree with the learned chambers judge that given the positive duty to inform resting on the Crown, it is no answer for it to say that the petitioners did not take affirmative steps in their own interests to be informed, conduct that the learned chambers judge described as possibly 'not ... entirely reasonable.'"[203] Since its failure to adequately consult with the Halfway River First Nation sufficed to render its infringement of the First Nation's treaty rights unjustified, the Crown – or, more accurately, its agents – had failed to uphold its honour. And so, the chambers judge did not, Finch J.A. concluded, err in holding that the Crown, by the district manager's approval of CP212, had unjustifiably infringed the Halfway River people's constitutionally protected right to hunt in the Tusdzuh.

Huddart J.A., disagreeing with Finch J.A., held that the chambers judge should not have applied the *Sparrow* test in her analysis of the district manager's decision. Basically, she thought that its application was premature. Huddart J.A.'s disagreement with Finch J.A. flowed from her view "that the chambers judge was wrong when she found that 'any interference' with the right to hunt constituted ... [a *prima facie*] 'infringement' of the treaty right requiring justification."[204] Contrary to the chambers judge's interpretation, Huddart J.A. could not "read either *Sparrow* or *Badger* to support that view."[205] An analysis of these and other cases, she insisted, revealed that whether interference with a treaty or Aboriginal right constituted infringement depended on the degree and significance of the interference. The chambers judge's immediate inference of *prima facie* infringement of the Halfway River people's treaty right to hunt was therefore unwarranted.[206] Since her inference was unwarranted, *prima facie* infringement had not been established. But the Crown could not rightly be pressed to justify an infringement that had not been established. Thus, Huddart J.A. concluded, the chambers judge's application of the justification stage of the *Sparrow* infringement-justification analysis was premature.

According to the *Sparrow* doctrine of infringement, the First Nation, as the party claiming that its Aboriginal or treaty rights had been infringed, bears the onus of proving *prima facie* infringement. It is tempting to suppose that Huddart J.A. also faulted the chambers judge for not concluding that the evidence did not support a finding of *prima facie* infringement. To put it another way, it is tempting to suppose that she faulted the chambers judge for not applying the first stage, the infringement stage, of the *Sparrow* infringement-justification analysis. The supposition itself presupposes that Huddart J.A. believed that had the chambers judge properly applied the infringement stage of the analysis, she would have realized that the second, justification stage had no application.

That was not Huddart J.A.'s position, however. To her mind, the *Sparrow* analysis had no, and therefore not even partial, application. The problem was not that the Halfway River First Nation had failed to discharge its evidentiary burden with regard to *prima facie* infringement but the deeper problem that the district manager had failed in his duty to consult the First Nation as to the nature and scope of its treaty and Aboriginal rights. Thanks to the inadequacy of his consultation efforts, what understanding of Halfway River's rights he had acquired fell short of what was needed to support a reliable determination as to whether the Crown's proposed use of the Tusdzuh was infringing or not. On top of that, courts "particularly in the context of judicial review ... [rely] heavily upon the findings of the decision maker."[207] Thus, the chambers judge, like the district manager, lacked the information needed to determine whether or not the Halfway River First Nation's rights would be infringed. Absent such information, application of the *Sparrow* infringement-justification analysis was simply premature.

Huddart J.A. did, however, agree with Finch J.A. on the general point that the *Sparrow* analysis could be applied in judicial review in certain circumstances. As long as the consultation process yielded adequate information about the nature and scope of the First Nation's Aboriginal or treaty rights and the impact of the Crown's proposed use on those rights, the analysis could be applied.

The fourth and final subordinate question on which the Court of Appeal split two to one was this: What is the legal responsibility of administrative decision makers to inform themselves of and determine Aboriginal and treaty rights issues? Finch and Huddart JJ.A. agreed both that decision makers such as the district manager who approved CP212 bear fiduciary and constitutional responsibilities to the First Nations peoples who may be affected by their decisions and also, but only generally speaking, on the content of those responsibilities. As Huddart J.A.'s position is the more fully articulated of the two and the main target of Southin J.A.'s criticisms, I will refer only to her discussion in what follows. I will present Southin J.A.'s criticisms last.

But first a few prefatory remarks. Section 35(1) of the *Constitution Act, 1982* constitutionally obliges the Crown to recognize and affirm Aboriginal and treaty rights in its dealings with First Nations peoples. Recognition and affirmation does not mean, however, that the Crown can never infringe those rights. But when it does infringe, it must do so according to constitutional norms. Those norms prescribe certain limits. The Crown's position of fiduciary in relation to Aboriginal peoples provides the main limiting principle – that is, infringement is justifiable only if it is consistent with the Crown's fiduciary position.[208]

When the Crown chooses to pursue an infringing course of action, it must satisfy its relevant fiduciary obligations in order to satisfy its constitutional obligation to recognize and affirm a First Nation's Aboriginal or treaty rights. As their satisfaction is a condition necessary for the satisfaction of the Crown's constitutional obligation, the relevant fiduciary obligations are – albeit indirectly – constitutional obligations. But the Crown also has fiduciary obligations that exist independently of its constitutional obligations under s. 35(1). They are engaged to some extent in all of the Crown's dealings with Aboriginal peoples, and thus not only when it is pursuing an infringing course of action. Clearly, then, the Crown's constitutional obligations under s. 35(1) do not exhaust its fiduciary obligations.

As an agent of the Crown, the district manager who approved CP212 bore both constitutional and fiduciary responsibilities to the Halfway River First Nation. With regard to the first set of responsibilities, the district manager was, Huddart J.A. observed in agreement with Finch J.A., "under a positive obligation to the Halfway River First Nation to recognize and affirm its treaty right to hunt in determining whether to grant Cutting Permit 212 to Canfor."[209] More specifically, "[t]his constitutional obligation required him to interpret the *Forest Act* and the *Forest Practices Code* so that he might apply government forest policy with respect for Halfway's rights."[210]

But "[t]he District Manager was also required to determine the nature and extent of the treaty right to hunt so as to honour the Crown's fiduciary obligation to the First Nation."[211] Huddart J.A.'s point in adding this remark was not merely to say that the district manager, faced with a possibly infringing use of the Tusdzuh, was constitutionally obliged to ensure that his decision was consistent with the Crown's fiduciary position, and was therefore constitutionally obliged to determine the nature and extent of the Halfway River people's treaty right for the sake of determining whether it would be infringed. It was to say that the district manager, faced with a possibly infringing use of the Tusdzuh, had a fiduciary obligation to look after the Halfway River people's interests in the decision-making process. It was part of his fiduciary obligation, Huddart J.A. implied, to determine the nature and extent of their treaty right.

The district manager's prior determination of the nature and extent of the treaty right was required for his subsequent determination not only of whether the Crown's contemplated use of the Tusdzuh was infringing but also of whether the contemplated use was compatible with the Halfway River people's rightful use. The latter determination was, Huddart J.A. insisted, a crucial factor in shaping such decision-making processes. For if a decision maker determines that the Crown's proposed use is compatible with a First Nation's rightful use of the land, his or her task becomes one of allocating "the use of the land ... among competing, perhaps conflicting, but ultimately compatible uses among which the land could be shared."[212] But if the decision maker determines that the Crown's proposed use is incompatible with the First Nation's rightful use, his or her main task becomes one of determining whether the Crown's assertion of exclusive use is justifiable.

All the aforesaid determinations rest on the prior determination of the nature and scope of the Aboriginal or treaty right possibly affected by the Crown's proposed use. But before the decision maker can properly make that prior determination, he or she must have information about the First Nation's Aboriginal or treaty rights. Generally speaking, information about the nature of the right will not suffice. The decision maker also requires information about the scope of the right. Often, a right's scope must be inferred from the First Nation's exercise of the right. Also, when the right concerns land or resources, the right's exercise finds expression in use. Thus, the decision maker will often require information about a First Nation's use of the land or resources before he or she can accurately gauge the right's scope. Only when the decision maker has an adequate understanding of the nature and scope of the First Nation's Aboriginal or treaty right can he or she determine whether the impact of the Crown's proposed use on the First Nation's right is infringing or not and also whether it is compatible or incompatible with the First Nation's rightful use.

Given that the decision maker is obliged on both fiduciary and constitutional grounds not to make a decision that infringes on Aboriginal or treaty rights unjustifiably, and given that the decision maker cannot satisfy his or her fiduciary and constitutional obligations unless he or she has made an accurate determination as to the nature and scope of the rights possibly affected, an inescapable problem presents itself: How is the decision maker to acquire the requisite information about the First Nation's Aboriginal or treaty rights? Huddart J.A.'s solution was simple and practical. Referring to the *Sparrow* infringement-justification analysis, she said: "Because only the First Nation will have information about the scope of their use of the land, and of the importance of the use of the land to their culture and identity, if the *Sparrow* guidelines are to organize the review of an administrative decision it makes good sense to require the First Nation to establish the scope of the right at the first opportunity, to the decision-maker himself during the consultation he is required to undertake, so that he might satisfy his obligation to act constitutionally."[213] Thus, although the decision maker is responsible for initiating consultation, the First Nation, she suggested, should be responsible for supplying him or her with the requisite information about its Aboriginal or treaty rights. The First Nation's reciprocal duty should, Huddart J.A. further suggested, carry consequences for any future judicial review proceedings:

> The requirement that a decision-maker under the *Forest Act* and the *Forest Practices Code* consult with a First Nation that may be affected by his decision does not mean the First Nation is absolved of any responsibility. Once the District Manager has set up an adequate opportunity to consult, the First Nation is required to co-operate fully with that process and offer the relevant information to aid in determining the exact nature of the right in question. The First Nation must take advantage of this opportunity as it arises. It cannot unreasonably refuse to participate ... In my view, a First Nation should not be permitted to provide evidence on judicial review it has had an appropriate opportunity to provide to the decision-maker, to support a petition asserting a failure to respect a treaty right.[214]

Summing up the key points, then, Huddart J.A. held that the Crown, and therefore the Crown's appointed decision maker, owed both fiduciary and constitutional duties to the Halfway River First Nation. Satisfaction of those duties "required [the district manager] to initiate a process of adequate and meaningful consultation with Halfway to ascertain the nature and scope of the treaty right at issue."[215]

Southin J.A. deeply disagreed with Huddart J.A.'s position, arguing that it was too burdensome to the province's resource-related decision-making system and that its economic implications were devastating. On the first point, she said:

> With respect, to create a system in which those appointed to administrative positions under the *Forest Act* or any other statute of British Columbia regulating Crown land in the Peace River are expected to consult 'to ascertain the nature and scope of the treaty right at issue' and to determine 'whether the proposed use is compatible with the treaty right' is to place on our civil servants a burden they should not have to bear – a patchwork quilt of decision making by persons appointed not for their skill in legal questions but for their skill in forestry, mining, oil and gas, and agriculture.[216]

On the second point, she wrote: "Not only is this burden on the civil servants unfair to them, but also it ladens the people of British Columbia with burdens heavy to be borne, burdens which no other province's people have to bear, even though the other provinces, except Newfoundland, also have First Nations."[217] Adding a rhetorical flourish, she emphasized the economic implications of the aforesaid burden: "If my colleagues are right, British Columbia, which was once described as the spoilt child of Confederation, is about to become the downtrodden stepchild of Confederation."[218]

Before closing this section, I want to make one final observation about the *Halfway River* case. In the proceedings before the chambers judge, the Halfway River First Nation claimed not only treaty rights to hunt, trap, and fish in the Tusdzuh but also Aboriginal rights to utilize the area for spiritual and religious purposes. The fact that the Halfway River First Nation was claiming Aboriginal rights of a practical religious nature implied that it considered the Tusdzuh area sacred on practical religious grounds at least. Dorgan J., the chambers judge, virtually ignored the Aboriginal rights claim to focus her attention on the treaty right to hunt.[219] At the Court of Appeal, Huddart J.A. alone discussed (albeit briefly) the Halfway River First Nation's claim to Aboriginal rights of a spiritual and religious nature in the Tusdzuh area.[220]

Unlike the chambers judge, Huddart J.A. did not assume that the Halfway River people's ancestors had surrendered all of their Aboriginal rights for treaty rights. Thus, she was open to the possibility that the Halfway River First Nation still possessed Aboriginal rights of a practical religious nature in the Tusdzuh area. That meant that besides the still-lingering question of whether Canfor's proposal to log the area would interfere with the First Nation's treaty right to hunt, there was another equally significant unanswered question, namely, whether it would interfere with Halfway River's Aboriginal spiritual and religious rights in the area. For its part, the Halfway River First Nation had asserted not merely that CP212 would interfere with its Aboriginal spiritual and religious rights but that it would infringe against them to the point of exclusion of their exercise.[221]

Huddart J.A. was fairly sympathetic to this assertion. Indeed, she believed that Canfor's interference with the Halfway River people's Aboriginal spiritual and religious rights in the Tusdzuh might be more culturally disruptive and damaging than its interference with their treaty right to hunt.

That she held this belief can be inferred from her response to Finch J.A.'s discussion of the chambers judge's finding that the Halfway River people's "preferred means are to exercise their rights to hunt, trap and fish in an unspoiled wilderness in close proximity to their reserve lands."[222] Based partly on her finding that CP212 represented a denial of their preferred means, the chambers judge had drawn the conclusion that the proposed interference with the Halfway River First Nation's treaty rights constituted *prima facie* infringement. On appeal, the Ministry of Forests attacked the conclusion by, among other things, attacking the chambers judge's finding. In response, Finch J.A. began by willingly conceding that the chambers judge's finding was mistaken. As he put it, "in my respectful view, the learned chambers judge overstated the petitioners' position in holding that they were entitled to exercise their 'preferred means of hunting' by doing so in an 'unspoiled wilderness.' The Tusdzuh was not unspoiled wilderness in 1996 when the district manager approved C.P.212, nor was it unspoiled wilderness in 1982 when treaty rights received constitutional protection. This was a wilderness criss-crossed with seismic lines, where oil and gas exploration and mining had taken place."[223] As for her characterization of their preferred means, he had this to say: "Nor do I think 'preferred means' should be taken to refer to an area, or the nature of the area, where hunting or fishing rights might be exercised. Those words more correctly refer to the methods or modes of hunting or fishing employed."[224] Nonetheless, contrary to the Ministry of Forests' submission, the chambers judge did not, he thought, err "in concluding that approval of C.P.212 constituted *prima facie* infringement of the Treaty 8 right to hunt because the proposed activity would limit or impair in some degree the exercise of that right."[225]

Commenting on Finch J.A.'s analysis of the phrase "preferred means" in an aside, Huddart J.A. said:

> Given the significance of particular land to aboriginal culture and identity, I would not preclude "preferred means" from being extended to include a preferred tract of land. Proof may be available that use of a particular tract of land is fundamental to a First Nation's collective identity, as it is to many indigenous cultures. While it may be that "preferred area" for hunting is not relevant [to determining whether interference rises to the level of *prima facie* infringement], "preferred area" for religious and spiritual purposes is likely to be.[226]

On Huddart J.A.'s analysis, then, the Halfway River First Nation might reasonably have claimed that it used the Tusdzuh for religious and spiritual purposes, that its religious and spiritual practices in the area were integral to its distinctive culture, that those practices were an exercise of unextinguished Aboriginal religious and spiritual rights in and to the area, and finally that the Tusdzuh was the place best suited to the exercise of those rights. They might even have made the stronger claim that the Tusdzuh was the only place in which they could exercise certain of their existing Aboriginal religious and spiritual rights. Assuming the validity of these or similar claims, Canfor's interference with the Halfway River people's religious and spiritual uses of the Tusdzuh could easily, as Huddart J.A. suggests, constitute a denial of their preferred means of exercising their rights, and therefore a *prima facie* infringement. Whether the infringement would be to the exclusion of the Halfway River people's exercise of their (assumed) Aboriginal religious and spiritual rights would primarily depend upon the nature of the rights and the ethic associated with the Tusdzuh as a sacred place.

It should be noted, finally, that Huddart J.A.'s comment assumes that the Tusdzuh may be more fundamental to the Halfway River people's collective identity as a place of practical religious significance than as a place of sustenance. It is worth reflecting on this assumption in comparison with Taylor J.'s assumption in the *Twin Sisters* case that the Twin Sisters area – although it had a theological/cosmological significance to the Saulteau First Nation – would have been more fundamental to the Saulteau people's culture and identity if it had greater practical religious significance and/or sustenance use.[227] I shall return to these matters later in Chapter 5.

The Strategy's Potential

The *Halfway River* and *Twin Sisters* cases each involved an attempt, and the earlier *Siska Creek* case a contemplated attempt, by one or more First Nations to protect a sacred site from impending resource exploitation activities by means of judicial review of how the provincial Crown conducted its decision-making process. For the Halfway River people, the sacredness of the Tusdzuh area appears to have been based primarily, if not wholly, on its practical religious purposes. For the West Moberly, Halfway River, Saulteau, and Kelly Lake Cree peoples, the sacredness of the Twin Sisters area was based primarily on its theological/cosmological significance. To the Siska Band, the Siska Valley was sacred on both practical religious and theological/cosmological grounds. In the Halfway River and Siska Creek cases, the threat to the sacred sites came from proposed logging and attendant road-building operations; in the Twin Sisters case, it came from an exploratory gas well and winter access trail. Of the three cases, only *Halfway River* resulted in an offending decision being quashed.

Earlier I spoke of these three cases as having employed a proto-Haida strategy. All three cases involved assertions of Aboriginal rights in relation to the use and/or integrity of sacred sites. (Admittedly, that aspect of *Halfway River* was muted in the chambers judge's judgment and in two of the three Court of Appeal justices' reasons for judgment.) In all three cases, First Nations submitted that their asserted rights should be given legal effect. Legal effect implies legal enforceability. Legal effect, as they argued the point, meant a fiduciary and/or constitutional duty on the part of the Crown to (at a minimum) meaningfully consult with them when considering embarking on or giving approval to a possibly infringing action. In all three cases, First Nations argued that the Crown had failed to fulfill its fiduciary and/or constitutional duty to consult, and therefore that its decision to approve the particular resource development should be quashed. Since the decisions of the British Columbia Court of Appeal in the *Taku River* and *Haida* cases have confirmed, first, that asserted but unestablished Aboriginal rights may trigger the Crown's fiduciary and constitutional duties of consultation and accommodation and, second, that issues about whether the Crown has fulfilled its duties can be decided on judicial review, the *Halfway River, Siska Creek*, and *Twin Sisters* cases can be seen, in retrospect, as involving attempts to employ a proto-Haida strategy to protect the use or integrity of sacred sites.

It would likely be misleading to say simply that they involved attempts to employ the Haida strategy. The Haida strategy has only recently taken clear shape. Prior to the Court of Appeal's decisions in the *Taku River* and *Haida* cases, courts (along with litigants and lawyers) were, generally speaking, labouring under too many confusions, especially as to the relevance, if any, of the *Sparrow* infringement-justification analysis to judicial review, to permit us to say that the Haida strategy was available to First Nations. In hindsight, it is apparent that Huddart J.A.'s analysis in *Halfway River* marked a judicial breakthrough.[228] One of her key insights was that it was premature to apply the *Sparrow* analysis on judicial review unless the chambers judge could first find that the decision maker had attempted both to consult with the potentially affected First Nation to ascertain the nature and scope of its rights and also to assess the impact of the proposed activity. Underlying this insight was her realization that *Sparrow* did not, contrary to the provincial Crown's claim, imply the proposition that the Crown's fiduciary and constitutional duty to consult is triggered only by the establishment of an Aboriginal (or, if disputed, a treaty) right in a court of law. As far as the courts in British Columbia are concerned, it was Rowles J.A. who finally put the proposition to rest in her judgment in *Taku River* in January 2002. There she demonstrated the proposition's inconsistency with the Supreme Court of Canada's decisions in *Sparrow, Delgamuukw,* and other cases.

Although it has now been fairly securely demonstrated that the aforesaid proposition – the Crown has neither a constitutional nor a fiduciary duty to consult with regard to the possible infringement of an Aboriginal right unless the right has been proved in a court of law – is inconsistent with *Sparrow, Delgamuukw,* and other Supreme Court decisions, what is not yet fully appreciated is the stronger claim that the *Sparrow* infringement-justification analysis implies that the Crown has a constitutional and/or fiduciary duty to consult if it wishes to undertake an activity that infringes an Aboriginal right *whether the right has been established or not.* (This is, I suggest, part of what Huddart J.A. was trying to show in *Halfway River.*)

Why this is so is not difficult to grasp. A court is not prompted to apply the *Sparrow* analysis unless a First Nation (or member of a First Nation) submits that the Crown has unjustifiably infringed its (or his or her) existing Aboriginal right(s). As a condition for establishing unjustifiable infringement, the First Nation must prove *prima facie* infringement. And as a condition for establishing *prima facie* infringement, the First Nation must prove that the purportedly unjustifiably infringed Aboriginal right existed prior to contact[229] (or, in the case of Aboriginal title, existed at the time at which the Crown asserted sovereignty over the land in question[230]). Proof of these things requires a court's determination of the nature and scope of the right claimed. If a previous court has not already made the determination, the court considering the First Nation's case will have to make it. Normally, since very few Aboriginal rights have been established in court, the court considering the First Nation's case will have to make the determination itself. (My subsequent remarks will presume the norm.) It follows, then, that when a First Nation submits that the Crown unjustifiably infringed its existing Aboriginal right, it is implying that the Crown infringed the right before it was established in court. The conclusion the First Nation is thereby asking the court to draw is that the Crown breached its constitutional duty to recognize and affirm its Aboriginal right – a right that had not yet been established. Speaking very generally, then, the Crown has a constitutional duty either to infringe Aboriginal rights justifiably or to not infringe at all. If it chooses to infringe, it has a constitutional duty to do so justifiably. But to fulfill its constitutional duty to infringe justifiably, it must act in a way that upholds the honour of the Crown. This entails a number of duties, among them, as both *Sparrow* and *Delgamuukw* point out, the duty to undertake meaningful consultation with a First Nation whose Aboriginal rights may be infringed. Whether the Crown fulfills its constitutional duty hinges on whether it fulfills this particular duty. But, as has just been noted, the Aboriginal rights in question are rights not yet established in court. Two important conclusions follow, therefore: (1) that the Crown has a constitutional duty to consult with regard to unestablished Aboriginal rights if it wishes to pursue an infringing activity, and (2) that it has, independently of its constitutional duty, a similar duty rooted in its honour.

As the British Columbia Court of Appeal's decision in the *Haida* case made clear, the Crown is obliged to undertake consultation with a view to finding a workable accommodation of First Nations' Aboriginal and treaty rights.[231] But if courts are going to hold the Crown to account for its accommodation efforts in advance of the establishment of the Aboriginal rights at stake, fairness requires that the Crown be given a reasonable opportunity to know about those rights, their existence, nature, and scope. Whether the Crown has a reasonable opportunity is partly the Crown's responsibility. If the Crown is contemplating an activity that may affect a First Nation's rights, it is the Crown's duty to initiate consultations. For its part, the First Nation has a reciprocal duty to participate in the consultation process with a view to having its rights accommodated.[232] As part of its reciprocal duty, it must assert its rights. Assertion alone does not suffice, however. The First Nation must also provide the Crown with some evidence of their existence, nature, and scope.[233] Courts are unlikely to seriously fault the Crown's accommodation efforts in cases where the First Nation has failed either to assert its Aboriginal rights or to provide the Crown with some evidence of their existence, nature, and scope.[234]

The Court of Appeal's *Haida* decision might mistakenly be taken to countenance the following argument. *Haida* shows that the Crown's constitutional and fiduciary duty to consult may be triggered by asserted Aboriginal rights. Taken together with the Supreme Court of Canada's *Sparrow* decision, it is clear that the Crown's constitutional and fiduciary duty to consult may be triggered by either asserted or established Aboriginal rights. But the Crown should not be held to account for its accommodation efforts (or lack thereof) unless it has a reasonable opportunity to know about the Aboriginal rights at stake. There are only two ways Aboriginal rights can be made known to the Crown: by a First Nation's assertion or by court establishment. The Crown's constitutional and fiduciary duty to consult is thus triggerable *only* by asserted or established Aboriginal rights. As a consequence, the argument concludes, the Crown has no legal duty to initiate consultation when contemplating an activity that may infringe unestablished Aboriginal rights unless they have been asserted.

That the Court of Appeal's *Haida* decision does not countenance the above argument can be seen by noting two things. First, Lambert J.A. (speaking for the Court on the issue of the Crown's duty) neither said nor implied that, absent court establishment, only asserted Aboriginal rights may trigger the Crown's constitutional and fiduciary duty to consult. His emphasis, like Rowles J.A.'s earlier emphasis in *Taku River,* was on asserted Aboriginal rights because the Crown, in the face of the facts that the First Nation had long asserted its Aboriginal rights (including title) and that it had a good *prima facie* case for its assertion, was maintaining that it had no constitutional or fiduciary duty to consult. Lambert J.A. found, contrary to the Crown's contention, that the Haida's asserted Aboriginal rights did trigger the Crown's constitutional and fiduciary duty to consult. That sufficed to settle the key issue. He had no reason, therefore, to propose that absent court establishment, only asserted Aboriginal rights may trigger the Crown's duty.

Moreover, if the issue had been raised, he would have had good reason not to adopt such a view. Section 35(1) of the *Constitution Act, 1982* enjoins the Crown to recognize and affirm Aboriginal rights. *A priori,* the Crown's constitutional duty to recognize and affirm Aboriginal rights includes anything the Crown must do to fulfill its duty. One of the things the Crown must do to fulfill its constitutional duty is make a reasonable effort to inform itself about Aboriginal rights that may be infringed by a contemplated activity. Clearly, as *Sparrow* suggests, if a court were to find that there was an Aboriginal right, that the right was infringed, that the Crown suspected or should have suspected that there was an Aboriginal right, and that the Crown did not initiate consultation, the court would be unlikely to be impressed by the argument that the Crown had no legal duty to consult on account of the fact that the First Nation had not yet asserted its Aboriginal right. The reason a court would be unlikely to be impressed is that the Crown had – as a condition necessary for fulfilling its constitutional duty to recognize and affirm Aboriginal rights – a duty to make a reasonable effort to inform itself about the Aboriginal right. In the (hypothetical) circumstances, a reasonable effort meant initiating consultation.

The main defect in the argument sketched earlier is that it fallaciously slips from the reasonable claim that the Crown cannot be faulted for its efforts *to accommodate* a First Nation's unestablished Aboriginal rights if the First Nation does not assert them to the questionable claim that the Crown cannot be faulted for its efforts (or lack thereof) *to consult* about unestablished Aboriginal rights if the First Nation has not previously asserted them. Besides the fact that it does not logically follow, the latter claim seems false. A First Nation may assert its Aboriginal rights before or after the Crown begins to consider undertaking a possibly infringing activity. Until it learns of the Crown's plans, it may have no pressing reason to assert any particular Aboriginal right. It would be arbitrary and fundamentally unfair were First Nations to be denied the right to be consulted about their unestablished Aboriginal rights simply because they had not yet asserted them. Furthermore, the Crown's subsidiary constitutional duty to make a reasonable effort to inform itself about any Aboriginal rights it may infringe appears to imply a corresponding subsidiary constitutional right on the part of First Nations to a reasonable opportunity to assert them.

As a way of trying to gauge the potential of the Haida strategy for protecting sacred sites, it is helpful to begin by reflecting on the difficulties First Nations are most likely to encounter in the consultation and accommodation phases of the Crown's decision-making process when the use or integrity of their sacred sites is at stake. As we have seen, if the Crown wishes to pursue an activity that infringes a First Nation's Aboriginal rights, it must fulfill its constitutional and fiduciary duty to consult with a view to accommodating those rights. As we have also seen, once consultation is underway, the First Nation has a reciprocal duty to participate with a view to having its Aboriginal rights accommodated. First Nations sacred sites have the potential to most severely test the limits of both the consultation and accommodation phases of the Crown's decision-making process.

During the consultation phase, if First Nations want their Aboriginal rights to be accommodated, they must both provide information about the existence, nature, and scope of their asserted Aboriginal rights and present an adequate *prima facie* case in support of their claims. First Nations who are not fully forthcoming about their Aboriginal rights run the risks of presenting a weak *prima facie* case and consequently of having their rights (at best) poorly accommodated or (at worst) not accommodated at all.[235] But First Nations can have good reasons to be less than fully forthcoming when it comes to the Aboriginal rights they associate with certain sacred sites. For a sacred site's ethic and extrinsic social/cultural factors can dictate restrictions on what sort of information may be shared and with whom it may be shared.

To have full information about a sacred site, one has to know several things, including its significance, its ethic, and its location. Basically, a sacred site's significance may be grounded in practical religious use or theological/cosmological meaning or both. For example, as I have already noted, the significance of the Tusdzuh to the Halfway River people appears to be grounded mainly in its practical religious use, while the significance of the Twin Sisters to the West Moberly, Halfway River, Saulteau, and Kelly Lake Cree peoples is grounded mainly in its theological/cosmological meaning. The significance of the Siska Valley to the Nlah7kápmx people is grounded in both its practical religious use and theological/cosmological meaning.

The ethic of a sacred site may dictate with whom a First Nation may share information. It may dictate that information about it is to be shared only with members of the particular First Nation community. It may even dictate that it is to be shared only with some members of the community. The ethic of a sacred site may permit information to be shared with people outside the community. It may permit it to be shared with anyone or with only some. Thus, for example, a sacred site's ethic may permit information about it to be shared with a respectful and trusted archaeologist or anthropologist. In any given case, how much information may be shared is determined by the site's ethic.

Sometimes factors extrinsic to a sacred site's ethic may dictate additional restrictions on who the information may be shared with and how much may be shared. And so, although a sacred site's ethic may permit information about it to be shared more widely, those who hold the information may have compelling prudential reasons not to share it more widely.[236] Often a concern that the site would be exposed to disrespect if the information were shared more widely is a motivation for not sharing it more widely. For First Nations, the concern is usually about people from outside their particular communities.[237] Sometimes, however, the concern is about certain people within their own communities. Sometimes the concern is even about the entire community. It is not unheard of for those responsible for a sacred site to refuse to hand their information on to anyone, preferring to let their knowledge die with them rather than expose the site to disrespect from their own people.[238]

Obviously, First Nations who are not fully forthcoming when consulted about the specific Aboriginal rights they associate with particular sacred sites increase the risk that they will present a weak *prima facie* case for those rights. A weak *prima facie* case can mean (at best) that the Crown is not obliged to be as accommodating of the use or integrity of the sacred site as it would have been had a stronger *prima facie* case been presented, or (at worst) that the Crown is not obliged to accommodate its use or integrity at all. If the Crown guarantees the requisite confidentiality during and after the consultation process, a First Nation's prudential concerns about a sacred site should be allayed sufficiently to allow it to provide the Crown with as much information as the site's ethic permits. But a sacred site's ethic may forbid sharing certain or even any information about it with outsiders. Then, the First Nation will be unable to be fully forthcoming when consulted about its specific Aboriginal rights in connection with the use or integrity of the sacred site. First Nations who find themselves in such a predicament will be forced to run the risks of presenting a very weak *prima facie* case for their Aboriginal rights – assuming they can even find an acceptable way to make a case for them – and thus of suffering tragic consequences with regard to the use or integrity of their particular sacred sites.

This predicament is a reflection of an irresolvable paradox at the heart of Canada's Aboriginal rights doctrine. Let me explain. We can assume that First Nations have certain specific Aboriginal rights associated with the use or integrity of at least some of their sacred sites. The content and scope of those specific rights is at least partly and probably largely determined by those sites' ethics. Where a sacred site's ethic places strict restrictions on information sharing, the content and scope of the associated Aboriginal right will reflect that fact. Thus, some of the Aboriginal rights connected with the use or integrity of sacred sites will include the right to secrecy or, more accurately, the right not to violate the duty to keep some or all information about the sites secret. The duty to keep some or all information about a site secret can require that the specific Aboriginal right associated with the site is itself kept secret. Some Aboriginal rights connected with the use or integrity of sacred sites will therefore include the right to keep those rights secret. Now, s. 35(1) obliges the Crown to recognize and affirm Aboriginal rights. The Crown's duty is premised on the possibility of it acquiring some awareness of the existence, nature, and scope of Aboriginal rights. But some Aboriginal rights connected to the use or integrity of sacred sites may preclude telling the Crown about the nature and scope or even (at the extreme) the existence of the right. It can turn out that a First Nation possesses a specific Aboriginal right (in relation to a particular sacred site) that is entitled to constitutional protection but that, by virtue of a subsidiary constitutional right not to violate the duty of secrecy, cannot ever enjoy such protection.

Working within the confines of Canada's Aboriginal rights regime, First Nations that find themselves faced with the dilemma just described have no way of escape. They may, however, be able to avoid the dilemma by asserting general rather than specific Aboriginal rights with regard to their sacred sites. A general Aboriginal right would be related to many sacred sites indifferently rather than to a single sacred site specifically. Such a general right's content and scope would be at least partly determined by the commonalities shared by the various sacred sites' ethics. If a First Nation can sufficiently define the nature and scope of such a general Aboriginal right, it should be able to present a reasonable *prima facie* case for the right without having to provide the Crown with specific information about the locations or significance of its particular sacred sites. If the First Nation does these things, the Crown will have a constitutional duty to respect the right. The Crown's duty to respect the general Aboriginal right should translate into a duty to seek to accommodate the various associated sacred sites. Since accommodation should normally be possible without it, the Crown should normally not need specific information about the locations or significance of particular sites in order to accommodate them.

As far as the protection of the use or integrity of a particular sacred site is concerned, a specific Aboriginal right is likely to afford more protection than a general Aboriginal right. Nonetheless, in those situations where a site's ethic strictly limits or forbids sharing information with outsiders, asserting a general Aboriginal right may be a First Nation's only way to gain Aboriginal rights-based protection for the site.

I said earlier that when a First Nation has an adequate *prima facie* case for a general Aboriginal right to the use or integrity of its sacred sites, the Crown should normally not need specific information about particular sacred sites to accommodate them. The Crown likely has a constitutional duty to try to accommodate those sacred sites connected with a First Nation's general Aboriginal right without requiring specific information about them. Certainly, Crown efforts to accommodate such sacred sites without requiring specific information about them would be consistent with its trust-like relationship with First Nations peoples. Indeed, Crown efforts to accommodate a First Nation's sacred sites without the assertion of an associated Aboriginal right would be consistent with this relationship. As recent experience in the United States has shown, it is open to the state as a fiduciary to take a more proactive approach to protecting off-reserve sacred sites. Thanks largely to former President Clinton's Executive Order 13007,[239] a number of sacred sites on federal lands have been accommodated without Native Americans having either to make a case for related Aboriginal rights or to disclose specific information about the location or significance of the sites.[240]

First Nations may, of course, claim other Aboriginal rights within the consultation process that can lend a measure of protection to the use or integrity of their sacred sites without having to advert to the sites as sacred places. A First Nation might claim, for example, a sustenance or cultural right in relation to an area that includes a sacred site. By gaining a measure of protection for the overall area, the First Nation would indirectly gain a measure of protection for the sacred site. A First Nation might also claim Aboriginal title over an area that includes a sacred site. Similarly, by gaining the protection that comes with a claim of Aboriginal title, the First Nation would indirectly gain a measure of protection for its sacred site.[241] These approaches to protecting sacred sites are of limited efficacy, however, for they rely on Aboriginal rights that are not defined in reference to the ethics of sacred sites. Consequently, the Crown's accommodation efforts, which are based on claimed Aboriginal rights, may fall far short of First Nations' needs and desires with regard to their undisclosed sacred sites.

First Nations sacred sites also have the potential to severely test the limits of the accommodation phase of the Crown's decision-making process. When consultation reveals that a proposed activity is likely to interfere with the use or integrity of a First Nation's sacred site (and that Aboriginal rights are likely at stake), the Crown will, as a matter of its constitutional and/or fiduciary obligations, become concerned with the general question of whether the proposed activity and the sacred site can be accommodated to one another. An answer to the general question presupposes an answer to the analytically prior question of whether the sacred site's ethic can accommodate the Crown's proposed activity.

What a sacred site's ethic may or may not permit depends on what aspect of the sacred site will be affected. A proposed activity may affect the practical religious use (including access) or integrity of a sacred site. The use of a sacred site depends on the site's integrity. When a site's integrity is too diminished, it becomes unfit for use. In some cases, a sacred site's integrity depends on its use. In such cases, if the use ends, the site loses its sacredness. A sacred site's integrity is a function of its physical and symbolic integrity, thus an activity that affects the integrity of a sacred site must affect its physical or its symbolic integrity. Generally speaking, it is possible to affect a site's physical integrity without necessarily affecting its symbolic integrity. There are limits, however. A site's physical integrity can be so degraded that it can no longer serve its practical religious or theological/

cosmological function within the community that considers it sacred – that is, it can no longer bear its former significance. It is also possible to affect a site's symbolic integrity without affecting its physical integrity, so a site's significance can be forgotten without its physical integrity being altered. An activity may therefore affect a sacred site by affecting its use, its physical integrity, or its symbolic integrity.

Every sacred site's ethic places limits on its physical alteration. Every sacred site's ethic also places limits on the kinds of activities that may be undertaken within its precincts. A sacred site's ethic may forbid an activity even though it has no effect on the site's physical integrity. It can be enough that the activity is incompatible with the site's significance. A sacred site's ethic may also place limits on how its significance is dealt with. As we have already seen, some sacred sites' ethics place limits on the dissemination of information about their significance. Such limits may have as much or more to do with protecting the site's symbolic integrity than they do with protecting its physical integrity.

Violations of a sacred site's ethic range from the relatively harmless to the utterly and irreparably destructive. Probably, the ethic of any sacred site is able to tolerate minor violations without the site's sacredness being diminished. Some more serious violations may defile a sacred site so as to diminish its sacredness without eliminating it. The most serious violations, however, are desecrations. Taking the word in its etymological sense, the desecration of a sacred site removes its sacred character. The effects of a site's desecration can be temporary or permanent.

Clearly, the Crown cannot adequately answer the question of whether a proposed activity can be accommodated with a First Nation's sacred site unless it first answers the analytically prior question of whether the sacred site's ethic can accommodate the proposed activity. If the proposed activity either does not violate the site's ethic or only minimally and relatively harmlessly violates it, the answer to the question is clear: the sacred site's ethic can accommodate the proposed activity. But what if the proposed activity defiles the First Nation's sacred site so as to diminish its sacredness without eliminating it? How will the Crown answer the question? Quite likely, the Crown will be tempted to distinguish between degrees of defilement. But would such an approach be consistent with the Crown's duty to deal with Aboriginal peoples in an honourable manner? A First Nation whose sacred site is at stake is unlikely to think so. Finally, what if the proposed activity desecrates the site? The desecration of a sacred site would put an end to the exercise of any Aboriginal rights dependent upon its sacredness. If the effect of the desecration is temporary, the exercise's cessation may be temporary. (Or it may not. Aboriginal practices all too often do not resume once interrupted.) If the effect is permanent, the exercise's surcease will be permanent and the Aboriginal rights effectively extinguished.[242] Obviously, a sacred site's ethic cannot accommodate an activity that desecrates it permanently. But what about an activity that desecrates it temporarily? If the Crown is willing to seriously contemplate going forward with such an activity, it will likely find significance in the distinction between short- and long-term temporary desecration. But such an approach would be difficult to reconcile with the honour of the Crown. Also, any First Nation whose sacred site is at stake is unlikely to agree that it is reconcilable.

The Haida strategy, as I am using the term, is a litigation strategy for protecting First Nations sacred sites threatened by activities – typically resource exploitation activities – that have received Crown approval. The strategy attempts to utilize judicial review in an effort to get the court to, among other things, quash the Crown's decision to approve an offending activity. Although it may incidentally include arguments claiming violations of administrative law principles, it essentially involves arguments claiming breach of one or both of the Crown's constitutional and fiduciary duties to consult in good faith and to seek a workable accommodation of the petitioning First Nation's claim for Aboriginal rights.

The chief issue before a reviewing court will be whether the decision maker breached the Crown's consultation and accommodation duties. Usually, the court's determination of the issue will be based on asserted rather than established Aboriginal rights (including Aboriginal title), for it will seldom have the benefit of a previous court's definition of the Aboriginal rights at stake. Nor will chambers judges be inclined to attempt such definitions themselves.[243] (Consequently, First Nations should not assume that they will be allowed to argue unjustifiable infringement of Aboriginal rights on judicial review.) My subsequent remarks will presuppose that the court's determination of the chief issue will be based on asserted rather than established Aboriginal rights.

Before a court can decide on judicial review whether the Crown fulfilled its duties of consultation and accommodation, it will have to make an assessment of the potential soundness of the First Nation's claim for Aboriginal rights. For, as Lambert J.A. said in *Haida,* "the scope of the consultation and the strength of the obligation to seek an accommodation will be proportional to the potential soundness of the claim for Aboriginal title and Aboriginal rights."[244] A claim that is supported by a decent *prima facie* case will engage the Crown's duties to consult and seek accommodation. The stronger the *prima facie* case, the more the Crown's duties will be engaged.

Since a reviewing court's determination of the chief issue – namely, whether the Crown has fulfilled its duties to consult and seek accommodation – will be based on its assessment of the potential soundness of the First Nation's assertion of Aboriginal rights, it is essential that First Nations fulfill their reciprocal duty to participate in the consultation process by both asserting their Aboriginal rights and trying to make their best case.[245] If the court finds that the petitioning First Nation was given an adequate opportunity to assert its Aboriginal rights and to make its best case but failed to take advantage of the opportunity, it will fault the First Nation rather than the Crown.[246] Given such a finding, the court will not be disposed to allow the First Nation to bring new evidence forward on judicial review that could have been supplied to the decision maker during consultations.[247]

Courts may, however, be more lenient in cases in which the Aboriginal rights asserted are connected to sacred sites. The court is unlikely to fault the First Nation for not providing the Crown with more information or for failing to present a decent *prima facie* case for its claim if a petitioning First Nation can show that (1) a sacred site's ethic allowed the sharing of information with the Crown's decision maker only if certain confidentiality conditions were met or that it had good prudential reasons for asking the Crown to meet certain confidentiality conditions, (2) it clearly communicated its needs or concerns to the Crown, and (3) the Crown did not make an adequate effort to accommodate its needs or concerns.[248] In the circumstances, the court might construe the Crown's failure to accede to the First Nation's confidentiality concerns as a breach of either its duty to consult in good faith or its duty to seek a workable accommodation or both.

The more difficult cases for judicial review will be those where the ethic of a sacred site forbids the First Nation to share what the Crown may consider a crucial piece of information. While the First Nation may be bound by the ethic of a sacred site not to reveal its exact location, the decision maker may find it difficult, if not impossible, to accommodate the proposed activity with the whole of the general area within which the site is located. While the First Nation may be bound by a sacred site's ethic not to reveal its particular significance, the decision maker may press for more than general information about its significance in an effort to understand the nature and scope of the Aboriginal right at stake, to accurately assess the impact of the proposed activity, and ultimately to seek a workable accommodation. It cannot be safely predicted how a court will decide between a First Nation's claim that the decision maker – by approving a particular activity that will seriously affect its sacred site – did not make a sufficient effort to accommodate its sacred site (as associated with an asserted Aboriginal right) and the Crown's claim that the First Nation – by withholding further information – did not participate fully in the consultation process. One thing seems clear, however. The court would likely decide in favour of the Crown were it to find either that the First Nation neglected to make it clear when consulted that the ethic of its threatened sacred site forbade sharing the information desired by the Crown or that it did not provide the Crown with evidence in support of its claim about the ethic of the site.

Just as there are unanswered questions about how the Crown's decision makers will approach the accommodation phase of the decision-making process when First Nations have asserted Aboriginal rights in connection with sacred sites, so too there are yet-to-be-answered questions about how courts will assess the Crown's accommodation efforts on judicial review.

As Huddart J.A. observed in *Halfway River,* accommodation is possible only where there is compatibility.[249] Compatibility does not preclude infringement, however. Thus, a Crown-proposed activity that is compatible with the exercise of an Aboriginal right may be infringing or non-infringing. As long as the activity does not exclude the exercise of the right, it is compatible with its exercise. If the activity is a short-term activity, it may temporarily exclude the exercise of the Aboriginal right without effectively extinguishing the right itself. In such a case, the activity is incompatible with the right's exercise but compatible with the right. An activity that is incompatible with either the exercise of an Aboriginal right or the right itself is infringing.

Courts will have difficulty squaring these notions of compatibility and infringement with the ethics of First Nations sacred sites and the Aboriginal rights asserted in connection with those sites. Any proposed activity that will affect a First Nation's sacred site will or will not violate the site's ethic. Obviously, if it will not violate the site's ethic, the activity is compatible with the site. If the activity will violate the site's ethic but relatively harmlessly, the activity can still be confidently said to be compatible. But if the activity defiles the sacred site by diminishing but not eliminating its sacredness, the answer is unclear. Is the activity compatible or incompatible with the site's ethic? *A priori,* the activity is both compatible in that the site remains sacred and incompatible in that it seriously harms it. Finally, if the activity desecrates the sacred site, it is clearly incompatible with the site's ethic. Given that accommodation presupposes compatibility, reviewing courts will find it difficult to assess Crown accommodation efforts that have resulted in the approval of activities that defile rather than desecrate First Nations sacred sites. It cannot be said in advance whether they will count such results as accommodations or not.

Reviewing courts will also have difficulty squaring the notion of infringement with the ethics of First Nations sacred sites and the Aboriginal rights asserted in connection with those sites. While courts are not likely to count a relatively harmless violation of a sacred site's ethic as a *prima facie* infringement, they may have trouble deciding how to classify more serious violations.[250] Should an activity that defiles a sacred site without desecrating it be classified as a *prima facie* infringement of the Aboriginal right asserted in connection with it? It is likely that courts will look upon desecrations, which are clearly incompatible with the ethics of sacred sites, as *prima facie* infringements of the relevant asserted Aboriginal rights. Perhaps they will also look upon activities that seriously diminish a site's sacredness without desecrating it as *prima facie* infringements.[251] If this is correct, we are left with the question of how courts will classify activities that defile a site without seriously diminishing its sacredness. Again, it cannot be said in advance how the courts will proceed. Nonetheless, should courts ultimately show themselves willing to entertain the idea that such activities may be non-infringing, they will be engaging in a patently unseemly calculus.

My discussion of the Haida strategy has placed considerable emphasis on the ethics of First Nations sacred sites. My primary justification for the emphasis is simply this: if a First Nation decides to petition for judicial review of a Crown decision on the grounds that the decision maker did not make sufficient efforts to accommodate asserted Aboriginal rights in relation to a sacred site, the court will need to know something about the site's ethic if it is going to form a sound judgment about whether the Crown's efforts satisfied its constitutional and/or fiduciary responsibility to seek accommodation. But, it should be noted, the court could coherently hold, on the one hand, that the sacred site's ethic was not accommodated in the least and, on the other hand, that the Crown's efforts satisfied its duty of accommodation were it to find that the First Nation (as a whole or in large part) no longer considered itself bound by and/or abided by the site's ethic.[252] Such a finding would imply – and so the court would likely infer – that the First Nation lacked a potentially sound claim for Aboriginal rights in connection with the sacred site in question. With regard to sacred sites and assertions of associated Aboriginal rights, then, First Nations cannot reasonably expect courts to hold the Crown to account for failing to accommodate what they themselves no longer respect.

As I have been using the term, the Haida strategy can be taken in a strict, less strict, and broad sense. In all three senses, a First Nation employs the strategy by petitioning for judicial review of a Crown decision that threatens one of its off-reserve sacred sites on the grounds that the Crown failed to fulfill its consultation or accommodation duties with regard to its asserted Aboriginal rights. Taken strictly, the Haida strategy involves a First Nation's assertion of a specific Aboriginal right in connection with a particular threatened sacred site. Taken less strictly, it may alternatively involve an assertion of a general Aboriginal right in connection with a number of sacred sites, at least one of which is threatened. Taken broadly, it involves an assertion of an Aboriginal right (including Aboriginal title) that may or may not be asserted in connection with a threatened sacred site but that is asserted (at least partly) for the sake of protecting a threatened sacred site.[253]

It remains to be seen whether First Nations will much employ the Haida strategy in their efforts to protect the use and integrity of their off-reserve sacred sites and whether they will succeed if they do. It will not always be evident, however, when First Nations are employing the Haida strategy in the broad sense of the term, for First Nations could employ it without ever alluding to the fact that their sacred sites are at stake. Consequently, we shall have to limit, generally speaking, our future assessments of frequency of employment and rate of success of employment of the Haida strategy to its strict or less strict senses.

Postscript

On 18 November 2004, shortly before this book went to press, the Supreme Court of Canada released its decisions in *Taku River Tlingit First Nation v. British Columbia*[254] and *Haida Nation v. British Columbia*.[255] The Court confirmed the position held by the British Columbia Court of Appeal whereby unestablished Aboriginal rights and title may engage the Crown's constitutional duties of consultation and accommodation, but it rejected the Court of Appeal's position that third parties may also owe such obligations.

Although Canada's highest court agreed with the Court of Appeal that the Crown's duties of consultation and accommodation may be engaged by unestablished Aboriginal rights and title, it disagreed with regard to the source of those duties. In place of the Crown's fiduciary relationship with Aboriginal peoples espoused by the Court of Appeal, the Supreme Court substituted the more primitive notion of the Crown's honour. But, as the Court explained, "the principle of the honour of the Crown grounds the Crown's duty to consult and if indicated accommodate Aboriginal peoples, even prior to proof of asserted Aboriginal rights and title."[256]

The Supreme Court of Canada's shift from the Crown's fiduciary relationship to the Crown's honour carries noteworthy consequences for the duty of accommodation. Where the Crown owes a fiduciary duty of accommodation to an Aboriginal group, as, for instance, when treaty rights are at stake, it is obliged to act with reference to the group's best interest.[257] But where its duty of accommodation is grounded directly in its honour, as when unproven Aboriginal rights and title are at stake, the Crown is obliged only to balance Aboriginal interests reasonably with competing interests.[258]

Although the points on which the Supreme Court of Canada departs from the British Columbia Court of Appeal's analysis are significant, the points on which it agrees are more significant. Therefore, since my discussion of the Haida strategy's potential for protecting First Nations sacred sites is based almost entirely on the points of agreement, and since nothing of importance in my discussion hangs on law now superseded, there has been no felt need to rework the final portion of this chapter.

How First Nations Sacred Sites Have Fared in Canada's Courts

In this chapter, I draw a number of conclusions about how Canada's courts have treated First Nations sacred sites. Most are critical. To be fair, many of the shortcomings I attribute to the courts have roots in the larger social/political system within which they operate. I also accept that today's courts are inheritors rather than creators of the ethically compromised position in which they find themselves vis-à-vis the First Nations peoples of Canada.[1] They are not, however, as some social critics would have it, the puppetry of greater social/political forces. They are – as human institutions whose functioning depends on human agency – complicit, and therefore responsible for their acts of complicity. Moreover, they are creatively complicit. That is, Canada's courts have developed their own unique ways of and fashioned their own unique tools for maintaining the multifarious subordination of First Nations peoples. That Canada's courts are still – despite their sometimes near-heroic efforts to lessen the injustice visited upon First Nations peoples – in the business of maintaining their subordination is seen perhaps most clearly in their treatment of First Nations sacred sites.

With Regard to the Results of Litigation

Of the cases I have discussed in this book, First Nations obtained the chief legal remedies they sought in only three: the *Meares Island*, *Deer Island*, and *Halfway River* cases. In the *Meares Island* and *Deer Island* cases, the Nuu-chah-nulth and Kwakwak'wakw, respectively, were granted interlocutory injunctions restraining road-building and logging activities. In *Halfway River*, the First Nation was granted an order quashing the Crown's decision to approve road building and logging in the Tusdzuh. In *Westar*, the Gitksan and Wet'suwet'en obtained only part of what they sought. They obtained an interlocutory injunction restraining road building and logging in the Shedin but were themselves restrained from interfering with the road building and logging in the Shegisic. Finally, in the *Lower*

Tsitika Valley, Ure Creek, High Falls, Siska Creek, and *Twin Sisters* cases, the First Nations were refused the relief they sought.

The sacredness of the areas in dispute was the most prominent feature in the five losing cases. In the *Meares Island, Deer Island,* and *Halfway River* cases, the sacredness of the areas (in whole or in part) was, as the courts dealt with them, merely one factor among many. Indeed, one can read the British Columbia Supreme Court and Court of Appeal decisions in the *Meares* case without ever realizing that the Nuu-chah-nulth were concerned with the protection of sacred sites on the island and that they had made their concern public. In *Halfway River,* whereas the Halfway River First Nation claimed that the Tusdzuh served sacred as well as sustenance purposes, the chambers judge focused her discussion on its sustenance purposes. There was no mention of sacredness in connection with the Shegisic or the Shedin in the *Westar* case.[2]

The fates of the sacred sites involved in the aforementioned cases have varied dramatically, ranging from the return of Deer Island and its sacred sites to Kwakwak'wakw control to the destruction of High Falls. Although the Kwakwak'wakw's case never came to trial, the interlocutory injunction helped protect Deer Island until its reserve land status was finally restored in 1997. Deer Island's sacred sites are now, therefore, under Kwakwak'-wakw control. Similarly, although the Nuu-chah-nulth's case remains adjourned (by agreement of the parties), the interlocutory injunction remains in place. Additionally, the Nuu-chah-nulth have signed an agreement in principle with Canada and the province that lends further protection to Meares Island and its sacred sites.[3] Since its decision to approve road building and logging in the Tusdzuh area was quashed, the Crown has made no further attempts to exploit the area's resources. The facts that the chambers judge's order was grounded in an analysis of the Halfway River First Nation's treaty rights and that the Court of Appeal upheld her decision will likely deter future Crown attempts.

Although the Saulteau First Nation and Kelly Lake Cree Nation failed in their efforts to have the Crown's decision to approve exploratory drilling and trail building in the Twin Sisters area quashed, and thus failed to gain the degree of protection for the Twin Sisters area that their beliefs about the area called for, the inner core of the area did, nonetheless, receive Protected Area designation in 1999.[4] (Apparently, it should be noted, the protection afforded by the designation accords with the West Moberly and Halfway River First Nations' beliefs about the area.) The Tlowitsis-Mumtagila, Lil'wat, and Siska Creek peoples failed in their efforts to stop the road building in and logging of Lower Tsitika Valley, Ure Creek, and Siska Creek, respectively. Although small consolation, some portions of the Lower Tsitika watershed were set aside as ecological reserves, the Ure

Creek logging road was rerouted to avoid further construction damage to an archaeologically significant site, and the forest plan for Siska Creek was modified to protect its culturally modified trees. The Poplar Point Ojibway were wholly unsuccessful in their attempts to stop the construction of the High Falls dam and consequent destruction of their sacred site. With the falls and rapids stilled, the designation of the upper slopes of the knoll overlooking the east bank of High Falls as an unapproved Aboriginal peoples cemetery – a designation given after the knoll had undergone extensive construction-related damage – was virtually no consolation.

Judged against the results, then, off-reserve sacred sites have not fared particularly well in Canada's courts in those cases in which First Nations have tried to leverage their Aboriginal and/or treaty rights into protection. Indeed, judged against the results, off-reserve sacred sites have fared increasingly badly as the years have passed. In a few cases, the use and integrity of the sites were fully protected (*Meares Island*, *Deer Island*, and *Halfway River*). Only one of those cases, however, was decided within the past decade (*Halfway River*). In three cases, all decided in the 1990s, the use of the sites was seemingly protected while their integrity was compromised (*Lower Tsitika Valley*, *Ure Creek*, and *Siska Creek*). In another case decided in the 1990s, the site was lost altogether (*High Falls*). Furthermore, those cases in which the use of the sites was seemingly protected but their integrity compromised may have been more damaging than appearances might suggest. This is because nothing in the judgments in those cases suggests that the courts were warranted in their twofold assumption that the effects to the physical and/or symbolic integrity of the sacred sites in question would neither destroy the sacred character of the sites nor diminish it to the point that the sites would no longer support practical religious use. Since the issue of whether the courts were warranted in their assumption is better dealt with below, I will turn to my next topic.

With Regard to the Reasoning of the Courts

Although it is important to investigate how First Nations sacred sites have fared in Canada's courts by looking at the results of litigation, it is ultimately more illuminating to investigate how they have fared by looking at the courts' reasoning about them. When courts are asked to make decisions about First Nations sacred sites, they are typically required to weigh or measure First Nations' interests in their sites against other interests or concerns (for example, economic concerns). But if they are to perform what I will call the measuring task adequately, courts need some understanding of the sacred sites they are to measure. And to understand a particular First Nation's sacred site is to understand the First Nation's perspective on the site. Thus, before courts can adequately measure First Nations' interests in their sacred sites, they must first gain an understanding of the perspectives of First Nations. What this suggests is that the courts' reasoning about First Nations sacred sites may be usefully analyzed with regard to their efforts to gain an understanding of the perspectives of First Nations on sacred sites and to fairly measure their interests in those sites against other interests or concerns.

Before I undertake such an analysis, I want to raise and briefly address a preliminary question: Are the courts open to claims of sacredness by First Nations? The question merits raising because of two facts: (1) that Canadian courts are functionally secular, and (2) that it is not humanly possible for judges to avoid bringing some of their own personal limitations, including biases concerning sacred matters, to the bench.

The relevance of the first fact is this. Canada is both a liberal-democratic state and a religiously pluralist society. Liberalism is well suited to religiously pluralist societies for the simple reason that liberal political and legal institutions are functionally secular. That is, they are designed not to favour one religion over another. Liberal institutions are, however, notorious for occasionally lapsing from not favouring one religion over another to disfavouring all. Such shifts from secular to secularist are endlessly – and not always unfairly – decried by religious groups the world over. There is an *a priori* concern, then, that Canada's courts may, in their secularist moments, adopt an excessively skeptical stance towards claims of sacredness by First Nations.

The relevance of the second fact is this. Judges may be personally biased against First Nations sacred sites. Their bias may stem from an anti-religious attitude, in which case they will be prejudiced against any First Nations sacred site that has religious associations. Their bias may also stem from an intolerant religious attitude, in which case they will be prejudiced against all sacred sites that fall outside their own particular religious traditions. Judges who consciously or not bring such attitudes to the bench will be biased against claims of sacredness by First Nations.

Such not uncommon concerns are ample justification for raising the question of whether the courts are open to claims of sacredness by First Nations. The case law, it must be admitted, provides some support to those who would answer in the negative. As the *High Falls* and *Halfway River* cases show, the courts can mute claims of sacredness. For the Poplar Point Ojibway, protecting the High Falls area as a sacred site was uppermost in their minds. Nonetheless, the judge who heard their initial petition for an interlocutory injunction all but ignored their religious or spiritual concerns, preferring to focus on their environmental concerns. In the other case, the Halfway River First Nation claimed that they utilized the Tusdzuh for practical religious purposes and that in so doing they were exercising unextinguished Aboriginal spiritual and religious rights in and to the area.

Their claim implied that they held the area (either in whole or in part) as sacred. The chambers judge, however, brushed aside their claim and focused instead on the Tusdzuh's sustenance values in relation to treaty rights. Except for Madam Justice Huddart, the Court of Appeal followed suit.

Too much, however, may be made of these cases. Courts are driven by legal issues. In both the *High Falls* and *Halfway River* cases, the chambers judges acknowledged that the petitioning First Nations wished to raise the issue of whether they had existing Aboriginal rights associated with the use or integrity of the sacred sites in question. In the *High Falls* case, the chambers judge concluded that the Poplar Point Ojibway were precluded from raising the issue by an agreement signed with Ontario's Minister of Natural Resources. (The same judge, it should be noted, did give prominence to their claim for the sacredness of the High Falls area when he heard their subsequent petition nearly a year later.[5]) In *Halfway River*, the chambers judge concluded that the Crown had failed to meaningfully consult with the Halfway River people about their treaty rights in the Tusdzuh. Given her conclusion, she was willing simply to assume that their Aboriginal rights had been extinguished. And so, while it is true that the First Nations' claims of sacredness were muted in both cases, they at least appear to have been muted more as a result of the courts' analyses of the relevant legal issues rather than as a result of a supposed lack of openness to such claims of sacredness.

The case law, moreover, more strongly suggests that the courts are generally open to claims of sacredness by First Nations. Claims of sacredness were front and centre in the *Lower Tsitika Valley*, *Siska Creek*, and *Twin Sisters* cases. The courts were accepting of those claims in all three cases.[6]

Understanding the Perspectives of First Nations
When a court is called upon to assess the impact of a Crown-sanctioned activity on a First Nation's sacred site, making a fair assessment requires the court to gain a good understanding of the First Nation's perspective on the site's ethic, its status, and the impact of the proposed activity. We may therefore evaluate the courts' overall efforts to gain an understanding of the perspectives of First Nations by evaluating their specific efforts with regard to each of the three areas.

Readers may have noticed that my list does not include the significance of a sacred site. Readers may even question its omission, thinking generally that some understanding of a sacred site's practical religious and/or theological/cosmological significance is necessary for understanding the site's ethic. For, it may be reasoned, how can one begin to understand why some activity does or does not count as a desecration without knowing something about the site's significance?

Let me respond first by granting that some understanding of a sacred site's significance is necessary for understanding its ethic. Certainly, some understanding of a site's significance is necessary to provide context for thinking about its ethic. For that purpose, however, information of a fairly general, even sketchy nature suffices.

What more is needed, then? Or, more to the point, to what purpose? One obvious purpose, especially within a courtroom, is to understand why certain types of activities do or do not count as defilements or desecrations. The goal is explanation or justification. Once adopted as a goal, the search for an explanation or justification for the rules governing a sacred site turns almost inevitably to the specifics of its significance, for, it is often assumed, specific and detailed information about a sacred site's significance is needed in order to explain or justify its governing rules or, in other words, its ethic.[7] The assumption seems reasonable because a sacred site's ethic depends upon its significance.

Let me deal with the purpose first and then with the assumption.

Simplifying somewhat, an ethic has two levels: surface and deep. At the surface, an ethic is a set of rules. Rules may be general or specific in scope. An ethic's rules tell whether certain types of activities are appropriate or not. They do not say, however, why one type is appropriate or not. To know why one type is appropriate or not, a person must delve into the deep level, the level of explanatory or justificatory principles.

In discussions of ethics, one should not lose sight of two obvious facts: (1) that we do not need to know why something is appropriate or not to know that it is appropriate or not, and (2) that we often know that something is appropriate or not without knowing why it is so. To put it slightly differently, it is an obvious fact both that we can know rules about what is and is not appropriate without knowing the explanation or justification for the rules, and also that we often know those rules without knowing their explanation or justification.

What, then, is the relevance of the aforementioned pair of facts to an understanding of sacred sites? In the first place, they show that people can know the rules governing the treatment of a sacred site without having to know the explanation or justification for the rules. Furthermore, they predict – what is, in fact, the case – that it is not uncommon for people to know the rules governing the treatment of a sacred site without knowing the explanation or justification for the rules. Finally, the two facts counsel that people's inability or apparent inability to articulate the explanation or justification for the rules governing a sacred site is not a secure basis for skepticism regarding their claim to know the rules governing the site.

Given that knowledge of the rules governing a sacred site does not depend upon knowledge of the explanation or justification for the rules, courts do not need to know why a First Nation counts a certain type of activity as a defilement or desecration of a sacred site to know that it counts it as such. Although the desire to know why a First Nation counts a certain type of activity as a defilement or desecration is natural, judges should not confuse their natural human desire for greater intelligibility with jurisprudential necessity. Generally speaking, a court that knows what sorts of activities a First Nation counts as defilements or desecrations of a sacred site has an adequate understanding of the First Nation's perspective on the site's ethic – that is, it has an understanding that should be good enough for its purposes.[8]

I have not, of course, said anything about the assumption that the explanation or justification for the rules governing a sacred site is located in the site's practical religious and/or theological/cosmological significance. It is, to say the least, a questionable assumption. Let me explain. It is true, it should be conceded, that a sacred site's ethic depends upon its significance inasmuch as its ethic is initially articulated in light of its significance, meant to accord with its significance, and meant to uphold its significance.[9] It does not follow from its dependence, however, that a sacred site's ethic is logically deducible from its significance. This is because a site's ethic concerns itself with what is and is not appropriate, appropriateness is a sort of consistency, and consistency, even from the logical point of view, is not reducible to deduction.[10] We should therefore not expect a sacred site's ethic to be logically deducible from its significance, although we should expect it to be consistent with its significance. Hence, it seems indeed possible that were we to know all there is to know about a sacred site's significance – together with the rules of deductive logic and their application – we still might not be able to come to know everything there is to know about its ethic. And so, as I stated at the outset of this paragraph, the assumption that the explanation or justification for the rules governing a sacred site is located in the site's significance is, at the very least, a questionable assumption.[11]

Returning to the main thread, the understanding of a First Nation's perspective on the particular significance of a sacred site that a court must have in order to make a fair assessment of the impact of a proposed activity does not require it either to acquire specific and detailed information about the site's significance or to uncover the explanation or justification for the site's ethic. Having general information about the site's significance should suffice to provide the court context for thinking about the site, its ethic, status, and so on. Knowing what types of activities the ethic permits and forbids should suffice for knowledge about the site's ethic. Such would constitute a good understanding of the site's ethic and a good understanding, other things being equal, is all that a court needs to begin the task of making a fair assessment of the impact of a Crown-sanctioned activity on a sacred site.

Unfortunately, the courts have exhibited a willingness to proceed with their analyses with a deficient knowledge of the ethics of First Nations sacred sites. In five of the cases I have discussed, First Nations forcefully submitted that the Crown's proposed activity would violate a sacred site (*Lower Tsitika Valley, Ure Creek, High Falls, Siska Creek,* and *Twin Sisters*). Their submissions presupposed the existence of associated ethics. Nonetheless, in only two of the five cases did the courts show some awareness of the proposed activity's inconsistency with the site's ethic (*High Falls* and *Twin Sisters*). Only in one of those cases, moreover, did the court eventually show an awareness of the First Nation's point of view about the consequences for the sacred site (*High Falls*). Because courts have proceeded with deficient knowledge of the ethics of sacred sites, they have failed to exhibit a good understanding of the perspectives of First Nations on the particular significance of their sacred sites.

Making a fair assessment of the impact of a Crown-proposed activity on a First Nation's sacred site also requires the court to gain some understanding of the First Nation's perspective on the site's relative status. Such an understanding involves some knowledge about the First Nation's views on sacred status generally as well as some knowledge about the particular site's status relative to the First Nation's other sacred sites.

To ascertain how a First Nation views sacred status generally, the court needs to inquire of the First Nation what difference it makes whether a site is accounted sacred or not. Thus far, courts have not explicitly posed the question. Perhaps, however, they have occasionally indirectly answered it. In a number of interlocutory proceedings, First Nations have submitted that the effects of the Crown's proposed activities on their sacred sites would amount to irreparable harm (*Lower Tsitika Valley, Ure Creek, High Falls,* and *Siska Creek*). Their claims suggest that sacred sites are sites that transcend pecuniary concerns, and therefore that one of the features that differentiates sacred sites from other sites is that their value is not approximable to, much less measurable by, monetary value. In some cases, the courts have accepted First Nations' submissions of irreparable harm in relation to their sacred sites (*Lower Tsitika Valley* and later *Siska Creek*), while in others, they have rejected them (*Ure Creek* and earlier *Siska Creek*). Those courts that have accepted their submissions appear to have at least impliedly recognized that the petitioning First Nations looked upon their sacred sites generally as sites transcending monetary value. Those that have rejected them, however, appear to have failed to appreciate the First Nations' perspectives on what is generally implied by sacred status.[12]

For many First Nations, sacred status often attaches to sites as integral wholes. Their holism can involve not merely the belief that the sacred site is not divisible into sacred and non-sacred parts but also the belief that what affects a part of the site affects the whole. From the holistic point of view, then, there are some activities that will violate a sacred site no matter how closely they are circumscribed. Thus, to a First Nation that views a sacred site holistically, it is senseless to ask it to identify the parts that will be violated by an activity that violates the whole. That is, however, precisely what some courts have asked First Nations to do (*Meares* [BCSC], *Ure Creek*, and later *Siska Creek*).[13] They have, it appears, failed to understand the First Nations' holistic perspective on the sacred sites in question. In a few cases, however, courts have recognized the First Nations' holistic perspective (*High Falls*, *Halfway River*, and earlier *Siska Creek*).[14] Indeed, in one case, a number of the chambers judge's conclusions were premised on the fact that the First Nation viewed the threatened area holistically (*Halfway River*).[15]

The courts' success in ascertaining First Nations' perspectives on the relative status of their sacred sites has been mixed. In five of the cases discussed earlier, First Nations asserted that the particular sacred sites they were trying to protect were highly sacred (*Lower Tsitika Valley*, *Ure Creek*, *High Falls*, *Siska Creek*, and *Twin Sisters*). They were saying, in other words, that the sites in question were among their most sacred. Despite their assertions, the courts in two cases inferred that the sites were not as sacred as the First Nations claimed. In the *Lower Tsitika Valley* case, MacKinnon J. interpreted the Tlowitsis-Mumtagila's late assertion of the valley's sacredness as a sign that the valley was not as sacred as the First Nation claimed.[16] In the later *Siska Creek* case, Sigurdson J. similarly concluded that the Siska Band's delays in pursuing its main action and in seeking an injunction after the logging company had been issued a cutting permit made its claims that the Siska Valley was highly sacred suspect.[17]

The inferences of MacKinnon J. and Sigurdson J. presupposed the following proposition: the more delay a First Nation shows in publicly defending a sacred site, the less sacred the site. The proposition is, as should now be clear, highly dubious. For one thing, the sacred site's ethic may limit what the First Nation may make public. For another, the First Nation may have prudential reasons for avoiding going public. Accordingly and more importantly, the proposition cannot credibly purport to reflect First Nations' perspectives on the relative status of their sacred sites.[18] Thus, applications of this rule of thumb are judicial impositions of an external viewpoint, pure and simple. They are more likely to distort than illuminate First Nations' perspectives on the relative status of their sacred sites.

Finally, making a fair assessment of the impact of a Crown-proposed activity on a First Nation's sacred site also requires the court to gain some understanding of the First Nation's perspective on how the activity will affect both the site and the society and culture with which the site is intertwined.

Basically, to gain a fair understanding of a First Nation's perspective on how a proposed activity will affect a sacred site, the court needs to find out two things: whether the activity's impact will count as a violation of the site's ethic and, if so, whether it will count as a serious violation. In five of the cases discussed, First Nations asserted that the proposed activities would seriously violate their sacred sites (*Lower Tsitika Valley*, *Ure Creek*, *High Falls*, *Siska Creek*, and *Twin Sisters*).[19] In four of those cases, the First Nations' claims notwithstanding, the courts persuaded themselves that the effects would not be serious. In the *Lower Tsitika Valley* case, the chambers judge formed the belief that the effects would not be serious based upon his dubious inference that the Lower Tsitika Valley was not as sacred as the Tlowitsis-Mumtagila claimed. In the *Ure Creek* case, the chambers judge held that, given that the Lil'wat's archaeological sites would be protected by provincial legislation, the road building and logging would still leave them free "to roam the area and absorb the spiritual surroundings."[20] In the early and later *Siska Creek* cases, the chambers judges found that the logging road and timber harvesting would not seriously interfere with the Siska Band's spiritual and religious practices. The chambers judge in the later *Siska Creek* case, like the chambers judge in the *Lower Tsitika Valley* case, believed that the effects would be insignificant based upon his dubious inference that the Siska Valley was not as sacred as the Siska Band claimed. Finally, in the *Twin Sisters* case, although the chambers judge agreed that the exploratory gas well would diminish the Saulteau and Kelly Lake Cree peoples' spiritual and religious connection to the Twin Sisters area, it would not, he held, eliminate it or prevent the exercise of any religiously significant practice in the area.[21] In all four of these cases, the courts assumed that the violations claimed by the First Nations would not render the sites unfit for practical religious use or eliminate their sacredness. One can read and reread the courts' reasons for judgment without finding even a hint that they took seriously the First Nations' views on the consequences of the claimed violations. The courts, therefore, and in the face of First Nations' claims to the contrary, unjustifiably assumed that the violations claimed by First Nations would neither render their sacred sites unfit for practical religious uses nor erase their sacredness.

Thus far, courts have devoted little attention to how the violations of sacred sites will affect First Nations' societies and cultures, much less to how First Nations view the matter. This is unsurprising, given their tendency to deprecate the seriousness of those violations. Generally speaking, the courts have pronounced on the impacts of Crown-proposed activities on off-reserve sacred sites, and thereby on First Nations peoples, with little to no idea of or concern for the social and cultural consequences for the peoples to be affected. Of the courts' members, Madam Justice Huddart is a rare exception. In her judgment in the *Halfway River* case, she clearly implied that a sacred site could be "fundamental to a First Nation's collective identity."[22] From this, it follows that a violation of a First Nation's sacred site can be an attack on its collective identity. Granted this, a serious violation of a First Nation's sacred site can be a serious attack on its collective identity. The courts in the *Lower Tsitika Valley*, *Ure Creek*, *High Falls*, *Siska Creek*, and *Twin Sisters* cases, however, seem never to have entertained the possibility that the effects of the proposed activities on the First Nations' sacred sites might seriously undermine those nations' besieged collective identities.

In the Twin Sisters case, Taylor J. implied that had the Saulteau and Kelly Lake Cree peoples utilized the Twin Sisters area for sustenance or practical religious purposes on a day-to-day or seasonal basis, he might have inferred that the area was fundamental to their collective identities.[23] As it was, the area served primarily a theological/cosmological function within their societies and therefore did not, he believed, suffice to make the area fundamental to their collective identities. Whether or not that was how the Saulteau and Kelly Lake Cree peoples viewed things, he did not ask.

Although one may be tempted to suppose that the courts would, were the issue to come up, subordinate an area's practical religious use to its sustenance use – saying that the latter is more fundamental to a First Nation's collective identity than the former – there is little in the judgments to support the supposition.[24] The chambers judge's decision in *Halfway River* might be read as lending support – although it would be a stretch, given that she neither explicitly nor impliedly raised the issue. In any case, at least one judge, Huddart J.A., has clearly implied that a site's spiritual or religious purposes could be at least as fundamental to a First Nation's collective identity as its sustenance purposes, if not more.[25]

Patently, how the courts choose to prioritize the sustenance, practical religious, and theological/cosmological values of sacred sites influences how they assess the impact of Crown-proposed activities on those sites. But making a fair assessment requires an understanding of First Nations' own priorities. Thus far, there is no indication that the courts have given more than scant attention to those priorities.

Judged against their specific efforts, then, the courts' overall efforts to gain an understanding of the perspectives of First Nations on sacred sites have been deplorably inadequate. Their specific efforts – when they have even made the efforts – to gain an understanding of the perspectives of First Nations on (1) the particular significance (including, most crucially, the ethic), (2) the relative status, and (3) the impact of the proposed activity on their sacred sites have failed more often than not. What this means, generally speaking, is that Canada's courts have made decisions about the sacred sites of First Nations without having adequately understood their perspectives on those sites. In the final analysis, they have made their decisions without having properly assessed the impact of the proposed activities on those sites.

Measuring First Nations Sacred Sites

Courts are called upon to assess the impact of Crown-proposed activities on First Nations sacred sites because they are first called upon to measure, weigh, or balance the interests (including rights) of First Nations against the interests (including rights) of others. Sacred sites are loci of competing and usually conflicting interests. But courts are not called upon simply to measure, weigh, or balance competing or conflicting interests; they are charged with measuring, weighing, or balancing them fairly. The main question I want to consider in this section is this: Have the courts fairly measured First Nations' interests in their sacred sites against the competing and usually conflicting interests of others? My answer, as I have already telegraphed, is no.

It should be noted at the outset that Canada's treatment of First Nations peoples presumes their subordination to the Canadian state, its political and legal structures and institutions.[26] Canada, like virtually all states in the western hemisphere, relies on its coercive power (embodied in its police and military forces) to maintain First Nations subordination. It must rely on its coercive power for the simple reason that First Nations subordination to the Canadian state is not, generally speaking, founded on First Nations consent.

Some readers may think that this claim is hyperbole. Proof that it is not is ready to hand. The proof is in the form of a thought experiment, the conclusion of which is verifiable through conversation with First Nations people. Suppose that tomorrow Canadian sovereignty over First Nations peoples and lands depended on First Nations consent. How many First Nations would give their consent? Some would, perhaps. Some definitely would not. Now, suppose more particularly that tomorrow Canada's exploitation of unsurrendered First Nations ancestral lands and waters depended on First Nations consent. How many First Nations would give their consent? Very likely, none. What this thought experiment shows is not merely that First Nations peoples would not, if given the choice tomorrow, consent to their subordination to the Canadian state but that they do not, generally speaking, consent to it now.[27] Absent First Nations consent, Canada must rely on its coercive power to maintain their subordination.

Canada's presumption of First Nations subordination is expressed in manifold ways. One way is by its sanction of non–First Nations interests in unsurrendered First Nations lands and resources. Another way is by its assertion of its courts' authority over First Nations peoples. Its courts' purported authority includes authority both to measure First Nations' interests in their sacred sites and to measure them against competing interests.

To those First Nations peoples who have never consented to incorporation into the Canadian project, Canada's assertion of its courts' authority over their affairs is unjust.[28] More specifically, to those First Nations peoples who have never formally agreed (through treaties) to share their ancestral lands, Canada's sanction of competing interests (especially competing interests in sacred sites) together with its assertion of its courts' authority to measure First Nations' interests (especially their interests in their sacred sites) against those competing interests is multiply unjust.

A similar point can be made in a way more familiar to Canadians. The Canadian state generally and its courts specifically suffer from a legitimacy problem in relation to First Nations peoples. Canada's legitimacy problem is particularly acute given its liberal democratic aspirations. The coercive subordination of whole peoples to the state is fundamentally at odds with liberal democratic values. It is, moreover, fundamentally at odds with liberal democratic notions of justice.

From the perspectives of both First Nations peoples and (insofar as they are committed to liberal democratic principles) Canadians, the unjust state of affairs described above precludes First Nations' interests in their sacred sites being fairly measured by the courts. Fairness implies justice. Justice legitimacy. The measurer cannot fairly measure what is not legitimately its to measure. Canada's courts could not, then, have fairly measured First Nations' interests in their sacred sites against competing interests.[29]

Although fairness writ large is precluded by a fundamental injustice at the heart of the Canadian project, there is still a point to inquiring whether the courts have *relative to the Canadian political/legal system* fairly measured First Nations' interests in their sacred sites against the competing and usually conflicting interests of others. That is, we may fruitfully inquire whether the courts have acted fairly in light of criteria internal to the Canadian system.

Have the courts, relatively speaking, fairly measured First Nations' interests in their sacred sites against competing interests? The fact that they have rendered their judgments without first taking care to understand the perspectives of First Nations peoples on their sacred sites implies that they have not. A fair measure of First Nations' interests in their sacred sites presupposes a decent understanding of those interests, and a decent understanding of those interests presupposes in turn an adequate understanding of First Nations' perspectives. Because of their failure to obtain an adequate understanding of First Nations' perspectives, the courts have been in no position to fairly measure First Nations' interests.

Manifestly, then, the courts have not – whether fairness is considered *simpliciter* or relative to the Canadian political/legal system – fairly measured First Nations' interests in their sacred sites against the competing interests of others.

But the foregoing analysis demonstrates something more. For the fact that Canada's courts have measured First Nations' interests in their sacred sites without having first acquired an adequate understanding of First Nations' perspectives indicates the presence of judicial bias. Generally speaking, it indicates a bias against First Nations and their interests in their sacred sites in favour of those claiming competing interests.

Accepting that such judicial bias exists, we may wonder what specific forms it takes. One candidate that would likely spring to many people's minds is a bias specifically against First Nations' spiritual and religious interests in their sacred sites. For a community's or people's spirituality and religion seem integral to its sacred sites.[30] The final question I want to consider in this section, then, is this: Have the courts shown a specific bias against First Nations' spiritual and religious interests in their sacred sites?

We should not assume that because the courts have exhibited bias generally against First Nations and their interests in their sacred sites, they must also be biased specifically against First Nations' spiritual and religious interests. For the courts may be biased generally against First Nations and their interests without being biased specifically against any particular interests. Alternatively, they may be biased specifically against one or more particular interests without being biased specifically against spiritual and religious interests. After all, a First Nation may have a variety of interests in a sacred site (including, for instance, sustenance and environmental interests) besides spiritual and religious.[31] The point, in any case, is that knowing that general judicial bias against First Nations and their sacred sites exists is not the same as knowing what specific forms it takes or indeed knowing whether it even takes any specific forms. Thus, the courts' general bias against First Nations and their interests in their sacred sites is not proof of a specific bias against First Nations' spiritual and religious interests.

Proof of specific bias would involve showing that the courts have not treated First Nations' spiritual and religious interests in their sacred sites as they have treated Canadian spiritual and religious interests in comparable Canadian sites. If it is shown that they have not, specific bias is proved. So the answer to the question of whether the courts have shown specific bias follows immediately from the answer to this question: Have the courts treated First Nations' spiritual and religious interests in their sacred sites as they have treated Canadian spiritual and religious interests in comparable Canadian sites?

Before we can say whether the courts have treated First Nations' spiritual and religious interests in their sacred sites as they have treated Canadian spiritual and religious interests in comparable sites, we must determine how they have treated First Nations' spiritual and religious interests in their sacred sites, and then how they have treated Canadian spiritual and religious interests in comparable Canadian sites.

At least since the *Meares Island* case, the courts have been in the habit of measuring First Nations' spiritual and religious interests in their sacred sites against economic and environmental concerns. Indeed, their main measures have been economic and environmental. Generally speaking, their adoption of such measures as their main measures has resulted in the subordination of First Nations' spiritual and religious interests to Canadian economic and environmental concerns. In what immediately follows, I shall discuss the courts' economic measure of First Nations sacred sites and then their environmental measure.

As is clear from the interlocutory injunction cases, the courts have by implication adopted the default position that serious economic consequences override First Nations' interests in their sacred sites. (I say "by implication" because it is implied by Esson's Rule.[32]) The courts define serious economic consequences in relation to the local, regional, or provincial economies. By default, First Nations' spiritual and religious interests in their sacred sites are subordinate to Canadian economic concerns.

What is not yet clear is how the courts will measure First Nations' spiritual and religious interests in their sacred sites against economic concerns when reviewing the Crown's efforts to accommodate First Nations' interests in their sacred sites. That they will take economic concerns into account is inescapable. For, as Lambert J.A. stated in *Haida:*

> It is an important fact that Weyerhaeuser employs something in the order of 200 workers in its Queen Charlotte Islands operations and has investments in plant, machinery and equipment in the Tree Farm Licence itself. Weyerhaeuser has a considerable business interest in the long term and short term continuance of its logging operations on T.F.L. 39 and the Crown must bear Weyerhaeuser's interest in mind as well as the interests of the Haida people when considering the overall public interest of the people of British Columbia in the Queen Charlotte Islands, or Haida Gwaii.[33]

It seems unlikely, however, that the courts in judicial review proceedings will adopt a position fully analogous to the position they have adopted in interlocutory injunction proceedings. For, were courts to adopt a general rule elevating economic concerns above First Nations' interests (whether or not they are spiritual and religious interests in their sacred sites), they would, in effect, be granting the Crown licence to violate its constitutional and fiduciary duties towards First Nations peoples.[34]

The second of the courts' two main measures of First Nations' interests in sacred sites is the environmental measure. In some judges' hands, environmental values have trumped the spiritual and religious values First Nations associate with their lands. For example, in the public mind, the *Meares Island* case was – or at least became – a fight first to preserve the island's ecology and only second to uphold Aboriginal rights and First Nations culture. Although most of the Court of Appeal justices in the *Meares Island* case saw things differently, Craig J.A. did not. In his reasons for judgment, he argued that since the logging of Meares Island would be environmentally sensitive, the Nuu-chah-nulth would likely suffer no serious harm.[35] His argument presupposed that environmental concerns outweighed the Nuu-chah-nulth's spiritual and religious as well as broader cultural concerns.

The chambers judges in the *Lower Tsitika Valley* and later *Siska Creek* cases apparently presupposed similar things. Their reasoning was basically this: given that the area in question is not highly sacred and given that the area's timber will be harvested in a way consistent with certain environmental values, the logging and road building will not seriously harm the First Nation's interests in the area. Their reasoning suggests that had certain environmental values not been respected, they might have concluded differently. This in turn suggests that they presupposed that environmental concerns outweighed the Tlowitsis-Mumtagila's and Siska Band's spiritual and religious concerns.[36]

Similarly, Kurisko J., in the first interlocutory proceeding involving the High Falls project, emphasized the Poplar Point Ojibway's (as well as the broader community's) environmental concerns while virtually ignoring the First Nation's spiritual and religious concerns over the impending loss of their sacred area.[37]

The courts have also subordinated First Nations' spiritual and religious interests in their sacred sites to environmental values in more subtle ways. In a few cases, they have indicated a preference for areas still untouched (or virtually untouched) by commercial resource exploitation over areas already exploited or developed. *Westar* provides a clear instance. There, the chambers judge and the majority of the Court of Appeal agreed that the Shedin, which was still untouched by commercial resource exploitation, should be protected pending the outcome of the *Delgamuukw* trial, while the Shegisic, which was already being logged, should not.[38] A similar assumption about the comparative worth of unexploited and exploited lands was at work in the chambers judge's decision in the *Halfway River* case, where she found significance in the fact that the Halfway River people looked upon the Tusdzuh region as "one of the last unspoiled areas of wilderness where they can exercise their traditional way of life."[39] What these cases suggest, is that courts favour sacred sites in commercially unexploited areas over sacred sites in already-exploited areas. It follows that those courts that have so favoured sacred sites in unexploited areas have presupposed that environmental concerns outweigh First Nations' spiritual and religious concerns.[40]

It should be noted that absent their apparent predilection for environmental values over First Nations' spiritual and religious values, courts might equally reasonably have inferred that because sacred sites in already-exploited areas are under greater threat, they are deserving of even greater protection than sacred sites in unexploited areas.

As the cases discussed show, courts have not only measured First Nations' spiritual and religious interests in their sacred sites against economic and environmental concerns but have also subordinated the former to the latter. The subordination is not necessarily an expression of a specific bias against First Nations' spiritual and religious interests, however. For if the courts have similarly subordinated Canadian spiritual and religious interests in their sacred sites to economic and environmental interests, they have treated First Nations' spiritual and religious interests as they have treated Canadian spiritual and religious interests.

Have the courts treated Canadian sacred sites similarly? With this question the inquiry into specific bias against First Nations' spiritual and religious interests in their sacred sites meets an insuperable obstacle. The basic problem is that the courts have never adjudicated upon Canadian sacred sites in circumstances in which economic or environmental concerns loom similarly large.[41] Given this problem, we cannot determine whether the courts' subordination of First Nations' spiritual and religious interests in their sacred sites to economic and environmental concerns expresses a specific bias against those interests.[42]

Although specific bias against First Nations' spiritual and religious interests in their sacred sites has not been proved, general bias has. The courts' failure to obtain an understanding of First Nations' perspectives on their sacred sites comparable to their understanding of the perspectives underlying competing interests in those sites demonstrates the presence of a general bias against First Nations and their interests in their sacred sites in favour of those claiming competing interests.

The absence of proof of specific bias is cold comfort, however. First of all, the courts have not been shown innocent of specific bias and, more important, their subordination of First Nations' spiritual and religious interests in their sacred sites to Canadian economic and environmental concerns raises suspicions. In other words, it raises the appearance of specific bias. Even if it is only appearance and not reality, the appearance is a serious concern. Courts within liberal democracies, like all liberal democratic political and legal institutions, cannot function properly without a large measure of collective faith in them, including faith in their fairness. The appearance of bias undermines such collective faith. The appearance of specific bias against First Nations' spiritual and religious interests undermines the collective faith of Canadians in their courts. It undermines, moreover, whatever collective faith First Nations peoples may have come to invest in Canada's courts.

Bias is said to be unfair or unjust because it produces unfairness or injustice. The courts' bias against First Nations and their interests in their sacred sites is therefore unfair because it has produced unfairness. In particular, the courts' bias has meant that the courts have not fairly measured

First Nations' interests in their sacred sites against the competing and usually conflicting interests of others.

For most of my discussion, I have been speaking of unfairness and therefore of bias relative to the Canadian political/legal system. There is, of course, a deeper unfairness and thus a deeper bias. This is summed up in Canada's presumption of First Nations subordination to the Canadian state, a presumption lacking First Nations consent and supported by coercion. The extent to which the relative unfairness and bias of which I have been speaking is an unavoidable result of the deeper unfairness and bias is a topic I shall touch upon in the next chapter.

As has been demonstrated in this section, then, First Nations sacred sites have fared poorly in the courts' reasoning about them in two respects. First, the courts have failed to gain an adequate understanding of First Nations' perspectives on their sacred sites. Second, and as a consequence of the first, they have not fairly measured First Nations interests in their sacred sites against the competing and usually conflicting interests of others.

The Results Reconsidered

First Nations sacred sites were involved in eight of the nine cases I have discussed. In those eight cases, First Nations tried to leverage their claims for Aboriginal and/or treaty rights into protection for their off-reserve sacred sites. The sacredness of the sites was prominent in five cases (*Lower Tsitika Valley, Ure Creek, High Falls, Siska Creek,* and *Twin Sisters*). First Nations lost in all five cases. Judged against the results, First Nations sacred sites have fared poorly in Canada's courts.

They have also fared poorly in the courts' reasoning about them. The courts' efforts to gain an understanding of the perspectives of First Nations on their sacred sites have been most inadequate. Because of this inadequacy, the courts' efforts to fairly measure First Nations' interests in their sacred sites against competing interests have also been inadequate. Given that, it is no surprise that they have fared so poorly in results.[43]

6
Tima Kwetsi – Epilogue

My discussion in Chapter 5 demonstrated that First Nations sacred sites have fared poorly in Canada's courts. My discussion in the introductory chapter demonstrated also that the existence, survival, and well-being of First Nations peoples are linked to the fate of their sacred sites, and thus that whatever threatens their sacred sites undermines their existence, survival, and well-being. By their failure to treat First Nations sacred sites fairly, Canada's courts have given their imprimatur to a continuation of one of colonialism's least remarked but most insidious assaults on indigenous peoples. If Canada's colonialist approach to First Nations sacred sites specifically and First Nations peoples generally is allowed to continue indefinitely unabated, the outcome is predictable. Colonialism's trajectory promises no future for indigenous peoples.

Although my main argument ended in the previous chapter, it is nonetheless fitting to offer a few final remarks on what Canada's courts might do to improve on their treatment of First Nations sacred sites and on what Canada itself has at stake in First Nations peoples' fight for their sacred sites.

Suggestions for Improvement

If Canada's courts are to improve on their treatment of First Nations sacred sites, they must gain a better understanding of what their sacred sites mean to First Nations peoples. For improvements to be lasting, the courts must come to recognize that First Nations sacred sites are crucial to the existence, survival, and well-being of First Nations peoples, and that, as such, Canada's treatment of First Nations sacred sites can implicate both constitutionally protected Aboriginal and/or treaty rights and the human rights of indigenous peoples under international law.[1] Accordingly, the courts should make that recognition their starting point.

The courts' failure to treat First Nations sacred sites fairly is largely traceable to their failure to obtain a decent understanding of First Nations' perspectives on their sacred sites. Therefore, the courts can both materially and relatively easily improve on their treatment of First Nations sacred sites by making the effort to better understand First Nations' perspectives, specifically on the ethics of the sacred sites in question, their status, and the impact of the allegedly offending activities.

As I explained in the previous chapter, a good understanding of First Nations' perspectives on the ethics of their sacred sites, their status, and the impact of the allegedly offending activities is a prerequisite to the courts making a fair assessment of the impact of an allegedly offending activity. As I also explained, the courts do not require a deep understanding of the site's significance and therefore should not press for specific and detailed information. (Indeed, the courts should take care not to press First Nations to violate the ethics of the sites they are being asked to defend.) General information should suffice for purposes of context. What is most crucial to their task in the initial stages of their analyses is a good understanding of the ethics of the sites.

How, then, can a court obtain a good sense of a sacred site's ethic? A simple way is to ask for examples of activities that are appropriate and inappropriate. With a few examples in hand, it should be able to analogize to other activities – including the purportedly offending activity – to determine whether they are consistent with the site's ethic. Normally, a few examples should provide the court with a reasonably good understanding of the First Nation's perspective on a site's ethic. Further understanding based on the principles explaining or justifying the site's ethic are, as I have previously demonstrated,[2] unnecessary and, even if obtained, unlikely to materially assist the court in its deliberations.

As part of their overall effort to better understand First Nations' perspectives on their sacred sites, the courts also need to gain a better understanding of First Nations' perspectives on the status of their sacred sites. Although such perspectives vary from First Nation to First Nation, there is considerable agreement on what sacred status – considered generally – entails. First Nations peoples agree, for instance, that their sacred sites transcend monetary valuation and that many are holistically sacred. Once the courts are aware of these facts, they can take steps to more faithfully measure, and therefore more fairly deal with, First Nations' interests in their sacred sites. Let me briefly explain how.

Aware that First Nations peoples consider their sacred sites beyond monetary valuation, the courts should, when called upon to deal with First Nations sacred sites in interlocutory and other proceedings, adopt the position that harm to a sacred site (including interference with access or use) is generally irreparable. That should be the default position and thus a standard part of judicial deliberations on sacred sites. Aware also that First Nations peoples often view their sacred sites holistically, the courts should be prepared and willing to deal with them as such. And so, having learned that a First Nation views a sacred site holistically, a court should not repeat the past mistake of some courts of asking it to distinguish between portions of the site deserving (or more deserving) and portions not deserving (or less deserving) protection. By taking even these small steps, the courts would be making a significant commitment to a more accurate and thus fairer representation of the perspectives of First Nations peoples on the status of their sacred sites.

It is not sufficient, however, for courts to practically demonstrate a better understanding of the perspectives of First Nations peoples on what sacred status generally entails. They should also strive to obtain and practically demonstrate a superior understanding of their perspectives on the relative status of *individual* sacred sites. A First Nation may hold some of its sacred sites as more and some as less sacred than others. Some courts have in the past concluded that a particular sacred site was less sacred than claimed based upon their assumption that were the site as sacred as claimed, the First Nation would have more expeditiously and/or more vigorously mounted a public defence. Armed with a better understanding of a sacred site's ethic, the limits its ethic may impose on the dispersal of information, and First Nations peoples' prudential concerns about sharing information on their sacred sites with outsiders, the courts should not again make the same manifestly faulty assumption about the relative status of individual sacred sites.[3]

By gaining a better understanding of First Nations' perspectives on both the particular significance (including especially the ethic) and the status of their sacred sites, the courts should have a better appreciation of their perspectives on the impact of allegedly offending activities. In several of the cases discussed in the previous chapter, courts disregarded First Nations' claims that the activities in dispute would seriously violate their sacred sites. In those cases, the courts were operating with a defective understanding of First Nations' perspectives on the particular significance and status of their sacred sites. With a better grasp of First Nations' perspectives on these matters, the courts should never again deal so dismissively with their claims of serious violations. They should more keenly appreciate the serious implications of threats to sacred sites for First Nations peoples and for their existence, survival, and well-being.

Thus, the courts can both materially and relatively easily improve on their treatment of First Nations sacred sites by making the effort to further their knowledge about First Nations' perspectives on their sites. Such improvement will not necessarily satisfy the courts' obligations of fairness, however. For fairness obliges them not only to make the effort to better understand First Nations' perspectives but also to acquire an understanding of those perspectives comparable to their understanding of the competing perspectives of government, developers, logging companies, and so on. To settle for less would be to violate fundamental obligations of fairness and thus to exhibit bias.

This presents a problem, however. Other than in rare instances in which a judge happens to be a member of the litigating First Nation, the courts cannot be expected to obtain an understanding of First Nations' perspectives fully comparable to their understanding of competing Canadian perspectives, for the judiciary does not share the cultural assumptions of First Nations peoples. It would seem, therefore, that no matter how far they delve into First Nations' perspectives, the courts will never understand them well enough to accurately and hence fairly measure First Nations' interests in their sacred sites against competing interests.

Fortunately, this problem is not a serious one. It appears serious only because the degree of comparability of understanding that courts must have before they can measure First Nations' interests accurately and fairly is exaggerated. Courts do not need a fully comparable understanding. That is, they do not need an understanding of First Nations' perspectives that is fully comparable to their understanding of competing perspectives before they can measure First Nations' interests accurately and fairly. What they need is a functionally equal understanding, and this they can obtain by acquiring a good grasp of the key features of First Nations' perspectives. The key features are nominally defined as those a court must understand before it can accurately and fairly measure First Nations' interests. They are, I suggest, summed up in First Nations' perspectives on the ethics of their sites, their status, and the impact of allegedly offending activities. A good grasp of these should usually suffice to provide the courts with a functionally equal understanding of First Nations' perspectives on their sacred sites.

A functionally equal understanding of First Nations' perspectives would not, however, automatically translate into judgments expressing a recognition of the importance of their sacred sites to First Nations peoples' existence, survival, and well-being. The main obstacle is the routine subordination of First Nations' spiritual and religious interests in their sacred sites to competing economic and environmental interests. Until this obstacle is removed, the courts' efforts to better understand First Nations' perspectives on their sacred sites will make little if any difference in terms of results.[4]

As I showed in the previous chapter, the courts – at least from the points of view of First Nations peoples – appear biased specifically against First Nations' spiritual and religious interests in their sacred sites. They have encouraged the appearance of specific bias by subordinating the spiritual and religious interests of First Nations peoples in their sacred sites to competing Canadian economic and/or environmental interests. The courts can remove the appearance of specific bias by clearly demonstrating that they do not – or at least would not – afford better treatment to the spiritual and religious interests of, say, Catholics, Jews, Muslims, or Sikhs in their sacred sites. If they cannot clearly demonstrate or convincingly argue the point, they should seriously entertain the possibility that they are biased specifically against First Nations' spiritual and religious interests and then set about rectifying the problem. This would require the courts to call a halt to their routine subordination of First Nations peoples' spiritual and religious interests in their sacred sites to Canadian economic and/or environmental interests.

Aside from the issue of whether First Nations' spiritual and religious interests in their sacred sites are victims of specific bias, their sacred sites implicate rights that should not be treated so lightly. First Nations sacred sites implicate both constitutionally guaranteed Aboriginal rights and the human rights of indigenous peoples under international law. The courts' routine subordination of First Nations' spiritual and religious interests in their sacred sites to the economic and/or environmental interests of others disrespects the legal magnitude of the rights at stake and thus undervalues what those rights are meant to protect.

With regard to their subordination of First Nations' spiritual and religious interests in their sacred sites to competing Canadian economic interests, the courts have the most room for improvement in their handling of First Nations sacred sites in interlocutory proceedings. First Nations' efforts to gain interlocutory protection for their sacred sites have tended to founder at the second stage of the courts' analyses, the balance of convenience test.[5] I have already suggested that by adopting the default position that harm to a sacred site is generally irreparable, the courts would be taking a significant step towards more accurately and more fairly representing the perspectives of First Nations peoples. If the courts were to adopt this as their default position, First Nations sacred sites would have a slightly better chance of passing the balance of convenience test. Even so, however, the courts are strongly disinclined to grant interlocutory protection to First Nations sacred sites when serious economic consequences would be engaged. Thus, as Esson's Rule stipulates, the harm, whether irreparable or not, that would befall a First Nation should interlocutory protection be denied a sacred site is generally outweighed by the harm that would befall the local, regional, or provincial economy should the protection be granted. Although there is, as Esson's Rule also provides, an exception for sites that qualify as sufficiently unique, in over a decade no sacred site has qualified as sufficiently unique.

The courts would be well motivated to treat First Nations sacred sites as sufficiently unique to qualify as an exception to the general rule that serious economic consequences override harm to petitioning First Nations. Let me explain why. Serious violations of the ethics of sacred sites are, legally speaking, irreparable. But they are more than irreparable. They pierce the hearts of First Nations peoples. They threaten the existence, survival, and, not least, well-being of First Nations peoples. What First Nations peoples have at stake in their sacred sites is more profound than what Canadians have at stake economically. The fact that Esson's Rule provides an exception to the general rule that serious economic consequences override harm to petitioning First Nations implies that the courts acknowledge that what a First Nation has at stake in a particular site may transcend and thus outweigh even weighty Canadian economic interests. Given their importance to the existence, survival, and well-being of First Nations peoples, the courts should recognize that what they have at stake in their sacred sites transcends Canadian economic interests. They should therefore consider stipulating that First Nations sacred sites are, provided that irreparable harm has been established, sufficiently unique to qualify as an exception to the general rule favouring Canadian economic interests over First Nations' interests.[6]

The courts have also subordinated First Nations' spiritual and religious interests in their sacred sites to Canadian environmental interests. As I detailed in the previous chapter, they have done this in at least two ways. They have assumed that proposed activities that meet provincial and/or federal environmental standards do not impact on First Nations sacred sites to their serious detriment. They have also assumed that First Nations sacred sites on exploited or developed lands are less deserving of protection than sites in environmentally pristine areas. With a better understanding of the perspectives of First Nations peoples on their sacred sites, especially their perspectives on the ethics of their sacred sites, the courts should see their way clear to jettisoning these mistaken assumptions. With a better understanding, they should see that just as the sacredness of First Nations sacred sites (although dependent on a measure of physical integrity) is not reducible to physical factors, so too the ethics of their sacred sites are not reducible to ordinary environmental ethics, much less to Canadian environmental ethics.

My suggestions for how Canada's courts might improve on their treatment of First Nations sacred sites have been limited to relatively simple and practical ways by which the courts might more closely approximate relative fairness, that is, fairness relative to the Canadian political/legal system. I have not, therefore, offered any suggestions for how they might work towards fairness writ large. Achieving fairness writ large would demand radical change. Most radically and fundamentally, it would require the courts not merely to question Canada's presumption of First Nations subordination to the Canadian state but to repudiate it. Canada's courts, however, have not yet come to a place where they are willing to address the issue full-square.[7] Nor have Canadians yet come to a place where they are willing not only to acknowledge the deep injustice still visited upon First Nations peoples but also to accept court-directed wholesale change in their relationship with them.[8] How Canadians, with some coaxing from their courts, might construct a post-colonialist relationship with First Nations peoples is a topic requiring its own book. Accordingly, my suggestions for how Canada's courts might improve on their treatment of First Nations sacred sites end here.

What Canada Has at Stake

Finally, I want to briefly consider what Canada has at stake in the struggle of First Nations to protect their sacred sites. Before I proceed, let me make my purpose transparent. My aim is to offer Canadians strong self-interested reasons for altering their treatment of First Nations sacred sites. To achieve this, I propose to show that Canada too has something profound at stake in the struggle of First Nations for their sacred sites.

Clearly, the fact that Canada's courts have failed to treat First Nations sacred sites fairly has serious implications for Canada's legal system. It also has serious implications for Canadian society. What those latter implications are and why they are serious can be understood most easily by reflecting on a prior fact, namely, that First Nations peoples have had to fight – and continue to have to fight – for their sacred sites. Let me elaborate.

First Nations peoples have had to fight to protect their sacred sites because their sites have been threatened. The threats have come mainly from resource exploitation and development. Because the threats have come from outside their communities, First Nations peoples have been provoked into fighting to protect them. Their fight, then, has been defensive. Although the threats to First Nations sacred sites have come from many sources, the ultimate and overall responsibility is Canada's, for those who have posed the threats have done so under the aegis of the Canadian state. Thus, in the final analysis, Canada has provoked First Nations peoples into fighting to protect their sacred sites.

It is a universally recognized truth that you can harm a person as much by attacking someone or something he or she cares deeply about as by directly attacking him or her. For many peoples, it is a truism to say that they care for their sacred things above others. First Nations peoples care deeply about their sacred sites. In effect, therefore, Canada's attacks on First Nations sacred sites are attacks on First Nations peoples. Certainly, they are *felt* by First Nations peoples as attacks on themselves.

It has long been a point of pride among Canadians that their history is virtually absent of conflicts with First Nations peoples approximating the Indian wars of nineteenth-century America. The pride of Canadians implies a correlative condemnation of America's attacks on its Native peoples. America's attacks were often direct attacks designed to inflict harm on and to force the submission or to cause the extermination of entire peoples. Canadians have rightly looked askance at their neighbour's behaviour.

But peoples, like persons, may bleed to death from one large or a thousand small cuts. Canada's attacks on First Nations sacred sites may not, it might be argued, qualify as large cuts, but they certainly do not qualify as small. Their sacred sites are too important to First Nations peoples for their defilement, desecration, and destruction to count as small cuts. By its attacks on First Nations sacred sites, Canada is causing palpable harm to

First Nations peoples. Taken together with the many other serious challenges facing contemporary First Nations communities, Canada's attacks on First Nations sacred sites pose an unacceptable risk to the well-being and future existence of those communities.

What is at stake for Canada? Nothing less, I suggest, than its national soul. How Canadians look upon their historical and current relationship with First Nations peoples and how they envision their future relationship are integral parts of their national self-image. Comparing themselves with the rest of the western hemisphere, they see themselves as having treated First Nations peoples relatively benignly. They are, however, also aware that their current relationship with First Nations peoples, like their past, is imperfect. Accordingly, Canadians have committed themselves to improving the relationship. These are integral parts of the Canadian self-image. Canada's role as assailant conflicts with that self-image.

Canada therefore faces a fundamental choice. It may either eliminate the inconsistency or attempt to live with it. It may eliminate the inconsistency in one of two ways: either by renouncing its role of attacker or by altering its national self-image to fit the role. The latter would be the loss of Canada's soul, but so too would be the attempt to live with the inconsistency, for it is already and will become increasingly difficult for Canada to live with the inconsistency without slipping into conscious hypocrisy. And the path of hypocrisy would still require Canada to alter its national self-image to fit its role of attacker. The difference between attempting to live with the inconsistency and ultimately adopting the stance of the hypocrite on the one hand, and eliminating the inconsistency by altering its national self-image to fit its role of assailant on the other, is not to be found in self-image but in the image projected to others. Consequently, the attempt to continue to live with the inconsistency would also be the loss of Canada's soul.

What Canada has at stake in the struggle of First Nations to protect their sacred sites is, then, nothing less than its national soul. Thus, Canada too has something profound at stake in their struggle. But a nation, unlike an individual, may lose its soul and later regain it as long as the nation continues to exist. Presumably, should Canada lose its national soul through its continued attacks on First Nations sacred sites, it might eventually regain it. But Canada's loss and possible recovery of its national soul is not a luxury First Nations peoples can afford. Canada's attacks on their sacred sites strike at the very roots of their collective ways of being, and therefore at their continued existence as indigenous peoples. Hence, what is at stake for First Nations peoples in their struggle to protect their sacred sites is yet more profound.

Notes

Introduction: What First Nations Peoples Have at Stake

1 See *The Mayagna (Sumo) Awas Tingni Community v. Nicaragua* (31 August 2001), Inter-Am. Ct. H.R. (Ser. C) No. 79, online: The Organization of American States <http://www.oas.org>.

2 *Ibid.* at para. 149.

3 As Pope John Paul II stated a decade earlier, "certain people, especially those identified as native or indigenous, have always maintained a special relationship to their lands, a relationship connected with the group's very identity as a people having their own tribal, cultural, and religious traditions. When such indigenous peoples are deprived of their land they lose a vital element of their way of life and actually run the risk of disappearing as a people." The excerpt can be found in Michael Stogre, *That the World May Believe: The Development of Papal Social Thought on Aboriginal Rights* (Sherbrooke, QC: Editions Paulines, 1992) at 182.

4 That their material and spiritual connections to the land are – and that indigenous peoples view them as – crucial to their existence, survival, and well-being is evidenced by the continuing struggle of those indigenous peoples who have been dispossessed of and removed from their traditional lands to maintain their material and spiritual connections. The Cherokee people are a well-known example.

5 Indigenous peoples also commonly refer to the spiritual realm to explain a host of related (believed) facts, e.g., that they have been providentially placed on their lands and that they and their lands have been carefully fitted to one another.

6 As Marie Battiste and James (Sa'ke'j) Youngblood Henderson put it, "[t]he core of Indigenous spirituality is that everything is alive." See their *Protecting Indigenous Knowledge and Heritage: A Global Challenge* (Saskatoon: Purich, 2000) at 100.

7 There is, it may be noted, potential here for paradox akin to the paradox presented by the Judeo-Christian doctrine that God is both immanent in creation and transcendent.

8 Because I have used the word, this is an appropriate place to observe that it is as much a mistake of *metaphysics* as it is of logic to think that statements about what a group collectively subscribes to necessarily purport to say what all of the group's members subscribe to and/or what each must subscribe to in order to count as a member. Neither the logic of ascriptions of collective intentionality nor the metaphysics of collective intentionality works that way. Hence, to say of a particular indigenous community that it believes, for instance, that it has been charged by the Creator with caring for the land is to say neither that all the community's members believe that their community has been so charged nor that only those who so believe are members of the community.

9 Although not a focus of my discussion, the importance of waters to the indigenous peoples of Canada generally and to First Nations peoples specifically should not be lost sight of. Speaking of the geographical distribution of Aboriginal communities within Canada, Frank Quinn states: "Invariably, these communities are strung out along lakes, rivers or estuaries. They can be found in every drainage system of the country." See his "As Long

as the Rivers Run: The Impacts of Corporate Water Development on Native Communities in Canada" (1991) 11 Canadian Journal of Native Studies 137 at 138-39.

10 A number of North American First Nations/Native American groups acting as – or with lawyers acting on their behalf as – *amici curiae,* submitted briefs to the Court, including the Assembly of First Nations, the Mohawk Community of Akwasasne, and the National Congress of American Indians.

Please note that when I speak of *First Nations* peoples, I refer primarily to those also known as *Indian* peoples. Although many of my general comments in the early chapters of this book apply to Canada's Aboriginal or indigenous peoples generally, and although most of my general comments in the later chapters potentially apply to Aboriginal or indigenous peoples generally, the cases I discuss in the middle chapters involve Indian peoples exclusively. By using the term *First Nations* to refer primarily to Indian peoples, I avoid overgeneralizing from the cases discussed here and allow my readers to extend my remarks, when appropriate, to the other Aboriginal or indigenous peoples who inhabit Canada.

11 Speaking generally of Aboriginal peoples but offering First Nations as examples, Patrick Macklem puts it this way:

> Aboriginal people have unique spiritual relationships with ancestral territories that transcend particular cultural customs, practices, and traditions that may be engaged in by communities on ancestral land. Examples abound of this deep connection between spiritual identity and land. Members of the Blackfoot Confederacy, for example, view the land as a gift from the Creator as a mother, a giver of life, and the provider of all things necessary to sustain existence. For the Gitksan in British Columbia, ownership of territory is a marriage of the chief and the land. Each chief has an ancestor who encountered and acknowledged the life of the land and received authority from such encounters. Although Aboriginal systems of belief are diverse, Aboriginal relationships with land are often structured by beliefs that manifest an overarching spiritual responsibility to protect, nurture, and cherish the earth as the giver of life.

See Macklem, *Indigenous Difference and the Constitution of Canada* (Toronto: University of Toronto Press, 2001) at 102.

12 As Brian Edward Brown puts it, "since the unique identity of the different Indian tribes is so often coherent with the land that animates and sustains their religious beliefs and practices, bureaucratic decisions to alter land sites are intrusive invasions of tribal self-understanding; the dissipation of tribal identity is the inherent consequence of land desecration." See his *Religion, Law, and the Land: Native Americans and the Judicial Interpretation of Sacred Land* (Westport, CT: Greenwood Press, 1999) at 6-7.

Chapter 1: The Outlines of a General Theory of Sacred Sites

1 For more information on Ista, see the Nuxalk Nation website at <http://www.nuxalk.org>.

2 David L. Carmichael, Jane Hubert, and Brian Reeves, "Introduction" in David L. Carmichael, Jane Hubert, Brian Reeves, and Audhild Schanche, eds., *Sacred Sites, Sacred Place* (London: Routledge, 1994) 1 at 3, put the point this way: "To say that a specific place is a sacred place is not simply to describe a piece of land, or just locate it in a certain position in the landscape. What is known as a sacred site carries with it a whole range of rules and regulations regarding people's behaviour in relation to it." Note that by speaking of a sacred site's ethic, I am not exempting law. Hence, as I am using the term, the ethic of a First Nation's sacred site may be wholly, partly, or not at all expressed in its laws.

3 By saying that the distinction depends upon a site's practical religious and/or theological/cosmological significance, I am not claiming that it is necessarily logically dependent, in the sense of being necessarily logically deducible therefrom. How a particular site's ethic relates to its significance can be a complex matter that cannot be captured by the easy reduction of "ought" (a site's ethic) to "is" (a site's significance) implicit in claims of logical deducibility. What I am claiming, however, is that a site's ethic is initially articulated

in light of its significance, is meant to accord with its significance, and is, moreover, meant to uphold its significance.

An analogy may serve to clarify my remark about the reduction of a site's ethic to its significance. For centuries, Catholics, east and west, considered it inappropriate to receive Communion from a priest in any other way than directly on the tongue. That was – and in many places still is – part of their ethic of Communion. Nonetheless, the claim that one *should* receive Communion only on the tongue is not logically deducible from standard Catholic eucharistic theology.

4 For example, Jane Hubert, "Sacred Beliefs and Beliefs of Sacredness" in Carmichael et al., *supra* note 2, 9 at 12, suggests this position in a passage in which she poses (without attempting to answer) a series of questions:

> It may be possible for archaeologists and other outsiders to come to recognize the characteristics of sacred sites in cultures other than their own, and to treat them with due respect. But does this imply a fundamental acceptance of the sacredness of the site, or is it merely the adoption, without conviction, of appropriate behaviour? Is it, in fact, possible for people who have different religious beliefs really to believe in the sacredness of the sites or objects that are part of another religion? What do we mean when we say that we believe in the sacredness of someone else's site? How far can we really believe in the sacredness of sites which relate to beliefs that we do not share? If we *treat* something as sacred, is that enough? Is it enough if we follow the rules set down by those whose sacred site it is — or is this merely paying lip service to their belief that it is sacred, rather than really believing it to be sacred ourselves? Can we say that something is sacred to someone else but not to us? Is that not the same as saying that it is not sacred? Could it be, on the other hand, that what is sacred to one person is in essence sacred?

Chapter 2: The Context in Which First Nations Carry Their Fight to the Courts

1 What has come to be known as the Oka crisis is the most dramatic (although not the only) recent example. The proximate cause of the crisis, which erupted in 1990 at Oka, Quebec, was a plan to extend an already contentious golf course onto a site sacred to the area's Mohawk people, a site that included an ancestral burial ground. For eleven weeks, Mohawk warriors, with the company of other Mohawk men, women, and children, engaged in an armed standoff first with provincial police and later with Canadian armed forces in a last-ditch effort to defend the sacred site. For a chronology of events, see Geoffrey York and Loreen Pindera, *People of the Pines: The Warriors and the Legacy of Oka* (Toronto: Little, Brown, 1991).

2 This policy had been articulated earlier in the *Royal Proclamation of 1763*. The *Royal Proclamation* (U.K.) is reprinted in R.S.C. 1985, App. II, No. 1. An accurate copy of the original is found in C.S. Brigham, ed., *British Proclamations Relating to America 1603-1783* in *Transactions and Collections of the American Antiquarian Society* (Worcester, MA: American Antiquarian Society, 1911) 212-18. For a helpful recent discussion of how the courts have dealt with the *Royal Proclamation,* see James I. Reynolds, "The Royal Proclamation 1763 and Section 35 of the Constitution Act 1982 – Solid Base or Shifting Sands?" in *Aboriginal Law Conference 2002: Determining, Defining and Proving Aboriginal Rights and Title* (Materials prepared for the Continuing Legal Education seminar *Aboriginal Law Conference 2002,* Vancouver, 1 March 2002) (Vancouver: Continuing Legal Education Society of BC, 2002), online: Ratcliff and Company <http://www.ratcliff.com/business/doc-reynolds.htm>, last accessed 12 February 2002.

The practice of setting aside lands for Indians predated the arrival of the British in New France and Acadia. For a brief overview of the history of reserve creation in Canada, see Chapter 4, 4.2, of *Restructuring the Relationship,* Part 2, *Report of the Royal Commission on Aboriginal Peoples: Looking Forward, Looking Back,* vol. 2 (Ottawa: Canada Communication Group, 1996).

3 The British signed a number of pre-Confederation treaties of peace and friendship with First Nations in Quebec and the Maritimes. Although reserves were subsequently created

in those areas covered by peace and friendship treaties, none were established by those treaties. That is because peace and friendship treaties were about political relationships rather than land.

4 The few exceptions are those reserves established on Vancouver Island by the Douglas Treaties and those in northeastern BC that followed adhesion to Treaty 8. Between 1850 and 1854, James Douglas, first as Hudson's Bay Company chief factor and then as the second governor of the Colony of Vancouver Island, signed fourteen agreements or treaties. The reserves created by the Douglas Treaties cover only roughly 3 percent of Vancouver Island (Robert White-Harvey, "Reservation Geography and the Restoration of Native Self-Government" [1994] 17 Dal. L.J. 587 at 601) and do not represent all of the Island's reserves. The federal government negotiated Treaty 8, which includes the northern half of Alberta and the northeastern quadrant of British Columbia, in 1899. It was not until the following year (or later in some cases) that BC's First Nations had the opportunity to join the treaty. Some of the BC First Nations who fell within the apparently intended area of Treaty 8 were never given the opportunity. Currently, eight BC Indian bands are parties to Treaty 8. For a discussion of the history of Treaty 8, see Arthur J. Ray, "Treaty 8: A British Columbia Anomaly" (1999) 123 BC Studies 5. For what is sure to become the authoritative work on reserve creation in BC, see Cole Harris, *Making Native Space: Colonialism, Resistance, and Reserves in British Columbia* (Vancouver: UBC Press, 2002).

5 Now often referred to as the *Constitution Act, 1867* (U.K.), 30 & 31 Vict. c. 3, reprinted in R.S.C. 1985, App. II, No. 5.

6 Sections 91(22) and (23), for instance, gave Parliament exclusive legislative authority over patents and copyrights, respectively.

7 The *Indian Act* has undergone numerous amendments in its 126-year history. Although not yet extending to many specifics, there is a growing consensus that it should undergo further, perhaps dramatic ones in the near future. For unfolding developments, see the Indian and Northern Affairs Canada website at <http://www.ainc-inac.gc.ca>.

8 The *Indian Act,* R.S.C. 1985, c. I-5, s. 2(1)(a) stipulates that "reserve"

    (a)   means a tract of land, the legal title to which is vested in Her Majesty, that has been set apart by Her Majesty for the use and benefit of a band.

9 The *band* classification is a legal/administrative one. Section 2(1) of the *Indian Act, ibid.,* defines "band" as follows:

    "band" means a body of Indians
    (a)   for whose use and benefit in common, lands, the legal title to which is vested in Her Majesty, have been set apart before, on or after September 4, 1951,
    (b)   for whose use and benefit in common, moneys are held by Her Majesty, or
    (c)   declared by the Governor in Council to be a band for purposes of this Act.

10 These earlier statistics were reported by Robert White-Harvey, *supra* note 4. To give some sense of the significance of these statistics, he drew the following comparisons (at 588). While Canada's Aboriginal peoples made up 3.5 percent of the total population (with the majority being First Nations and residing in the provinces) and while the province's reserves took up less than 0.5 percent of the land, Australia's aborigines made up 1.2 percent of the total population and held title to 10.3 percent of the country, and, closer to home, American Indians made up 0.8 percent of the total US population and held 2.8 percent of the land in the lower forty-eight states or 4 percent if Alaskan Native claims were included.

11 These are Department of Indian Affairs and Northern Development (DIAND) statistics. See DIAND's *Basic Departmental Data – 2001* (Ottawa: Minister of Indian Affairs and Northern Development, 2002) at 82. The document is also available at the Indian and Northern Affairs Canada website at <http://www.ainc-inac.gc.ca>.

DIAND observes that the 2,666 reserves comprising slightly over 3 million hectares (about 7.6 million acres) add up to an area approximately the size of Vancouver Island. A more informative and perhaps telling comparison is with the Navajo reservation in the American Southwest. Canada's 2,666 reserves add up to less than half the area of the Navajo reservation's 6.4 million hectares (16 million acres).

12 Legislation (like regulations and policy) tends to be aimed at broader categories, e.g., *heritage* or *cultural* rather than *sacred* sites specifically. Section 13(4) of BC's *Heritage Conservation Act* [*HCA*], R.S.B.C. 1996, c. 187, for instance, requires the minister to provide "an opportunity for consultation with the First Nations whose heritage site or object would be affected" before he or she may make certain decisions affecting the particular site or *object*. (Note: The *HCA* extends to heritage sites on private property.) Section 12(1) of the federal *Canada National Parks Act,* S.C. 2000, c. 32, for instance, says: "12. (1) The Minister shall, where applicable, provide opportunities for public participation at the national, regional and local levels, *including participation by aboriginal organizations, bodies established under land claims agreements* and representatives of park communities, in the development of parks policy and regulations, the establishment of parks, the formulation of management plans, land use planning and development in relation to park communities and any other matters that the Minister considers relevant" [emphasis added].

13 *Constitution Act, 1982,* being Schedule B to the *Canada Act 1982* (U.K.), 1982, c. 11 [*Constitution Act, 1982*].

14 *R. v. Sparrow,* [1990] 1 S.C.R. 1075 at 1091 [*Sparrow*]: "The word 'existing' makes it clear that the rights to which s. 35(1) applies are those that were in existence when the *Constitution Act, 1982* came into effect."

15 *R. v. Sioui,* [1990] 1 S.C.R. 1025 [*Sioui*].

16 *R. v. Sioui,* [1987] R.J.Q. 1722.

17 *Sioui, supra* note 15 at 1070.

18 *Ibid.* at 1032.

19 The Court, *ibid.* at 1069, said: "Given the nature of Indian religious rites and especially Indian customs at the time, any significant exercise of such rights would require territory extending beyond Lorette."

20 *Ibid.*

21 Provisions dealing with sacred sites not located on First Nations' lands will likely be a common feature of future treaties. For example, the *Sahtu Dene and Métis Comprehensive Land Claim Agreement* (Ottawa: Ministry of Indian and Northern Affairs, 1993) and the *Nisga'a Final Agreement* (Victoria: Ministry of Aboriginal Affairs, 1998) contain sections dealing with sacred sites not located on settlement lands. Both agreements or treaties stipulate that certain sites that are of historical or cultural significance, including certain sacred sites, and that are not located on settlement lands are to receive (in the former case) territorial or (in the latter case) provincial protection. (Note that treaty settlement lands are not governed by the *Indian Act* and therefore are not, technically speaking, reserve lands.)

The level of protection afforded to sacred sites not located on treaty settlement lands varies from province/territory to province/territory. The Nisga'a treaty, for example, contains a provision requiring British Columbia to designate as provincial heritage sites certain sites of cultural and historic significance outside Nisga'a Lands (see *Nisga'a Final Agreement,* c. 3, para. 95). Although this designation, bestowed under the *Heritage Conservation Act, supra* note 12, affords these sites some protection, it does not compel the province to prefer ongoing site integrity to, say, resource exploitation.

Recent developments in British Columbia may eventually lessen the value of provincial protection of sacred and other cultural sites not located on Nisga'a lands or other future settlement lands in the province. The government of BC, in an effort to trim the budget by $1.5 million, is planning to turn the management of a dozen provincial heritage sites over to the private sector. The goal currently is to increase the number to thirty. See "B.C. Wants Private Sector to Run Heritage Sites" *Globe and Mail* (8 August 2002) A9A.

22 See, e.g., *R. v. Catarat,* [1998] S.J. No. 601 at paras. 16ff and 63ff (Sask. Prov. Ct.) (QL). At

trial, the accused, two members of the Buffalo River Dene Nation, were acquitted of unlawfully entering the Cold Lake Air Weapons Range in northern Saskatchewan and unlawful hunting. The trial judge found, among other things, that the Buffalo River Dene Nation has an Aboriginal right to hunt moose at Watapi Lake (which falls within the Cold Lake Air Weapons Range) (para. 81), that the Watapi Lake area is a "spiritual place, highly significant to and valued by the Dene of Buffalo River" (para. 72), and that the taking of moose "is integral to Dene spirituality and connection to the land" (para. 73). In spite of the appearance of Aboriginal rights at trial, the case is really about treaty hunting rights – at least that is how the higher courts dealt with it. The Saskatchewan Court of Queen's Bench ([1999] S.J. No. 612) set aside the acquittals and referred the case back to trial. The Court of Appeal ([2001] S.J. No. 213) dismissed the conviction appeal. The Supreme Court of Canada ([2001] S.C.C.A. No. 382 [QL]) refused leave to appeal.

23 *R. v. Van der Peet*, [1996] 2 S.C.R. 507 [*Van der Peet*].

24 *Ibid.* at 549.

25 Here are the Court's words: "[I]n assessing a claim to an aboriginal right a court must first identify the nature of the right being claimed; in order to determine whether a claim meets the test of being integral to the distinctive culture of the aboriginal group claiming the right, the court must first correctly determine what it is that is being claimed" (*ibid.* at 551).

26 *Ibid.* Note that Lamer C.J.C., writing for the majority, derived the requirement from the reconciliation doctrine. The reconciliation doctrine is grounded in a purposive interpretation of s. 35(1): "[W]hat s. 35(1) does is provide the constitutional framework through which the fact that aboriginals lived on the land in distinctive societies, with their own practices, traditions and cultures, is acknowledged and reconciled with the sovereignty of the Crown" (*ibid.* at 539). He went on to add: "The substantive rights which fall within the provision must be defined in light of this purpose; the aboriginal rights recognized and affirmed by s. 35(1) must be directed towards the reconciliation of the pre-existence of aboriginal societies with the sovereignty of the Crown" (*ibid.*). Here, then, is how Lamer C.J.C. linked the aforementioned requirement to the doctrine of reconciliation: "The definition of an aboriginal right must, if it is truly to reconcile the prior occupation of Canadian territory by aboriginal peoples with the assertion of Crown sovereignty over that territory, take into account the aboriginal perspective, yet do so in terms which are cognizable to the non-aboriginal legal system" (*ibid.* at 551).

27 Here is how Lamer C.J.C. put it: "It is possible ... that the Court could be said to be 'reconciling' the prior occupation of Canada by aboriginal peoples with Crown sovereignty through either a narrow or broad conception of aboriginal rights; the notion of 'reconciliation' does not, in the abstract, mandate a particular content for aboriginal rights. However, the only fair and just reconciliation is ... one which takes into account the aboriginal perspective while at the same time taking into account the perspective of the common law. True reconciliation will, *equally*, place weight on each" [emphasis added] (*ibid.* at 551). In her dissent, L'Heureux-Dubé J. expressed her disagreement, saying simply: "[U]nlike the Chief Justice, I do not think it appropriate to qualify this proposition [i.e., that when defining Aboriginal rights, it is crucial 'to be sensitive to the aboriginal perspective itself on the meaning of the rights at stake'] by saying that the perspective of common law matters as much as the perspective of the natives when defining aboriginal rights" (*ibid.* at 589). Although she did not elaborate on her remark about the appropriateness of Lamer C.J.C.'s qualification, one obvious way in which it is inappropriate is in its paternalistic assumption that Aboriginal claimants should not be entrusted fully with the task of characterizing their rights as they see fit, whether for better or for worse.

The proposition referred to in the passage immediately above is stated in *R. v. Sparrow*, *supra* note 14 at 1112. It is noteworthy that Dickson C.J.C. and La Forest J. (writing for the Court in *Sparrow*), immediately prior to the remarks referred to by L'Heureux-Dubé J., cautioned courts about the application of common law concepts to Aboriginal rights. They wrote: "Courts must be careful, then, to avoid the application of traditional common law concepts of property as they develop their understanding of ... the '*sui generis*' nature of aboriginal rights" (at 1112).

28 See in this chapter note 36 for an example.

29 It is now retrospectively clear that Lamer C.J.C., in *Van der Peet, supra* note 23, had hoped that the inclusion of the Aboriginal perspective in a court's identification of the claimed Aboriginal right would, on the one hand, steer it away from overly specific or narrow descriptions and that the inclusion of the common law, on the other, would prevent it from overly general descriptions. (See the passage, where this hope is plainly presupposed, quoted in *supra* note 27.) It is difficult to imagine precisely how the common law is to perform this limiting function. (Which portions of the common law are to be applied and which not?) It seems more likely that it would be performed by invoking certain factors (e.g., integrity and distinctiveness) that are supposed to be taken into account only at the second stage but that nonetheless exert a prospective influence on a court's analysis at the identification stage. But then the court would be crafting its description to yield a predetermined outcome. Then the charge that the courts are really "'reconciling' the prior occupation of Canada through either a narrow or broad conception of aboriginal rights" – a charge that concerned Lamer C.J.C. – would seem to be true. (For the full quote, again see *supra* note 27.) What the charge insinuates is, of course, that the ultimate determining factors will be extralegal.

30 Here is how Lamer C.J.C. explained it: "The claimant must demonstrate that the practice, custom or tradition was a central and significant part of the society's distinctive culture. He or she must demonstrate ... that it was one of things that truly *made the society what it was*" (*Van der Peet, supra* note 23, at 553). A court will, when inquiring whether or not a claimed right is integral, take into account the activity's significance to the claimant's people. Nevertheless, it is open to the court to deny that a highly significant activity is integral (*ibid.* at 554). In other words, in the eyes of the court, the fact that an Aboriginal people considers an activity highly significant and accordingly integral to its culture does not suffice to make it integral to its culture.

31 The point is simply that "[i]t is those practices, customs and traditions that can be rooted in the pre-contact societies of the aboriginal community in question that will constitute aboriginal rights" (*ibid.* at 555-56).

32 In other words, the claimed right not only must be something integral to the claimant's culture, it must also itself be a distinctive part of, although not necessarily unique to, that culture.

33 *Van der Peet, supra* note 23 at 562.

34 *Sparrow, supra* note 14.

35 *Fisheries Act,* R.S.C. 1970, c. F-14.

36 Despite the fact that the BC Court of Appeal had set aside his conviction, Mr. Sparrow was before the Supreme Court of Canada appealing its decision, arguing that it had too narrowly characterized the right he was claiming. In other words, he was arguing that the Court of Appeal had mischaracterized the right he was claiming. It is important to note that the Supreme Court did not endorse the lower court's characterization of the claimed right. It merely adopted it as adequate for purposes of the appeal. It thus left open the possibility that Mr. Sparrow possessed a constitutionally protected right of yet greater scope. See *Sparrow, supra* note 14 at 1101.

37 Here is the way the Court put it: "The first question to be asked is whether the legislation in question has the effect of interfering with an existing aboriginal right. If it does have such an effect, it represents a *prima facie* infringement of s. 35(1)" (*ibid.* at 1111). The step from interference to *prima facie* infringement is not, logically speaking, immediate. The interference must have an "adverse impact" (*ibid.* at 1112). A number of questions may be asked to help the court determine whether the interference is adverse, including whether the limitation is unreasonable, whether the legislation/regulation imposes undue hardship, and whether the legislation/regulation denies to the holders of the right their preferred means of exercising that right (*ibid.*). The onus of proving *prima facie* infringement lies on the one(s) challenging the legislation/regulation (*ibid.*).

38 The retrial never occurred.

39 *Sparrow, supra* note 14 at 1109.

40 If s. 35(1) rights were construed as absolute, any infringing law would run afoul of s. 52 of the *Constitution Act, 1982, supra* note 13. Section 52(1) says:

> 52. (1) The Constitution of Canada is the supreme law of Canada, and any law that is inconsistent with the provisions of the Constitution is, to the extent of the inconsistency, of no force or effect.

41 The seminal case on the Crown's fiduciary duty to Aboriginal peoples is *Guerin v. The Queen*, [1984] 2 S.C.R. 335.

42 *Sparrow, supra* note 14 at 1109.

43 This is the test of justification as set forth by Lamer C.J.C. in *Delgamuukw v. British Columbia*, [1997] 3 S.C.R. 1010 at 1107-8 [*Delgamuukw*]. It differs in a couple respects from the test originally presented by then Chief Justice Dickson and Justice La Forest in *Sparrow*. There satisfaction of the first stage of the test required only a valid legislative objective. Although the Court held that "objectives found to be compelling and substantial" automatically qualified as valid, it did not say – unlike what Lamer C.J.C. said later in *Delgamuukw* – that only objectives that are compelling and substantial would satisfy the first stage of the justification test (*Sparrow, supra* note 14 at 1113). Also in *Sparrow*, satisfaction of the second stage of the test required that where there is a conflict of interests arising from the constitutional recognition and affirmation of Aboriginal rights, Aboriginal interests are to be given priority (*Sparrow, ibid.* at 1114-15). In *Delgamuukw*, Lamer C.J.C. softened the Crown's fiduciary obligations, asserting that "the fiduciary duty does not demand that aboriginal rights always be given priority" (*Delgamuukw, ibid.* at 1108-9).

On the surface, the shift from the *Sparrow* analysis of the first stage of the test for justification of infringement to the *Delgamuukw* analysis would appear to favour Aboriginal parties. That is not the case however. For an explanation combined with an important critique of Lamer C.J.C.'s *Delgamuukw* analysis, see Madam Justice Hanson's judgment *Mikisew Cree First Nation v. Canada (Minister of Canadian Heritage)*, [2001] F.C.J. No. 1877 at paras. 115-22 (F.C.T.D.) (QL), rev'd on other grounds 2004 F.C.A. 66 [*Mikisew Cree*]. Leave to appeal granted by the Supreme Court of Canada on 22 July 2004 ([2004] S.C.C.A. No. 112 [QL]). For further critical comment, see Patrick Macklem, "Recent Developments in Aboriginal Rights: A Thematic Overview" in *Aboriginal Law Conference 2002, supra* note 2 at 1.1.01.

44 *Delgamuukw, supra* note 43, at 1113: "There is always a duty of consultation." Prior to making a decision to pursue an infringing course of action, the Crown is obliged to consult with those whose Aboriginal rights will be affected in an effort to seek to accommodate their rights. Thus, the Crown's duty to consult implies a duty to seek accommodation. To date, the most explicit and detailed judicial articulation of the connection between the duty to consult and the duty to seek accommodation is found in the recent British Columbia Court of Appeal decision *Haida Nation v. British Columbia (Minister of Forests)*, [2002] B.C.J. No. 378 (B.C.C.A.) (QL) [*Haida Nation (Part 1)*]. On 19 August 2002, the Court of Appeal gave additional reasons for its judgment. See *Haida Nation v. British Columbia (Minister of Forests)*, [2002] B.C.J. No. 1882 (B.C.C.A.) (QL) [*Haida Nation (Part 2)*]. Leave to appeal to the Supreme Court of Canada was granted on 20 March 2003, S.C.C. Bulletin, 2003, at 442. The S.C.C. heard the appeal on 24-25 March 2004.

45 On 6 March 2002, the Haida Nation filed a lawsuit in the BC Supreme Court against the provincial and federal governments seeking a declaration of Aboriginal title and other Aboriginal rights for Haida Gwaii (the Queen Charlotte Islands) and surrounding waters.

46 *Delgamuukw, supra* note 43 at 1080.

47 Because the Supreme Court of Canada, in *Delgamuukw*, defined Aboriginal title in advance of future Aboriginal title litigation, trial level courts do not – as they do in other Aboriginal rights litigation – have to identify/describe the nature of the right claimed before applying the test of Aboriginal title. That test differs from the *Van der Peet* integral-to-a-distinctive-culture test in several respects. For one, it is an *occupancy* test rather than an integral-to-a-distinctive-culture test. For another, unlike other Aboriginal rights (excepting Métis rights), where the critical date is contact, the critical date for establishing Aboriginal title is sovereignty. For these and the remaining criteria, see *Delgamuukw, ibid.* at 1097-1107.

48 *Ibid.* at 1111.

49 See page 17 in this volume.

50 For a right to have *legal effect,* as I am using the term, the state must recognize the holder's right and, based on its recognition, ensure that the holder of the right may freely and fully exercise the right and, as a necessary adjunct, that the holder has effective judicial recourse when his or her right is violated.

It is as yet little remarked that the fact that the Aboriginal rights of Canada's Aboriginal peoples are largely without legal effect is at odds with recent developments in international law on the rights of indigenous peoples. For those developments, see especially (1) *The Mayagna (Sumo) Awas Tingni Community v. Nicaragua* (31 August 2001), Inter-Am. Ct. H.R. (Ser. C) No. 79; (2) *Mary and Carrie Dann v. United States* (27 December 2002), Inter-Am. Comm. H.R., Case 11.140, Report No. 75/02, *Annual Report of the Inter-American Commission on Human Rights: 2002,* OEA/Ser.L/V/II.117/doc.1, rev.1; and (3) *Maya Indigenous Communities of the Toledo District v. Belize* (24 October 2003), Inter-Am. Comm. H.R., Case 12.053, Report No. 96/03.

51 In *Van der Peet, supra* note 23 at 559, Lamer C.J.C. wrote:

> [A]boriginal rights are constitutional rights, but that does not negate the central fact that the interests aboriginal rights are intended to protect relate to the specific history of the group claiming the right. Aboriginal rights are not general and universal; their scope and content must be determined on a case-by-case basis. The fact that one group of aboriginal people has an aboriginal right to do a particular thing will not be, without something more, sufficient to demonstrate that another aboriginal community has the same aboriginal right. The existence of the right will be specific to each aboriginal community.

The case-by-case approach to establishment means that establishing all the Aboriginal rights of Canada's indigenous peoples is an impossibility, practically speaking. And this in turn means that, under Canada's current Aboriginal rights regime, most Aboriginal rights will never, and indeed cannot ever, be given legal effect through the courts. Will Kymlicka understates the reality, observing only that "the task of defining Aboriginal rights remains largely unfinished." See his *Finding Our Way: Rethinking Ethnocultural Relations in Canada* (Oxford: Oxford University Press, 1998) at 2.

52 *Canadian Charter of Rights and Freedoms,* Part I of the *Constitution Act, 1982,* being Schedule B to the *Canada Act 1982* (U.K.), 1982, c. 11.

53 Note that I am not saying that Canada's *treaty rights* regime is moribund.

54 *Taku River Tlingit First Nation v. Tulsequah Chief Mine Project,* [2002] B.C.J. No. 155 (B.C.C.A.) (QL) [*Taku River (BCCA)*]. Leave to appeal to S.C.C. granted on 14 November 2002, S.C.C. Bulletin, 2002, at 1591. The S.C.C. heard the appeal on 24-25 March 2004. The *Taku River* case revolved around the decision of two provincial ministers to approve the reopening of a mine in northwestern British Columbia. The project included the construction of a 108-kilometre road for purposes of mine access and ore transport through the pristine heart of Taku River Tlingit traditional territory. The Tlingit applied to the BC Supreme Court for judicial review of the decision and were granted an order quashing the ministers' approval of the project. See *Taku River Tlingit First Nation v. Tulsequah Chief Mine Project,* [2002] B.C.J. No. 1301 (B.C.S.C.) (QL) [*Taku River (BCSC)*]. The province and mining company subsequently appealed the chambers judge's decision to the BC Court of Appeal. For further details, see Chapter 4.

55 *Haida Nation (Part 1), supra* note 44. The *Haida* case concerned a series of decisions by a provincial minister to replace a tree farm licence on Haida Gwaii (Queen Charlotte Islands) and to approve a transfer of the licence from MacMillan Bloedel to Weyerhaeuser. The Haida Nation applied to the BC Supreme Court for judicial review where the chambers judge dismissed their petition. See *Haida Nation v. British Columbia (Minister of Forests),* [2002] B.C.J. No. 2427 (B.C.S.C.) (QL) [*Haida Nation (BCSC)*]. The Haida then appealed the decision to the BC Court of Appeal. For further details, see Chapter 4.

56 *Haida Nation (Part 1), supra* note 44 at para. 52. The legal character of these duties derives from s. 35(1) of the *Constitution Act, 1982,* while their equitable character derives from the Crown's fiduciary relationship to Aboriginal peoples. It is easily, but should not be, lost

sight of that the duties to consult and to seek accommodation represent merely the minimum, and therefore not necessarily all, the Crown is obliged to do in its fiduciary capacity.
57 *Ibid.* at para. 51.
58 Its remote aim is to encourage negotiations. It is clear that most members of the Court of Appeal have formed an unflattering opinion of the province's approach to the ongoing treaty negotiations in BC. In *Taku River (BCCA), supra* note 54 at para. 96, Southin J.A. (dissenting) seems to suggest that according interim effect to asserted Aboriginal title will result in "endless litigation." At para. 174, Rowles J.A. (writing for the majority) countered by arguing, in effect, that to deny interim effect to Aboriginal title "would effectively end any prospect of meaningful negotiation or settlement of aboriginal land claims." In *Haida Nation (Part 1), supra* note 44 at para. 10, Lambert J.A. (writing for the Court) expanded on Rowles J.A.'s earlier argument: "The issue is an important one. If the Crown can ignore or override aboriginal title or aboriginal rights until such time as the title or rights are confirmed by treaty or by judgment of a competent court, then by placing impediments on the treaty process the Crown can force every claimant of aboriginal title or rights into court and on to judgment before conceding that any effective recognition should be given to the claimed aboriginal title or rights, even on an interim basis."
59 *Haida Nation (Part 1), supra* note 44 at para. 14. In *Halfway River First Nation v. British Columbia (Ministry of Forests),* [1999] B.C.J. No. 1880 at para. 161 (B.C.C.A.) (QL) [*Halfway River (BCCA)*], the BC Court of Appeal, in a 2-to-1 decision, held that First Nations have a reciprocal duty "to express their interests and concerns once they have had an opportunity to consider the information provided by the Crown, and to consult in good faith by whatever means are available to them. They cannot frustrate the consultation process by refusing to meet or participate, or by imposing unreasonable conditions." Presumably, they have a reciprocal duty also in relation to the Crown's duty to seek an accommodation, that is, a duty to participate in the consultation process in an effort to have their concerns, interests, and rights accommodated. That they have such a reciprocal duty is confirmed by *Heiltsuk Tribal Council v. British Columbia (Minister of Sustainable Resource Management),* 2003 B.C.S.C. 1422 [*Heiltsuk*]. There Gerow J. decided, contrary to the Heiltsuk Tribal Council's request, neither to quash a number of provincial government decisions to issue licences aimed at the construction and operation of an Atlantic salmon hatchery within Heiltsuk territory nor to bar future issuance of approvals or licences relating to the hatchery chiefly because she found that the Heiltsuk had been "unwilling to enter into consultation regarding any type of accommodation concerning the hatchery" (at para. 108).
60 For critical analyses, see Taiaiake Alfred, "Deconstructing the British Columbia Treaty Process" (Paper prepared for the Assembly of First Nations, August 2000). The Delgamuukw/Gisday'wa National Process, online: <http://www.delgamuukw.org/research/bctreaty process.pdf>, last accessed 14 May 2004, and James Tully, "Reconsidering the B.C. Treaty Process" in *Speaking Truth to Power II: A Treaty Forum* (Vancouver, BC: British Columbia Treaty Commission, 2001) 3.
61 *The Changing Landscape: BC Treaty Commission Annual Report, 2002* at 9, online: British Columbia Treaty Commission <http://www.bctreaty.net>.
62 Here is how the British Columbia Claims Task Force originally described them: "Interim measures agreements may affect the management and use of lands, sea, and resources and the creation of new interests. They may facilitate the access to and development of resources, often a useful means of dealing in a preliminary or experimental way with a contentious issue, or provide transition to implementation of the treaty." See the *Report of the British Columbia Claims Task Force* (28 June 1991) at 23; also available online: Ministry of Attorney General, Treaty Negotiations Office <http://www.gov.bc.ca/tno/rpts/bcctf/toc.htm>, last accessed 17 May 2004.
63 In March 2001, Cowichan Tribes and Hulqu'minum Treaty Group on Vancouver Island signed a two-year renewable agreement with BC and Canada to protect 1,700 hectares (4,420 acres) of off-reserve Crown land referred to as the Hill 60 sacred site. The Hill 60 site is sacred to a number of the area's First Nations. The site has deep symbolism, which is expressed in their creation stories. This is the first interim agreement explicitly designed

to protect a sacred site. The shared expectation is that the agreement will be integrated into a final comprehensive agreement. For further details, see the BC Treaty Commission's *Annual Report 2001* and May 2002 *Update,* online: BC Treaty Commission <http://www.bctreaty.net>.

64 In its 1991 *Report, supra* note 62 at 23, the BC Claims Task Force recommended, as the sixteenth of its nineteen recommendations, that "[t]he parties negotiate Interim Measures Agreements *before* or during the treaty negotiations when an interest that is being affected could undermine the process" [emphasis added].

65 For statements explaining why the aforementioned First Nations have chosen not to participate in the BC Treaty Process, see the Union of British Columbia Indian Chiefs website at <http://www.ubcic.bc.ca>.

66 There are no treaty processes in place in Nova Scotia, New Brunswick, and Prince Edward Island. In 2001, the Mi'kmaq of Nova Scotia, the province of Nova Scotia, and the government of Canada signed an Umbrella Agreement meant to guide negotiations of a Framework Agreement. The later agreement will create the process within which treaty negotiations will take place. For the *Mi'kmaq-Nova Scotia-Canada Umbrella Agreement* (June 2002) see the Government of Nova Scotia website at <http://www.gov.ns.ca/abor/pubs/umbrella_june_2002.pdf>, last accessed 17 May 2004.

   Although treaties were signed in the eighteenth century between the British Crown and the Mi'kmaq and Maliseet peoples, they were designed chiefly to establish relations of peace and friendship and did not involve the cession of land. There is therefore a strong likelihood that Aboriginal title survives throughout most of the Maritimes. For a thorough discussion of these matters, see Thomas Isaac, *Aboriginal and Treaty Rights in the Maritimes: The* Marshall *Decision and Beyond* (Saskatoon: Purich, 2001).

67 In January 2004, the Iroquois Confederacy reached an agreement with the city of Hamilton, Ontario, which, among other things, lends protection exceeding that given by the Ontario *Cemeteries Act* (Revised), R.S.O. 1990, c. C.4, to burial sites located in the Red Hill Creek Valley. Negotiation of the agreement was occasioned by the city's plan to build an eight-kilometre expressway through the valley. Despite its opposition to the expressway's construction, the Iroquois Confederacy negotiated the agreement in an effort to forestall or otherwise mitigate the negative effects of the already-advancing construction. For further information, see John Milton, "Results of Hamilton's Negotiations with the Haudenosaunee Council," Hamilton Independent Media Center (18 February 2004), online: Hamilton Independent Media Center <http://hamilton.indymedia.org/feature/display/5714/index.php>, last accessed 18 October 2004

68 Although seldom expressed, such skepticism is typified by the stance taken by former BC Supreme Court Chief Justice McEachern who, speaking frankly in his *Delgamuukw* decision, said that "the evidence does not disclose the beginning of the Gitksan and Wet'suwet'en people. Many of them believe God gave this land to them at the beginning of time. While I have every respect for their beliefs, there is no evidence to support such a theory and much good reason to doubt it": *Delgamuukw v. British Columbia,* [1991] 3 W.W.R. 97 at 130 [*Delgamuukw (BCSC)*]. It might be objected that McEachern's remark misses the point of the oral accounts and that subsequent to the Supreme Court of Canada's remarks on oral history in its *Delgamuukw* decision (*supra* note 43), judges are less likely to repeat his mistake. This objection would, however, miss my point, which can be easily grasped by asking oneself this question: How many lawyers and judges would accept as true the claim *as understood by the Gitksan and Wet'suwet'en who believe* that God gave their land to them at the beginning of time? If the answer is "few," then it must be conceded that McEachern's stance typifies the sort of skepticism I am discussing.

69 The deep (but false) assumption is that a site's sacredness is wholly dependent on the grounds for its sacredness. The assumption is false because believing that a site is sacred is partly constitutive of its sacredness. Recall that unless a people represents or symbolizes a site as sacred, it cannot be sacred to them. Representing a site as sacred is, it seems, partly constitutive of its sacredness. Believing that a site is sacred is a way of representing it as sacred. And so, once belief in a site's sacredness is sufficiently established, the belief, and therefore the site's sacredness, acquires a measure of independence from the grounds

for its sacredness. The site's sacredness, just like the belief in its sacredness, can therefore survive shifting and uncertain grounds.

Chapter 3: In Canada's Courts: The Meares Strategy

1 There are, of course, other litigation strategies available that do not involve Aboriginal or treaty rights. For example, in the *Kitkatla* case, the Kitkatla Band advanced a constitutional division of powers argument in a failed attempt to protect a number of culturally modified trees (sacred objects). See *Kitkatla Band v. British Columbia (Minister of Small Business, Tourism and Culture)*, [2002] 2 C.N.L.R. 143 (S.C.C.), aff'g [2000] 2 C.N.L.R. 36 (B.C.C.A.), aff'g [1999] 2 C.N.L.R. 176 (B.C.S.C.). Although *Kitkatla* was focused on sacred objects, the case has implications for sacred sites. For some of those implications together with an insightful critique of the Court of Appeal's decision, see Catherine Bell, "Protecting Indigenous Heritage Resources in Canada: A Comment on *Kitkatla v. British Columbia*" (2001) 10 Int'l J. Cult. Prop. 246.

2 These figures are mentioned by Gibbs J. in *MacMillan Bloedel v. Mullin*, [1985] 2 C.N.L.R. 26 at 30 (B.C.S.C.) [*Meares (BCSC)*].

3 Here are the portions of the declaration most relevant to my purposes: "Let it be known as of April 21, 1984, we the Clayoquot Band, do declare Meares Island a Tribal Park. [Our goals include:] (1) Total preservation of Meares Island based on title and survival of our Native way of life; (2) Preserve Meares Island as the island is an economic base of our people to harvest natural unspoiled Native foods ... (6) Protection of all sacred burial sites on Meares." The entire declaration can be found in *Meares Island: Protecting a Natural Paradise* (Tofino: Friends of Clayoquot Sound, 1985) at 15.

4 "Nuu-Chah-Nulth Annual Assembly," *Meares Island* (pamphlet) (Tofino: Friends of Clayoquot Sound, n.d.).

5 "Friends of Clayoquot Time-Line," online: Friends of Clayoquot Sound <http://www.focs.ca/1clayoquot/timeline.htm>, last accessed 14 May 2004.

6 This paragraph is a fair summary of Gibbs J.'s presentation and the law as it currently stands.

   Note that outside BC, courts prefer to say that there are three tests: the serious/fair question test, the irreparable harm test, and the balance of convenience test. The leading case on the three-stage approach is *RJR MacDonald v. Canada (Attorney General)*, [1994] 1 S.C.R. 311. McLachlin J.A. (as she then was), in *B.C. (A.G.) v. Wale*, [1987] 2 W.W.R. 331 at 343 (B.C.C.A.), aff'g [1991] 1 S.C.R. 62, commented on the difference as follows: "While I prefer to view the requirement of irreparable harm as integral to the assessment of the balance of convenience between the parties, the practical effect of the two approaches is the same." Her claim of integrality appears exaggerated given that in the paragraph immediately following (at 344) she observes that the irreparability requirement is only a general rule. Perhaps, however, she meant (in the comment quoted above) to say that the irreparability *test*, rather than irreparability itself, is integral to the balance of convenience test.

   Theoretically speaking, the "BC view" makes better sense than the "three-stage view." The irreparability criterion represents only a general, not a universal, rule. Consequently, the irreparability inquiry is not on all fours with the serious question and balance of convenience inquiries. It makes better sense, therefore, to think of irreparability as one, albeit the most important, of the factors to be taken into account in assessing the balance of convenience.

7 *Meares (BCSC)*, *supra* note 2 at 37.

8 It should be kept in mind that *Meares (BCSC)* was decided twelve years before the Supreme Court of Canada finally offered its first delineations of Aboriginal title in *Delgamuukw*. In 1985, the extent and content of Aboriginal title (like Aboriginal rights generally) were, jurisprudentially speaking, largely open questions. Nearly two decades later, the questions are not entirely closed. Thus, for example, although Gibbs J. confidently asserted, in the face of the Nuu-chah-nulth's claim to the contrary, that the province has the power to infringe Aboriginal title by legislation of general application (*Meares [BCSC]*, *supra* note

2 at 46), the issue remains unresolved. For a brief statement of the problem, see Lambert J.A.'s remarks, *Haida Nation v. British Columbia (Minister of Forests)*, [2002] B.C.J. No. 1882 at paras. 77-79 (B.C.C.A.) (QL) [*Haida Nation (Part 2)*].

9 As his authority, Gibbs J. cited *Calder v. Attorney General of British Columbia* (1969) 8 D.L.R. (3d) 59 (B.C.S.C. [Calder]). There, speaking of the Nisga'a people's claim to Aboriginal title, the trial judge concluded that "if there ever was such a thing as aboriginal title in ... the delineated area, such has been lawfully extinguished *in toto* [by colonial ordinances and proclamations made prior to the union of the colonies of Vancouver Island and British Columbia in 1866]" (at 82). Subsequently, the British Columbia Court of Appeal, in *Calder* (1970), 13 D.L.R. (3d) 64, affirmed the trial judge's decision. Although the Supreme Court of Canada, in *Calder*, [1973] S.C.R. 313, dismissed the Nisga'a appeal, it did so on technical rather than substantive grounds: the Nisga'a had failed to obtain the then-requisite Lieutenant Governor's permission to pursue its litigation against the provincial Crown. On the issue of whether Nisga'a Aboriginal title had been extinguished, six of the Court's seven justices split evenly, with the seventh judge declining to address the substantive issue.

10 *Forest Act*, R.S.B.C. 1979, c. 140.

11 See *supra* note 8.

12 The Supreme Court of Canada did not begin directing trial courts to adjust the rules of evidence to accommodate the oral histories of Aboriginal claimants until its 1996 *Van der Peet* decision. See *R. v. Van der Peet,* [1996] 2 S.C.R. 507 at 558-59 [*Van der Peet*].

13 *Meares (BCSC), supra* note 2 at 52.

14 *Ibid.* at 38-39.

15 *Ibid.* at 52.

16 *Ibid.*

17 This meant that MacMillan Bloedel was permitted to return to the island to remove equipment and materials it had previously put there and to remove spikes that had been driven into trees by protestors.

18 Seaton J.A. was relying on the statement of Justice Dickson (as he then was), in *Kruger v. The Queen,* [1978] S.C.R. 104 at 109, that "claims to aboriginal title [in British Columbia] are woven with history, legend, politics and moral obligations. If the claim of any Band in respect of any particular land is to be decided as a justiciable issue and not a political issue, it should be so considered on the facts pertinent to that band and to that land, and not on any global basis."

19 *MacMillan Bloedel v. Mullin,* [1985] 2 C.N.L.R. 54 at 65 (B.C.C.A.) [*Meares (BCCA)*].

20 *Ibid.*

21 *Ibid.* at 68.

22 *Ibid.* at 69.

23 Here are Seaton J.A.'s words: "I am concerned too about this. In the first year more of Meares Island will be logged than has been logged in the whole of its history. Each year the effect would be cumulative. Just to log the first hectare there must be loggers and their equipment. Approval has already been given for miles of roads, a parking area, dumping grounds, log storage area and docks" (*ibid.* at 72).

24 *Ibid.*

25 *Ibid.* at 67-68.

26 *Ibid.* at 73.

27 *Calder, supra* note 9.

28 *Meares (BCCA), supra* note 19 at 76.

29 His words echoed Seaton J.A.'s:

Each application [for an injunction] will depend upon its own individual circumstances, and the factors to be taken into account in weighing the balance of convenience will vary from area to area. The cumulative effect of granting applications will not be overlooked. Of course, the balance of convenience on any subsequent application would have to be weighed in the light of the cumulative effect upon the industry and the economy. Furthermore, if an injunction is granted here it is because there are special circumstances in this case, which are unlikely to give rise to other injunctions, especially a rash of them. The bona fides of any particular application will weigh heavily in the balance. (*Ibid.* at 77-78)

30 *Ibid.* at 78.
31 *Ibid.* at 79.
32 *Ibid.*
33 *Ibid.*
34 Note that Macdonald J.A. assumed without argument that the Nuu-chah-nulth would not suffer irreparable harm.
35 Curiously, Macdonald J.A. neglected to mention that courts have the power to issue interim injunctions for a set period of time.
36 *Meares (BCCA), supra* note 19 at 87.
37 *Ibid.*
38 *Ibid.* at 89.
39 *Ibid.*
40 *Hunt v. Halcan Log Services,* [1987] 34 D.L.R. (4th) 504 [*Hunt*].
41 *Westar Timber v. Ryan; Formula Contractors v. George;* and *Gwoimt v. Westar and Formula* (20 October 1988), Vancouver C882521, C884927, and C885035 (B.C.S.C.) [*Westar (BCSC)*].
42 *Hunt, supra* note 40 at 506.
43 *Ibid.* at 509.
44 *Ibid.* at 506.
45 Halcan's rights of ownership were rooted in the province's land title legislation and ultimately in s. 92(13) of the *British North America Act,* which gave the provinces exclusive jurisdiction over land. Trainor J. found that how those rights related to the Kwak-wak'wakw's claimed rights under s. 35(1) of the *Constitution Act, 1982* and how s. 91(24) of the *British North America Act,* which gave Parliament exclusive jurisdiction over lands reserved for Indians, factored in and raised serious constitutional questions for trial.
46 *Hunt, supra* note 40 at 514.
47 *Ibid.* at 515.
48 Here is the passage from Seaton J.A.'s judgment that Trainor J. relied on:

It has also been suggested that a decision favourable to the Indians will cast doubt on the tenure that is the basis for the huge investment that has been and is being made. I am not influenced by the argument. Logging will continue on this coast even if some parts are found to be subject to certain Indian rights. It may be that in some areas the Indians will be entitled to share in one way or another, and it may be that in other areas there will be restrictions on the type of logging. There is a problem about tenure that has not been attended to in the past. We are being asked to ignore the problem as others have ignored it. I am not willing to do that. (*Meares [BCCA], supra* note 19 at 73)

49 *Hunt, supra* note 40 at 515.
50 *Ibid.* at 516.
51 *Delgamuukw v. British Columbia,* [1991] 3 W.W.R. 97 at 163 [*Delgamuukw (BCSC)*].
52 *Ibid.* at 117.
53 The trial ultimately took 374 days, running from 11 May 1987 until 30 June 1990. Chief Justice McEachern delivered his judgment on 8 March 1991.
54 This is how the Court of Appeal referred to them.
55 This and other parts of both writs are quoted in *Westar Timber v. Gitksan Wet'suwet'en Tribal Council,* [1990] 1 C.N.L.R. 151 at 174-76 (B.C.C.A.) [*Westar (BCCA)*].
56 *Crown Proceedings Act,* R.S.B.C. 1979, c. 86.
57 *Delgam Uukw v. British Columbia* (5 December 1986), Vancouver 006460 and 006495 (B.C.C.A.).
58 Since Formula's rights were dependent on Westar's, he often subsumed Formula's action under Westar's. His practice was followed by the Court of Appeal.
59 *Westar (BCSC), supra* note 41 at 8.

60 *Ibid.*
61 *Ibid.* at 8-9.
62 *Ibid.* at 9.
63 *Ibid.* at 10.
64 *Ibid.*
65 *Ibid.*
66 Macdonell J. (optimistically) believed that the decision might be delivered in the fall of 1989.
67 The main case relied upon was *Attorney General of Manitoba v. Metropolitan Stores*, [1987] 2 S.C.R. 110.
68 *Westar (BCCA), supra* note 55 at 162.
69 *Forest Act,* R.S.B.C. 1979, c. 140.
70 *Westar (BCCA), supra* note 55 at 165.
71 *Ibid.*
72 *Ibid.*
73 *Ibid.* at 168.
74 To punctuate his conclusion, he added: "[I]t is now four years since this court gave judgment in the Meares Island case and ... the experience in that period does not bear out the fear that that decision would spawn a rash of injunctions which would cripple the economy of the province. The number of applications has not been great. Most have failed" (*ibid.* at 168-69).
75 *Ibid.* at 170.
76 *Ibid.* at 171-72.
77 *Ibid.* at 173.
78 *Ibid.*
79 *Ibid.* at 182.
80 *Ibid.* at 185.
81 Interestingly, in a later proceeding, the Gitksan and Wet'suwet'en claimed among their Aboriginal rights connected to the Shedin,

> the right to hunt large game, the right to fish, the right to gather and use medicinal plants and herbs, the right to use fresh water for spiritual needs, the right to cut trees for cabins and for poles, the right to cedar for bent boxes for storage of goods, long houses and poles, the right to swamp areas for dyes, the right to hunt small fur-bearers like the fisher, the right to have cache sites for food, the right to protect ancient village sites and the right to protect and maintain habitat areas for large game, small fur-bearers and fish, and the right to the protection of spawning streams.

See *House of Gwoimt v. Skeena Cellulose,* [1995] B.C.J. No. 783 at para. 18 (B.C.S.C.) (QL) [*House of Gwoimt*]. On a related note, it was later learned that there were three Aboriginal archaeological sites in the vicinity of the proposed Babine River bridge (*ibid.* at para. 14).
82 *Clayoquot Indian Band v. British Columbia,* [1986] B.C.J. No. 3169 (B.C.S.C.) (QL).
83 On 10 March 2001, as part of stage 4 of the six-stage BC treaty process, negotiators for the Nuu-chah-nulth Tribal Council signed an agreement in principle with Canada and British Columbia. Among other things, the agreement says that the Nuu-chah-nulth "will hold the 7,800 hectare [20,280 acre] Meares Island in joint trust with British Columbia." The trust is contingent on a final agreement. Ministry of Indian and Northern Affairs, Information Bulletin, "Nuu-Chah-Nulth, Canada, British Columbia Initial Agreement-in-Principle" (10 March 2001), online: Indian and Northern Affairs Canada <http://www.aincinac. gc.ca/nr/prs/j-a2001/ncn_e.pdf>, last accessed 14 May 2004.
84 Ministry of Indian and Northern Affairs, News Release, "Kwakiutl First Nation Settlement Agreement Reached" (24 April 1997), online: Indian and Northern Affairs Canada <http://www.ainc-inac.gc.ca/nr/prs.j-a1997/apr24.html>, last accessed 26 June 2002.
85 It was later suggested that at the time "Westar was encountering other difficulties and was then in the process of withdrawing from logging activities." See *House of Gwoimt, supra* note 81 at para. 17.

86 The law had changed due to the Court of Appeal's *Delgamuukw* decision. If the *Westar* injunction were to continue, it would have had to do so on the basis of non-exclusive Aboriginal rights. Hunter J. concluded that there was not a fair question to be tried "because the plaintiffs' [the Gitksan's and Wet'suwet'en's] rights are not exclusive, that is, they do not have the right to exclude all others from using the land and resources which would be the effect of continuing the injunction" (*ibid.* at para. 28). Neither, he added, did the balance of convenience favour continuing the injunction. Supporting that conclusion, Hunter J. found that Skeena's limited timber harvesting in the Shedin would not significantly interfere with the Gitksan's and Wet'suwet'en's Aboriginal rights, that Skeena's rights in the area and its local employment would be at risk if the injunction were not discharged, that the province had recently committed itself to a policy of meaningful consultation in an effort to respect Aboriginal rights, and finally that the BC treaty negotiation process – in which the Gitksan and Wet'suwet'en were participants – allowed for the adoption of interim agreements "including co-management programs, which can be employed to protect priority areas or increase participation of First Nations in decision-making processes" (*ibid.* at para. 32).
   A subsequent application for leave to appeal and a stay of proceedings was denied. See *House of Gwoimt v. Skeena Cellulose*, [1995] B.C.J. No. 2967 (B.C.C.A.) (QL).

87 I ultimately take issue with this way of putting it. For my reasons, see starting page 70, this volume.

88 This view of the Meares Island case is, I will argue, mistaken. Again, see page 70ff, this volume.

89 Recall that Esson J.A. acknowledged that there were likely other areas within Gitksan and Wet'suwet'en territory similar to the Shedin.

90 By saying that they did not explicitly argue the point, I do not mean to suggest that they – really their counsel – implied it instead.

91 *Tlowitsis Nation and Mumtagila Nation v. MacMillan Bloedel*, [1991] 2 C.N.L.R. 164 (B.C.S.C.) [*Tlowitsis-Mumtagila (BCSC)*].

92 *Ibid.* at 169.

93 *Ibid.* at 170.

94 *Ibid.*

95 *Ibid.*

96 *Ibid.* at 170-71.

97 *Meares (BCCA), supra* note 19 at 78. For more of the larger passage quoted by MacKinnon J., see *supra* note 29.

98 To be fair, MacKinnon J.'s reasons were particularly confusing on the point. Unfortunately, the Court of Appeal in its subsequent comments (see the following paragraph), because it failed to articulate the confusion and identify its source, left the impression that it misunderstood – or, worse, that it was dodging – the Tlowitsis-Mumtagila counsel's argument.

99 *Tlowitsis-Mumtagila v. MacMillan Bloedel*, [1990] B.C.J. No. 2499 at 8 (B.C.C.A.) (QL).

100 *Tlowitsis-Mumtagila v. MacMillan Bloedel*, [1991] 4 W.W.R. 83 at 96 (B.C.C.A.).

101 *Ibid.*

102 For example, through a series of amendments to the *Indian Act,* the potlatch was outlawed in Canada from 1884 to 1951.

103 In total, nine people were found guilty of criminal contempt. Eight of the nine were sentenced to one month's imprisonment. The ninth, who had previously, in a different incident, been found guilty of contempt, was sentenced to six months' imprisonment. All nine sentences were suspended on condition of keeping the peace and adhering to the court's orders. See *International Forest Products v. Pascal*, [1991] B.C.J. No. 718 & No. 719 (B.C.S.C.) (QL) [*Pascal*].

104 See the text version of a pamphlet produced by the Lil'wat Peoples Movement in 1991, available on the website of Settlers in Support of Indigenous Sovereignty at <http://sisis. nativeweb.org/lilwat/pam.html>, last accessed 17 May 2004.

105 *Mount Currie Indian Band v. International Forest Products*, [1991] B.C.J. No. 703 at 3-4 (B.C.S.C.) (QL) [*Mount Currie*].

106 Here are McEachern C.J.'s words: "I find the evidence establishes beyond question that

the Crown, in the colonial period, clearly and plainly intended to, and did, extinguish any aboriginal right of ownership which existed in the colony" (*Delgamuukw [BCSC]*, *supra* note 51 at 408).

107 Here again are McEachern C.J.'s words: "In the face of this [the fact that many cases have found provincial laws regulating basic Aboriginal sustenance rights to be valid], and in view of the fact that Indians have always had access to all vacant Crown land, it is difficult to understand how, apart from the question of priorities, an aboriginal sustenance right in such a remote land could be an exclusive right. If it was exclusive originally, it has been changed throughout history" (*ibid.* at 395).

108 *Mount Currie, supra* note 105 at 2.

109 Here are McEachern C.J.'s words: "In my judgment, s. 35 ... does not apply to the question I am considering [i.e., whether the Crown's promise that vacant Crown lands could be used for Aboriginal purposes subject to the general law, so long as such lands were not dedicated to an adverse purpose] because it only recognizes and affirms aboriginal rights which I have excluded in this case" (*Delgamuukw [BCSC], supra* note 51 at 414).

110 *Ibid.* at 425. Note that McEachern C.J. did not limit usufructuary rights to sustenance-related rights. He also included the more general category of cultural rights (*ibid.* at 423) and the specific category of the right to use the land and its resources for spiritual purposes (*ibid.* at 421).

111 *Mount Currie, supra* note 105 at 4.

112 *Ibid.*

113 See page 29 in this volume for Gibbs J.'s statement.

114 *Mount Currie, supra* note 105 at 4.

115 *Heritage Conservation Act*, R.S.B.C. 1979, c. 16.

116 *Mount Currie, supra* note 105 at 5.

117 *Ibid.*

118 *McCrady v. Ontario*, [1991] O.J. No. 1722 (Ont. Ct. Gen. Div.) (QL) [*McCrady (1991)*].

119 In his final report on his archaeological investigation of the High Falls area in 1992, this is how Professor Scott Hamilton described the area's significance to the Poplar Point Ojibway: "It is a place of great power, where quiet contemplation permits one (who is in the right frame of mind) to hear the voices of the dead. In such a place one may learn from the dead, and draw comfort from their presence. Such a sacred place is not to be profaned with the activities of everyday life. Consistent with this meaning of a sacred place, several individuals pointed out that, as children, their Elders emphatically told them not to play at places such as High Falls. It was a place of mystery and potentially dangerous supernatural power." This and other excerpts of Professor Hamilton's final report are quoted in *Poplar Point Ojibway Nation v. Ontario*, [1993] O.J. No. 601 at 16-18 (Ont. Div. Ct.) (QL) [*Poplar Point*].

120 *Lovelace v. Ontario*, [2000] 1 S.C.R. 950 (Appellant's factum at para. 17). The factum is available on the Native Law Centre of Canada's website at <http://www.usask.ca/nativelaw/factums/view.php?id=18>, last accessed 14 May 2004.

121 For the *Indian Act*'s definition, see Chapter 2, note 9.

122 The minister's information appears to have been derived from the (slender) fact that "the whole area had been extensively logged in the 1930's" without there being any records of any burial sites (*Poplar Point, supra* note 119 at 5).

123 The NLSAA is a coalition of First Nations and Métis communities in the region north of Lake Superior. At the time of the blockade, it included twenty-four such communities (*ibid.* at 6).

124 *McCrady (1991), supra* note 118 at 3.

125 *Ibid.*

126 The entire agreement is quoted in *Poplar Point, supra* note 119 at 6-8.

127 *Ibid.* at 7.

128 *Ibid.* at 8.

129 *Ibid.* at 9.

130 No further steps were taken regarding the application for judicial review.

131 A statement of claim was never filed.

132 *McCrady (1991), supra* note 118 at 2.

133 *Ibid.*
134 *Delgamuukw (BCSC), supra* note 51 at 231.
135 McCrady (1991), *supra* note 118 at 2.
136 *Ibid.*
137 *Ibid.* at 3.
138 *Ibid.* at 5.
139 *Ibid.* at 6.
140 *Ibid.*
141 Section 71(4) of the *Cemeteries Act* (Revised), R.S.O. 1990, c. C.4, defines an "unapproved aboriginal peoples cemetery" as "land set aside with the apparent intention of interring therein, in accordance with cultural affinities, human remains and containing remains identified as those of persons who were one of the aboriginal peoples of Canada." Beginning with a comment on this section of the *Act,* John Borrows explains why such legislation discourages First Nations peoples from sharing their knowledge of their burial sites, even when they are under threat:

> [T]he legal order frustrates First Nations participation in decision making with respect to Indigenous burial sites. Not marked in conventional Western ways, these sites are considered by the Cemeteries Act to be "unapproved Aboriginal cemeteries." This offensive designation of the places in which our ancestors rest grants to the Provincial Director of Cemeteries sole discretion to determine how to treat the remains of those so interred. Since burial sites are sacred to the Anishinabek [Ojibway], as they are to most people, the director's broad discretion creates a powerful disincentive for Aboriginal people to reveal their knowledge about them. Why would any Anishinabek person want to reveal where a sacred site is, only to have someone else decide how to treat the area? Most people would prefer to take their chances with developers and hope that they have the decency to respect burial sites. At least developers can be appealed to on a personal basis, whereas appeals to the Director of Cemeteries can be bureaucratic, formalistic, and humiliating. Aboriginal participation ... is severely hindered by a system that devalues First Nations knowledge of spiritual and historic sites. Such environmental racialization also hinders environmental protection because so many storied sites can be lost.

See his *Recovering Canada: The Resurgence of Indigenous Law* (Toronto: University of Toronto Press, 2002) at 41-42.
142 In his final report, this is what Professor Hamilton had to say on the matter:

> Last year the Elders of the Poplar Point First Nation warned that burials were located in the High Falls locality. They were not prepared to specify precise locations since, in their view, such disclosure would compromise the sacred character of the area, and leave it vulnerable to looters. The dam construction proceeded, and the discovery of at least one burial confirms the credibility of the Elders' assertions. From my perspective, it is far better to err on the side of caution, and assume that more than one burial lay in the most favoured localities overlooking the falls.

For this and other portions of Professor Hamilton's report, see *McCrady v. Ontario,* [1992] O.J. No. 2321 at 8 (Ont. Ct. Gen. Div.) (QL) [*McCrady (1992)*].
143 Moreover, the Ministry of Natural Resources was willing to deal with the site as an unapproved Aboriginal peoples cemetery in spite of the fact that only one set of human remains had been found (*Poplar Point, supra* note 119 at 19).
144 Sections 72(1)-(3) of the *Cemeteries Act, supra* note 141, state:

> (1) The Registrar, on declaring a burial site to be an unapproved peoples cemetery or an unapproved cemetery, shall serve notice of the declaration on such persons or class of persons as are prescribed;

(2) all persons served with notice under subsection (1) shall enter into negotiations with a view of entering into a site disposition agreement;

(3) If a site disposition agreement is not made within the prescribed time, the Registrar shall refer the matter to [binding] arbitration.

145 *Poplar Point, supra* note 119 at 17.
146 *Ibid.* at 18.
147 *McCrady (1992), supra* note 142 at 1.
148 The motion was brought under the *Cemeteries Act* and thus did not depend on a claim of Aboriginal rights. Thus the application did not involve what I have been calling the Meares strategy.
149 *Poplar Point, supra* note 119 at 21.
150 See *ibid.*
151 Ontario's Living Legacy website at <http://www.ontariolivinglegacy.com/ollsearch/ Nipigon/ Chapter%201.pdf>, last accessed 14 May 2004. For a brief but excellent overview of how Canada's hydroelectric projects have affected First Nations and other Aboriginal peoples, see James B. Waldram, *As Long as the Rivers Run: Hydroelectric Development and Native Communities in Western Canada* (Winnipeg: University of Manitoba Press, 1988) at 7-17. Although it was peripheral to his discussion, Waldram occasionally mentions the impact of hydroelectric projects on sacred sites.
152 *Siska Indian Band v. British Columbia (Minister of Forests),* [1999] B.C.J. No. 2354 (B.C.S.C.) (QL) [*Siska (1999)*].
153 As Sigurdson J. put it, "[t]he Siska Band has, for many years, opposed all logging in the Watershed and, in the past, has sought to have it preserved as a park, an ecological reserve or to have it placed in the Provincial Protected Area Strategy" (*ibid.* at para. 5).
154 *Siska Indian Band v. British Columbia (Minister of Forests),* [1998] B.C.J. No. 1661 at para. 4 (B.C.S.C.) (QL) [*Siska (1998)*].
155 *Ibid.* at para. 5.
156 Pat Venditti, "Siska First Nation Blockade Begins to Stop Watershed Destruction," Forest Action Network (6 October 1999), online: Forests.org <http://www.forests.org/archive/ canada/siskafir.htm>, last accessed 17 May 2004.
157 See page 44, this volume.
158 As of summer 2004, J.S. Jones Timber Limited (now Teal Cedar Products Limited) is still in business and continues to operate a mill at Boston Bar.
159 *Westar (BCCA), supra* note 55 at 168.
160 *Ibid.*
161 That is what John J.L. Hunter suggests in his "Advancing Aboriginal Title Claims after Delgamuukw: The Role of the Injunction" (Paper presented at the Continuing Legal Education Conference on Litigating Aboriginal Title, June 2000), online: Davis and Company <http://www.davis.ca/publications/2000-06_advancing_aboriginal_title_claims_injunctions.pdf>, last accessed 14 May 2004.
162 Note that Seaton J.A. explicitly made this point. For his words, see page 33, this volume.
163 Since it is not a crucial point, I concede that Deer Island *may* fit. The Shedin does not, however. The chambers judge in the *Westar* case concluded that an injunction protecting the Shedin would not cause serious economic consequences for the logging company, the region, or the province. The majority of the Court of Appeal, which included Esson J.A., held that he did not err in his conclusion.
164 Supposing – what is debatable – that serious negative public interest concerns were engaged in the case, the *Hunt, supra* note 40, case would be an example of a case where uniqueness sufficient to override those concerns was established.

Chapter 4: In Canada's Courts: The Haida Strategy
1 See page 151, this volume.
2 *Taku River Tlingit First Nation v. Tulsequah Chief Mine Project,* [2002] B.C.J. No. 1301 at para. 14 (B.C.S.C.) (QL) [*Taku River (BCSC)*].

3   *Ibid.* at para. 3.
4   See the *Report and Recommendations of the Tulsequah Chief Project Committee with Respect to: A Decision on a Project Approval Certificate by the Minister of Environment, Lands and Parks and the Minister of Energy and Mines and Minister Responsible for Northern Development* (March 1998), online: Environmental Assessment Office <http://www.eao.gov.bc.ca>, last accessed 14 May 2004.
5   See the *Report and Recommendations of the Taku River Tlingit First Nation with Respect to a Decision on a Project Approval Certificate by the Minister of Environment, Lands and Parks and the Minister of Energy and Mines* (6 March 1998), online: Environmental Assessment Office <http://www.eao.gov.bc.ca>, last accessed 14 May 2004.
6   Here is how a report prepared for the Environmental Assessment Office on the Tlingits' behalf described the relationships:

> For the Taku River Tlingit, use of the land within their traditional territory is much more than a set of activities. At the heart of their land use is a system of social and economic relationships, values and ideas that define them as a people and that are recognized in their constitution. The traditional land use activities of hunting, trapping, fishing and collecting plants are not ends in themselves, but the means by which their social and economic system, and the values and ideas associated with it, are sustained and renewed. In this respect they are basic to the very organization and viability of their community.

See Lindsay Staples and Nick Poushinsky, *Determining the Impact of the Tulsequah Chief Mine Project on the Traditional Land Use of the Taku River Tlingit First Nation* (Report prepared for the Environmental Assessment Office, August 1997) at 12, online: Environmental Assessment Office <http://www.eao.gov.bc.ca>, last accessed 14 May 2004.

7   The modern era of treaty negotiations in Canada traces its origins to 1973, when the federal government announced its willingness to negotiate Native claims. See Department of Indian Affairs and Northern Development, Communiqué 1-7339, "Statement Made by the Honourable Jean Chrétien, Minister of Indian Affairs and Northern Development, on Claims of Indian and Inuit People" (8 August 1973). The following year, the federal government opened its Office of Native Claims. The province of BC remained decided against joining in treaty negotiations until 1990. See Ministry of Native Affairs, News Release 90:20, "Province Accepts Recommendations of Premier's Council on Native Affairs" (9 August 1990). Based upon the principles set forth in the 1991 *Report of the British Columbia Claims Task Force* (28 June 1991), online: Ministry of Attorney General, Treaty Negotiations Office <http://www.gov.bc.ca/tno/rpts/bcctf/toc.htm>, last accessed 17 May 2004; and the *British Columbia Treaty Commission Agreement* (21 September 1992), online: BC Treaty Commission <http://www.bctreaty.net>, last accessed 10 May 2004, the BC Treaty Commission was established in 1992. The BC Treaty Commission, which oversees tripartite negotiations between Canada, British Columbia, and First Nations, opened its doors for business in 1993. The Taku River Tlingit First Nation was at stage 4 of its negotiations – the negotiation of an agreement in principle – when it petitioned the BC Supreme Court for judicial review in 1998. The federal and provincial governments, adhering to their shared policy of refusing to negotiate treaties with First Nations that pursue Aboriginal rights litigation, immediately suspended treaty negotiations with the Tlingits.
8   *Taku River (BCSC), supra* note 2 at para. 17.
9   All nine grounds are fully reproduced in *Taku River Tlingit First Nation v. Tulsequah Chief Mine Project,* [2002] B.C.J. No. 155 at para. 31 (B.C.C.A.) (QL) [*Taku River (BCCA)*].
10 *Taku River Tlingit First Nation v. Tulsequah Chief Mine Project,* [1999] B.C.J. No. 984 at para. 2 (B.C.S.C.) (QL), leave to appeal the Supreme Court chambers judge's order to refer issues requiring determination of the Tlingits' Aboriginal rights to the trial list refused [1999] B.C.J. No. 1665 (B.C.C.A.), application to review the Court of Appeal chambers judge's decision to refuse leave to appeal the Supreme Court chambers judge's order dismissed [1999] B.C.J. No. 2204 (B.C.C.A.).
11 *Ibid.* at para. 12.

12 *Ibid.* at para. 28.

13 *Taku River (BCSC), supra* note 2 at para. 125.

14 *Ibid.* at para. 120.

15 *Ibid.* at para.130.

16 *Ibid.*

17 *Ibid.* Kirkpatrick J.'s formulation of the Crown's constitutional duty echoes language used by Lamer C.J.C. in *Delgamuukw v. British Columbia*, [1997] 3 S.C.R. 1010 at 1113 [*Delgamuukw*], where he wrote that "even in these rare cases when the minimum acceptable standard [for the Crown to satisfy its fiduciary obligations and thus to proceed justifiably when infringing Aboriginal title] is consultation, this consultation must be in good faith, *and with the intention of substantially addressing the concerns of the aboriginal peoples whose lands are at issue*" [emphasis added].

18 *Ibid.* at para. 134.

19 *Ibid.* at para. 137.

20 The Tlingits also cross-appealed. They submitted that the chambers judge erred by (1) failing to find that the latter stages of the Crown's decision-making process gave rise to a reasonable apprehension of bias, (2) consequently failing to find that the presence of a reasonable apprehension of bias so tainted the process as to render the ministers' decision void and unamenable to reconsideration, and (3) referring the matter back to the ministers for their reconsideration. See *Taku River Tlingit First Nation v. Tulsequah Chief Mine Project*, [2000] B.C.J. No. 2024 at para. 15 (B.C.C.A.) (QL).

21 *Taku River (BCCA), supra* note 9 at para. 90.

22 *Ibid.*

23 I say the Court *appeared* to agree because Rowles J.A., who wrote the majority judgment, does not state explicitly that she agreed with Southin J.A., who wrote in dissent, that the chambers judge erred in finding that the Crown had breached its administrative law duties. Indeed, Rowles J.A. does not, logically speaking, imply it. Nonetheless, what she does say on the matter clearly presupposes it. Here are her words: "It is on the question of whether the chambers judge erred in deciding that the Ministers of the Crown were under a [constitutional and/or fiduciary] duty or obligation to take into account the Tlingits' aboriginal rights before deciding to issue the Project Approval Certificate that I respectfully disagree with my colleague, Madam Justice Southin, whose draft reasons I have had the advantage of reading" (*ibid.* at para. 108).

24 I say that it *appeared* to agree because although Southin J.A. agreed with the majority that the Crown had a duty to consult with the Tlingits, she did not say explicitly whether the duty is constitutional, fiduciary, or something else. Since she concluded, however, that the consultation process provided by the *Environmental Assessment Act*, R.S.B.C. 1996, c. 119, met "*the demands of Delgamuukw*" (*ibid.* at para. 99 [emphasis added]), she suggested that there was a constitutional duty at play in the decision-making process.

25 *Ibid.* at para. 94.

26 For the relevant portion of her judgment, see *ibid.* at paras. 153-94.

27 *Ibid.* at para. 173. The second half of Rowles J.A.'s remark is an exact quote of the words of Dickson C.J.C. and La Forest J. in *R. v. Sparrow*, [1990] 1 S.C.R. 1075 at 1107-8 [*Sparrow*]. Besides *Sparrow*, Rowles J.A. mentioned two other Supreme Court of Canada decisions in support of her claim: *Guerin v. The Queen*, [1984] 2 S.C.R. 335 [*Guerin*], and *Nowegijick v. The Queen*, [1983] 1 S.C.R. 29.

28 *Sparrow, supra* note 27 at 1105. Lamer C.J.C. briefly expanded on the remark in *Delgamuukw, supra* note 17 at 1123-24.

29 *Taku River (BCCA), supra* note 9 at para. 174. For the missing premises in Rowles J.A.'s argument, see Lambert J.A.'s elaboration in *Haida Nation v. British Columbia (Minister of Forests)*, [2002] B.C.J. No. 378 at para. 10 (B.C.C.A.) (QL) [*Haida Nation (Part 1)*]. Lambert J.A.'s elaboration is quoted above, in Chapter 2, *supra* note 58.

30 *R. v. Van der Peet*, [1996] 2 S.C.R. 507 at 548 [*Van der Peet*].

31 Prior to the *Constitution Act, 1982*, Parliament had the power to unilaterally extinguish both Aboriginal and treaty rights. On its power to extinguish Aboriginal rights, see *Van der Peet, ibid.* at 538. On its power to extinguish treaty rights, see *R. v. Marshall*, [1999] 3

S.C.R. 456 at para. 48. Of course, Parliament's extinguishment power included the power to otherwise interfere with or sanction interference with Aboriginal and treaty rights howsoever it pleased.

32 *Van der Peet, supra* note 30, and *Delgamuukw, supra* note 17 at 1066.

33 In *R. v. Côté,* [1996] 3 S.C.R. 139 at 174, Lamer C.J.C. wrote: "The entrenchment of aboriginal ancestral and treaty rights in s. 35(1) has changed the landscape of aboriginal rights in Canada. As explained in the *Van der Peet* trilogy, the purpose of s. 35(1) was to extend constitutional protection to the practices, customs and traditions central to the distinctive culture of aboriginal societies prior to contact with Europeans." In *R. v. Adams,* [1996] 3 S.C.R. 101 at 121, he spoke in a similar vein of s. 35(1)'s "noble purpose of preserving the integral and defining features of distinctive aboriginal societies." Lamer C.J.C.'s unstated assumption is that s. 35(1)'s protective purpose is part of its ultimate reconciliation purpose.

34 *Delgamuukw, supra* note 17 at 1107.

35 *Sparrow, supra* note 27 at 1119.

36 *Taku River (BCCA), supra* note 9 at para. 194.

37 *Ibid.* at paras. 183 and 187.

38 *Ibid.* at para. 160. The point is most explicit in *Van der Peet, supra* note 30 at 538: "s. 35(1) did not create the legal doctrine of aboriginal rights; aboriginal rights existed and were recognized under the common law."

39 For the full text of s. 52(1), see Chapter 2, note 40.

40 *Sparrow, supra* note 27 at 1109-19.

41 *Van der Peet, supra* note 30 at 584, per L'Heureux-Dubé J.

42 *Sparrow, supra* note 27 at 1095.

43 *Ibid.* at 1099.

44 *Ibid.* at 1112 and 1120.

45 *Ibid.* at 1121.

46 Lamer C.J.C., speaking of the what the Crown's role as fiduciary demands in cases of infringement, observed in *Delgamuukw, supra* note 17 at 1113: "There is always a duty of consultation."

47 *Taku River (BCCA), supra* note 9 at para. 191.

48 *Ibid.* at para. 192.

49 *Ibid.* at para. 193.

50 *Ibid.* at para. 199.

51 *Ibid.* at para. 201.

52 *Delgamuukw, supra* note 17 at 1113.

53 *Taku River (BCCA), supra* note 9 at para. 190.

54 *Ibid.* at para. 207. On 13 December 2002, the Minister of Sustainable Resource Management and the Minister of Energy and Mines announced that they had, after reconsidering the Tulsequah Chief Mine Project as the British Columbia Court of Appeal had ordered, issued a new Project Approval Certificate. See Ministry of Sustainable Resource Management and Ministry of Energy and Mines, News Release 2002SRM0044-001098, "Strict Rules Key to Tulsequah Mine Approval" (13 December 2002), online: <http://www2.news.gov.bc.ca/nrm_news_releases/2002SRM0044-001098.htm#>, last accessed 28 April 2004. On 24 and 25 March, the Supreme Court of Canada heard the appeal from the BC Court of Appeal's decision.

55 For background information on TFL 39, see BC Ministry of Forests, Ken Baker, Deputy Chief Forester, *Tree Farm Licence 39: Rationale for Allowable Annual Cut (AAC) Determination* (21 November 2001), online: BC Ministry of Forests <http://www.for.gov.bc.ca/hts/tfl/tfl39/tsr2/rationale.pdf>, last accessed 14 May 2004.

56 *Haida Nation v. British Columbia (Minister of Forests),* [1995] B.C.J. No. 2411 at para. 2 (B.C.S.C.) (QL) [*Haida Nation (1995)*].

57 *Ibid.*

58 *Ibid.* at paras. 1 and 2a.

59 In their petition, the Haida submitted that their Aboriginal title constituted an *encumbrance* within the meaning of s. 28 of the *Forest Act,* R.S.B.C. 1979, c. 140, and thus that

the Minister of Forests had acted outside his statutory power by issuing TFL 39 in 1981 and 1995, at least insofar as the licence purported to encompass portions of Haida Gwaii. Section 28(1)(b)(i) stipulates that a TFL entered into under the act shall describe a tree farm licence area composed of "(i) an area of Crown land, the timber on which is not otherwise encumbered, determined by the minister." On 8 June 1995, Chief Justice Esson (who had been appointed Chief Justice of the BC Supreme Court in 1989) ordered the issue of "whether the interest claimed by the Petitioners, namely aboriginal title ... is capable of constituting an encumbrance within the meaning of section 28" tried as a preliminary issue of law (*ibid.* at para. 3). On 20 November 1995, Cohen J., the chambers judge, released his decision holding that the Haida's Aboriginal title was not capable of constituting an encumbrance under the act (*ibid.*). The Haida appealed. On 7 November 1997, the BC Court of Appeal issued its judgment. The Court – composed of Justices Esson (who had been reappointed to the Court of Appeal the previous year), Southin, and Huddart – was unanimous in holding that the Haida's claimed Aboriginal title, *if it exists*, constitutes an encumbrance under the act. See *Haida Nation v. British Columbia (Minister of Forests)*, [1997] B.C.J. No. 2480 at para. 6 (B.C.C.A.) (QL) [emphasis added]. For the subsequent significance of the phrase "if it exists," see pages 92-93, this volume.

60 *Haida Nation v. British Columbia (Minister of Forests)*, [2002] B.C.J. No. 2427 at para. 54 (B.C.S.C.) (QL) [*Haida Nation (BCSC)*].

61 *Ibid.* at para. 42.

62 *Forest Act*, R.S.B.C. 1996, c. 157. Section 35(1)(b)(i), the relevant section, is the same as s. 28(1)(b)(i) in the earlier version of the act. For s. 28(1)(b)(i), see *supra* note 59.

63 *Haida Nation (BCSC)*, *supra* note 60 at para. 10.

64 *Ibid.*

65 *Ibid.*

66 *Ibid.* at para. 12.

67 *Ibid.* at para. 17.

68 *Ibid.* at para. 27.

69 *Ibid.* at para. 28.

70 *Haida Nation (Part 1)*, *supra* note 29 at para. 1.

71 *Ibid.* at para. 2.

72 See *supra* note 59.

73 *Haida Nation (Part 1)*, *supra* note 29 at para. 5.

74 *Ibid.* at para. 29.

75 *Ibid.*

76 *Ibid.* at para. 48. In their appeal, the Haida had "confined their claim to the 1999 and 2000 renewal of T.F.L. 39 and the transfer of the beneficial interests in T.F.L. 39 from MacMillan Bloedel to Weyerhaeuser" (*ibid.*).

77 *Ibid.* at para. 52.

78 *Ibid.* at para. 46.

79 *Ibid.* at para. 49.

80 *Ibid.* at para. 51.

81 *Ibid.*

82 *Ibid.* at para. 55.

83 *Ibid.*

84 *Ibid.* By omitting mention of the duty to seek accommodation, Lambert J.A. was not suggesting that the duty fell outside his conclusion's scope. As he made clear later in *Haida Nation v. British Columbia (Minister of Forests)*, [2002] B.C.J. No. 1882 at para. 60 (B.C.C.A.) (QL) [*Haida Nation (Part 2)*], "every obligation of consultation must carry with it an obligation to seek accommodation."

85 *Haida Nation (Part 2)*, *ibid.* at para. 116, Finch C.J.B.C (concurring in result with Lambert J.A.). In *Haida Nation (Part 1)*, *supra* note 29 at para. 26, Lambert J.A. noted that "Weyerhaeuser employs something in the order of 200 workers in its Queen Charlotte Islands operations and has investments in plant, machinery and equipment and in the Tree Farm Licence itself. Weyerhaeuser has a considerable business interest in the long term and short term continuance of its logging operations on T.F.L. 39."

86 *Haida Nation (Part 1), supra* note 29 at para. 62.
87 *Haida Nation (Part 2), supra* note 84 at para. 93.
88 *Ibid.* at para. 120, per Finch C.J.B.C.
89 In additional reasons released on 19 August 2002, the Court narrowed the declaration to say "that the Crown provincial had in 2000, and the Crown and Weyerhaeuser have now, legally enforceable duties to the Haida people to consult with them in good faith and to endeavour to seek workable accommodations" (*Haida Nation [Part 2], supra* note 84 at para. 104). Although the Court remained unanimous that the Crown had and continued to have constitutional and fiduciary duties to consult with the Haida and to seek to accommodate their interests, it split two to one on whether Weyerhaeuser had similar duties. Low J.A., shifting to dissent, thought that the Court, in its original judgment, had ventured outside the pleadings and gone beyond the evidence to fashion its original remedy and thus had erred in extending the duties to Weyerhaeuser (*ibid.* at paras. 131-40). For the majority's legal justifications for ascribing consultation and accommodation duties to Weyerhaeuser, see especially Lambert J.A.'s summary at paras. 98-101 and Finch C.J.B.C.'s brief comment at para. 123 (*ibid.*). For what led to the Court's issuance of additional reasons, see paras. 1-22 of Lambert J.A.'s judgment (*ibid.*).
90 In its *Report and Recommendations, supra* note 5, the Taku River Tlingits spoke of the "[p]otential direct and indirect impacts [of the project] on specific cultural and sacred sites" (at 26). In its original petition for judicial review, the Haida submitted, among other things, that logging within Block 6 "would adversely affect, impair or otherwise interfere with ... areas of particular or special cultural and spiritual significance." See *Haida Nation (1995), supra* note 56 at para. 2a.
91 The full text of the treaty is set out in *Halfway River First Nation v. British Columbia (Ministry of Forests),* [1999] B.C.J. No. 1880 at para. 205 (B.C.C.A.) (QL) [*Halfway River (BCCA)*].
92 *Ibid.*
93 *Halfway River First Nation v. British Columbia (Ministry of Forests),* [1997] B.C.J. No. 1494 at para. 35 (B.C.S.C.) (QL) [*Halfway River (BCSC)*].
94 *Ibid.* at para. 48.
95 *Ibid.* at para. 68.
96 *Ibid.* at para. 82.
97 See page 17, this volume.
98 *Halfway River (BCSC), supra* note 93 at para. 87. Dorgan J. was paraphrasing the Supreme Court of Canada in *Sparrow, supra* note 27, which said at 1112: "[I]t is possible, and, indeed, crucial, to be sensitive to the aboriginal perspective itself on the meaning of the rights at stake."
99 *R. v. Badger,* [1996] 1 S.C.R. 771 [*Badger*].
100 *Ibid.* at 793.
101 *Halfway River (BCSC), supra* note 93 at para. 101. Dorgan J.'s attribution of this assumption to Cory J. in *Badger, supra* note 99, was later criticized by Madam Justice Huddart in *Halfway River (BCCA), supra* note 91 at para. 186.
102 *Halfway River (BCSC), supra* note 93 at para. 106.
103 *Ibid.*
104 *Ibid.* at para. 111.
105 *Ibid.* at para. 113.
106 *Ibid.* at para. 114.
107 *Ibid.* at para. 115.
108 *Ibid.* at para. 116.
109 *Ibid.* at para. 117.
110 *Ibid.* at para. 118.
111 *Guerin, supra* note 27.
112 *Badger, supra* note 99 at 820-21.
113 *Halfway River (BCSC), supra* note 93 at para. 132.
114 *Ibid.* at para. 133. Here are her references: *R. v. Jack* (1995), 16 B.C.L.R. (3d) 201 (C.A.); *R. v. Noel,* [1995] 4 C.N.L.R. 78 at 95 (N.W.T. Terr. Ct.); and *Delgamuukw v. B.C.,* [1991] 3 W.W.R. 97 at 423 (B.C.S.C.).

115 *Ibid.* at para. 145.
116 *Ibid.* at para. 158.
117 *Ibid.*
118 *Ibid.* at para. 160.
119 *Ibid.* at para. 162.
120 The petition for judicial review was never heard.
121 *Siska Indian Band v. British Columbia (Minister of Forests)*, [1998] B.C.J. No. 1661 at para. 2 (B.C.S.C.) (QL) [*Siska (1998)*].
122 *Ibid.* at para. 7.
123 *Crown Proceedings Act*, R.S.B.C. 1996, c. 89.
124 *Siska (1998)*, *supra* note 121 at para. 12.
125 *Ibid.*
126 Recall that it was because they were similarly barred from enjoining Crown officials in the *Delgamuukw* action that the Gitksan and Wet'suwet'en decided to launch the *Westar* case. See page 39, this volume.
127 *Siska (1998)*, *supra* note 121 at para. 15.
128 *Ibid.* at para. 16.
129 *Ibid.* at para. 17.
130 See page 105, this volume.
131 *Sparrow* was concerned with Aboriginal rights generally, *Delgamuukw* with Aboriginal title specifically. The Court in *Delgamuukw* adapted the *Sparrow* test for justifiable infringement to Aboriginal title cases. For a brief discussion of the relationship between the *Sparrow* and *Delgamuukw* tests, see Chapter 2, note 43.
132 *Siska (1998)*, *supra* note 121 at para. 18.
133 *Ibid.* at para. 20.
134 Apparently, the Siska Band's counsel had neglected to argue specifically that the road building would harm the band's intangible interests in the Siska Valley.
135 *Siska (1998)*, *supra* note 121 at para. 22.
136 For a brief but helpful summary of the demographics of these communities (except the Halfway River First Nation), see c. 7 of the *Application for the Wolverine Coal Project*, available at the Environmental Assessment Office website at <http://www.eao.gov.bc.ca/epic/output/documents/p162/d13660/ 1036444873915_16af42884ae64e0f8553d621be48be92.pdf>, last accessed 3 March 2004.
137 There are, for example, some burial sites in the area.
138 *Kelly Lake Cree Nation v. Canada (Ministry of Energy and Mines)*, [1998] B.C.J. No. 2471 at para. 23 (B.C.S.C.) (QL) [*Kelly Lake Cree Nation*].
139 As quoted in *ibid.* at para. 40.
140 *Ibid.*
141 *Ibid.* at para. 46.
142 Here is how Taylor J. explained the breakdown:

> The reasons for this conflict regarding the information sharing agreement arose out of a misunderstanding between MEM and the SFN [Saulteau First Nation] as to the effects of the information sharing agreement. The view of the government was that the agreements were political agreements or protocols between governments. From the perspective of the SFN, they provided a legal binding right ... [that] information acquired during the TUS ... would remain solely with the SFN. In essence what MEM sought was a protocol. What the SFN sought was an agreement that preserved information and the title over the information to itself. (*ibid.* at para. 57)

143 See TSSMC, *Twin Sisters Special Management Committee Recommendations for Management Objectives and Strategies for the Special Management Zones and Proposed Protected Area* (21 October 1997) at 2, online: BC Ministry of Sustainable Resource Management, Dawson Creek Land and Resource Management Plan, Appendix J <http://srmwww.gov.bc.ca/lrmp/dawson/toc.htm#toc>, last accessed 14 May 2004.
144 *Ibid.* at 2-3.

145 In 1999, the Klin-se-za became one of sixteen new protected areas created under the Dawson Creek Land and Resource Management Plan. The plan is available online: BC Ministry of Sustainable Resource Management, *supra* note 143.

146 The final report (*supra* note 143) was signed by all the original participants except the Saulteau First Nation. It should be noted that not long after the teleconference, an election was held and Mr. Stewart Cameron replaced Mr. Napolean as Chief of the Saulteau First Nation.

147 *Kelly Lake Cree Nation, supra* note 138 at para. 71.

148 *Ibid.* at para. 86.

149 The Kelly Lake Cree Nation commenced proceedings on 15 July 1996. Among other things, they sought declarations of their Aboriginal title and other rights and the Crown's breach of its fiduciary and other duties. They also sought an order to allow them to adhere to Treaty 8. The litigation is ongoing. For what has transpired thus far, see *Kelly Lake Cree Nation v. Canada,* [1998] 2 F.C. 270 & [2000] F.C.J. No. 1942 (T.D.) (QL).

150 The Ministry of Forests was also named as a respondent because of its approvals of a master licence to cut and a cutting permit allowing Amoco to fell timber in order to construct a winter trail to the well site. The approval was granted subsequent to MEM's approval of the Mount Monteith project. Because Taylor J. determined that the Ministry of Forests' decisions would rise or fall based on MEM's decision, he largely ignored the former decisions. I shall continue to do the same.

151 *Kelly Lake Cree Nation v. Canada (Ministry of Energy and Mines),* [1998] B.C.J. No. 3207 at para. 1 (B.C.S.C.) (QL).

152 *Ibid.* at para. 2.

153 *Ibid.*

154 *Ibid.* at para. 5.

155 *Ibid.* at para. 6.

156 *Ibid.* at para. 15.

157 *Kelly Lake Cree Nation, supra* note 138 at para. 27.

158 *Ibid.* at para. 28.

159 *Ibid.* at para. 30.

160 *Ibid.* at para. 168.

161 *Ibid.* at para. 173.

162 *Ibid.* at para. 174.

163 *Ibid.* at para. 184.

164 *Ibid.* at para. 162.

165 Taylor J. rejected the argument that by filing a federal land claim, the Kelly Lake Cree Nation had asserted rights to the area in such a way as to trigger a duty to consult (*ibid.* at para. 164).

166 *Ibid.* at para. 165.

167 *Ibid.*

168 *Ibid.* at para. 241.

169 *Ibid.* at para. 243.

170 *Ibid.*

171 The Saulteau First Nation filed its claim in March 1997. The claim encompassed the entire Twin Sisters area as originally defined by the CMAC.

172 *Kelly Lake Cree Nation, supra* note 138 at para. 245.

173 *Ibid.*

174 *Delgamuukw, supra* note 17 at 1113, per Lamer C.J.C.

175 *Kelly Lake Cree Nation, supra* note 138 at para. 248.

176 *Ibid.*

177 *Canadian Charter of Rights and Freedoms,* Part I of the *Constitution Act, 1982,* being Schedule B to the *Canada Act 1982* (UK), 1982, c. 11. For an illuminating discussion of how US courts have – largely dismissively – dealt with the arguments of Native American tribes claiming that the integrity of their off-reservation sacred sites should be protected as part of their free exercise of religion under the First Amendment, see Brian Edward Brown, *Religion, Law, and the Land: Native Americans and the Judicial Interpretation of Sacred Land* (Westport, CT: Greenwood Press, 1999). For a helpful overview of how the religious freedom

claims of indigenous peoples with regard to their sacred sites have fared in Australia, Canada, New Zealand, and the United States, see Richard B. Collins, "Sacred Sites and Religious Freedom on Government Land" (2003) 5 U. Pa. J. Const. L. 241.

178 Here are Taylor J.'s words: "It is not that in fact anyone can be said to have actually gone there on any consistent basis, as might one visit a temple, shrine or church. While there is a vague reference to sun dances having been performed some 50 years ago, there is simply a dearth of evidence as to any practices being carried out in any of the areas defined by the TSSMC" (*Kelly Lake Cree Nation, supra* note 138 at para. 192). Taylor J.'s handling of the evidence of infrequent visitation to the Twin Sisters area and the lack of evidence regarding practical religious uses of the area betrays a lack of understanding. As for the lack of evidence regarding practical religious usage, he should have been aware of the fact that, generally speaking, First Nations are justifiably reticent about providing information about their religious practices. And as for the evidence of infrequent visitation, he might have asked himself – since he brought up the comparison to temples, shrines, and churches – how often, to take just one example, individual Muslims make the *hajj* to Mecca. The fact that individual Muslims might visit Mecca only once (if at all) in a lifetime does not lessen its practical religious importance.

179 Taylor J. was apparently unaware of the widespread idea that sacrilege can render a sacred site unsuitable for practical religious purposes. If a Catholic church, for example, has been profaned by some activity sufficiently contrary to its sacred character, it is, as a matter of canon law, unfit for practical religious purposes (e.g., Mass). The building must be reconsecrated before it can again be put to practical religious use. The integrity of the building as a sacred place is thus a precondition for the exercise of certain religious rights and freedoms therein.

180 *Kelly Lake Cree Nation, supra* note 138 at para. 195.

181 *Ibid.*

182 *Ibid.* at para. 251.

183 See page 117, this volume.

184 *Halfway River (BCCA), supra* note 91 at para. 203.

185 For Dorgan J.'s discussion of the administrative law issues, see pages 99ff, this volume.

186 *Halfway River (BCCA), supra* note 91 at para. 65.

187 *Ibid.* at para. 72.

188 *Ibid.* at para. 85.

189 *Ibid.* at para. 203.

190 *Ibid.* at para. 233.

191 *Ibid.* at para. 234.

192 *Ibid.* at para. 53. Rule 52(11)(d) of the *Supreme Court Rules* (B.C. Reg. 221/90) says that the Court may "order a trial of the proceeding, either generally or on an issue, and order pleadings to be filed, and may give directions for the conduct of the trial and of pre-trial proceedings, and for the disposition of the application."

193 *Ibid.*

194 *Ibid.* at para. 55.

195 *Ibid.* at para. 56.

196 *Ibid.* at para. 133.

197 *Ibid.* at para. 135.

198 *Ibid.* at para. 138.

199 *Ibid.* at para. 144. It is true that the chambers judge held, as a matter of interpretation, that Cory J. had assumed in *Badger, supra* note 99, that any interference with the right to hunt under Treaty 8 constituted a *prima facie* infringement. Logically speaking, however, her conclusion that the district manager's approval constituted *prima facie* infringement of the Halfway River First Nation's treaty right to hunt did not depend on the proposition that any interference constituted *prima facie* infringement. If it had, there would have been no point to her asking, as she did, whether Canfor's logging of the Tusdzuh would be a reasonable limit on the treaty right, whether it would cause undue hardship, and whether it denied the Halfway River people's preferred means of exercising their right. As was pointed out in note 37 of Chapter 2, these are all questions suggested by the Supreme

Court of Canada in *Sparrow* to help courts decide whether interference with an Aboriginal right rises to the level of *prima facie* infringement. Careful analysis of her discussion shows that she introduced the aforesaid proposition only to counter Canfor's claim that the geographical limitation on the right to hunt implied that taking up surrendered land for timber harvesting *could not* constitute *prima facie* infringement of the right. Basically, she was arguing, relying on the Supreme Court of Canada's authority, that *prima facie* infringement by timber harvesting was not precluded by the treaty right's geographical limitation. For my summary of her reasoning, see pages 102ff, this volume.

200 *Halfway River (BCCA), supra* note 91 at para. 157.

201 Curiously, Finch J.A. had formed the mistaken belief that the chambers judge had not addressed any of the first three questions. She had not, it is true, addressed the third question, which is not surprising as the question was not one of those listed in *Sparrow*. She did, however, address the first and second questions. For her responses to the first and second questions, see page 104 of this volume.

202 *Halfway River (BCCA), supra* note 91 at para. 165.

203 *Ibid.* at para. 166.

204 *Ibid.* at para. 186.

205 *Ibid.*

206 As I have already stated (*supra* note 199), I think that this portrayal of the chambers judge's reasoning is inaccurate.

207 *Halfway River (BCCA), supra* note 91 at para. 180.

208 Consistency with the Crown's fiduciary position does not suffice to render an infringement justifiable, however. For, as Lamer C.J.C. insisted in *Delgamuukw*, the infringement must also be in pursuit of a substantial and compelling legislative objective. For the relevant passage in *Delgamuukw*, see *supra* note 17.

209 *Halfway River (BCCA), supra* note 91 at para. 178.

210 *Ibid.*

211 *Ibid.*

212 *Ibid.* at para. 175. In reviewing allocation decisions that involve infringement, courts will, Huddart J.A. said, focus on the Crown's fiduciary and constitutional duty to accommodate the First Nation's rightful use (*ibid.* at para. 190). For the relationship between the duty to consult and the duty to seek accommodation, see Chapter 2, note 44.

213 *Ibid.* at para. 180. It is worth noting that later, in her dissent in *Paul v. British Columbia (Forest Appeals Commission)*, [2001] 89 B.C.L.R. (3d) 210 (B.C.C.A.), Huddart J.A. paused to challenge the provincial government's assumption that it was constitutionally obliged to recognize and affirm only those Aboriginal rights that had been established in court. Importantly, she refuted the assumption and incidentally the claim that the assumption found some support in the Supreme Court of Canada's *Sparrow* and other decisions, saying (at 245), that "we know from *R. v. Sparrow* and *R. v. Gladstone* [citations omitted] that this assumption is flawed. In those seminal cases, infringements or potential infringements of aboriginal rights were found to have occurred at times when the rights in question had not been proven. Legal duties arise from legal rights. Proof of the right is required in the process of establishing a breach that gives rise to a remedy. Lack of proof does not mean the right and the duty do not exist. Legal proceedings simply enforce the duty and give a remedy for a breached right."

214 *Halfway River (BCCA), surpra* note 91 at para. 182.

215 *Ibid.* at para. 191.

216 *Ibid.* at para. 229.

217 *Ibid.* at para. 231. Southin J.A.'s unfairness argument glaringly ignores the fact that the current relationship between the province and First Nations is an expression of a history that differs significantly from the history of other parts of Canada.

218 *Ibid.* at para. 232. John A. Macdonald is reputed to have called BC "the spoilt child of Confederation."

219 She apparently believed that Treaty 8 had "extinguished any non-Treaty Aboriginal Rights Halfway may have had prior to entering into the Treaty" (*Halfway River [BCSC], supra* note 93 at para. 91).

220 Southin J.A. incorporated the claim into her reasons for judgment by quoting Chief Metecheah's deposition (*Halfway River [BCCA], supra* note 91 at para. 209). Understandably, however, given her view that such Aboriginal and treaty rights issues should not have been dealt with on judicial review, she did not discuss the claim. Finch J.A. ignored the claim completely.

221 As Huddart J.A. perceptively noted, "[i]t is implicit in Halfway's submission that the proposed lumbering use is incompatible with its rights or at least would be found to be so if the District Manager had full information and properly considered the scope of its treaty right to hunt and of its aboriginal right to use the particular tract in question for religious and spiritual purposes" (*ibid.* at para. 181).

222 For the context of the chambers judge's statement, pages 102ff., this volume.

223 *Halfway River (BCCA), supra* note 91 at para. 140.

224 *Ibid.* at para. 141.

225 *Ibid.* at para. 142.

226 *Ibid.* at para. 187.

227 See page 119, this volume. In *Kitkatla Band v. British Columbia (Minister of Small Business, Tourism and Culture)*, [2000] 2 C.N.L.R. 36 (B.C.C.A.) at 64, Hall J.A. articulated a position similar to Taylor J.'s, saying that "one's lineage and heritage in the general sense is an important circumstance for us all but objects and sites ... do not appear to me to rise to the level of importance of territorial rights or 'way of life' rights – such latter subjects in the Aboriginal field as hunting and fishing rights and practices for instance."

228 See pages 131ff., this volume.

229 *Van der Peet, supra* note 30 at 554-55.

230 *Delgamuukw, supra* note 17 at 1097.

231 Lambert J.A., in *Haida Nation (Part 1), supra* note 29 at para. 48, found that the Crown, over a certain period of time, "had an obligation to consult the Haida people ... *about* accommodating the aboriginal title and aboriginal rights of the Haida people" [emphasis added].

232 See *Heiltsuk Tribal Council v. British Columbia (Minister of Sustainable Resource Management)*, 2003 B.C.S.C. 1422 [*Heiltsuk*].

233 Lambert J.A., *Haida Nation (Part 1), supra* note 29 at paras. 49-51, implied that the First Nation must have an adequate *prima facie* case for its asserted right. The Haida, he found, had "a good *prima facie* case." Lambert J.A. also implied that the Crown could be held responsible for evidence it has acquired or could reasonably have acquired independently of consultation with the First Nation (*ibid.* at para. 49). The province's new consultation guidelines reveal that it is fully cognizant of the fact that it could be held so responsible. See the *Provincial Policy for Consultation with First Nations* (October 2002) at 14, 18, 20, 25, 26; online: Ministry of Sustainable Resource Management <http://www.gov.bc.ca/srm>, last accessed 17 May 2004.

234 My discussion presupposes that the petitioner is a First Nation. When the petitioner is, say, a corporation challenging a decision not to give the go-ahead to a particular resource exploitation activity because of concerns over Aboriginal rights, a reviewing court may find fault with both the Crown for failing to fulfill its consultation and/or accommodation duties and the First Nation for failing to fulfill its reciprocal duties. That is what happened in *Husby Forest Products v. Minister of Forests*, 2004 B.C.S.C. 142 [*Husby*]. The case centred around a provincial government decision to refuse a cutting permit to Husby, a logging company with a forest licence for Graham Island, on the grounds that it would infringe certain Aboriginal rights asserted by the Haida Nation. Garson J. decided to remit the decision for reconsideration on the basis of her findings that the Haida had failed "to clearly define the nature and scope of the aboriginal right they claimed was being infringed" (at para. 94) and, in consequence, that the Crown's decision maker failed chiefly, among other things, to identify the nature and scope of the asserted right in reference to the allegedly conflicting activity.

235 As Lambert J.A., *Haida Nation (Part 1), supra* note 29 at para. 51, explained, "the scope of the consultation and the strength of the obligation to seek an accommodation will be proportional to the potential soundness of the claim for aboriginal title and aboriginal rights."

236   Indigenous communities around the world often find that deliberations about (1) whether or not it is permissible to reveal information about a sacred site to outsiders and (2) if so, whether or not it should be revealed can be agonizing and deeply divisive. See, e.g., Margaret Simons's detailed account of how such deliberations affected the Ngarrind-jerri people of South Australia, *The Meeting of the Waters: The Hindmarsh Island Affair* (Sydney, Australia: Hodder, 2003).

237   Examples are easily found. I shall mention only one. Until fairly recently, the Sto:lo, a Coast Salish people, tended to maintain a tradition of silence about their sacred sites, not saying anything about them to their non-Aboriginal neighbours. In many cases, their silence was dictated not by the ethics of the sacred sites but by a concern over disrespect. Although disrespect remains a concern, the Sto:lo have decided that the mounting damage and destruction of their sacred sites outweighs the concern over disrespect and thus have made significant information about their sacred sites public. Gordon Mohs, "Sto:lo Sacred Ground" in David L. Carmichael, Jane Hubert, Brian Reeves, and Audhild Schanche, eds., *Sacred Sites, Sacred Places* (London: Routledge, 1994) 184 at 200-1, supplies the startling statistics and their explanation: "As regional developments have increased in scope and magnitude in recent years, conservation concerns have become more acute. With urbanization, damage to Sto:lo spiritual sites has been extensive. Of 200 spiritual sites identified to date, about 50 sites have been destroyed and 50 damaged or disturbed. Another 25 face ongoing disturbance or potential destruction from development. This represents over 50 percent of all documented Sto:lo spiritual sites ... the majority of existing sacred sites (about 65 percent) are not found on reserve lands." I am assuming that the Sto:lo did not violate or at least did not seriously violate the ethics of their sacred sites by revealing information about them.

238   The failure or refusal to hand the knowledge of sacred sites on to the next generation is part of the larger phenomenon of the failure or refusal to hand on traditional knowledge generally. See, e.g., Canada, Department of Indian Affairs and Northern Development, and Intellectual Property Policy Directorate, Industry Canada. *Intellectual Property and Aboriginal People: A Working Paper* (Paper written for Research and Analysis Directorate by Simon Brascoupé and Karin Endemann) (Ottawa: Minister of Public Works and Government Services, 1999) at 2.

239   Executive Order 13007 (U.S.), "Protection and Accommodation of Access to 'Indian Sacred Sites'" (24 May 1996), 61 FR 26771; 29 May 1996. The key section is s. 1:

> Section 1. *Accommodation of Sacred Sites* ...
> (a)   In managing Federal lands, each executive branch agency with statutory or administrative responsibility for management of Federal lands shall to the extent practicable, permitted by law, and not clearly inconsistent with essential agency functions, (1) accommodate access to and ceremonial use of Indian sacred sites by Indian religious practitioners and (2) avoid adversely affecting the physical integrity of such sacred sites. Where appropriate, agencies shall maintain the confidentiality of sacred sites.

240   E.g., the Blackfeet have a number of off-reserve sacred sites in the Badger–Two Medicine area south of Glacier National Park in Montana. Proposed seismic testing and exploratory gas wells posed a threat to the sites. The superintendent of the Lewis and Clark National Forest suspended the drilling permits without the Blackfeet having to disclose the exact locations of their sacred sites. See Andrew Gulliford, *Sacred Objects and Sacred Places: Preserving Tribal Traditions* (Boulder: University Press of Colorado, 2000) at 116. On the west side of the Montana Rockies, the Blackfeet's neighbours, the Kootenai, have similarly successfully protected off-reserve sacred sites on federal lands by indicating only their general locations. See Rebecca S. Timmons, "Kootenai – Ksanka – Kunaitupii" in Brian O.K. Reeves and Margaret A. Kennedy, eds., *Kunaitupii: Coming Together on Native Sacred Sites: Their Sacredness, Conservation and Interpretation* (Proceedings of the First Joint Meeting of the Archaeological Society of Alberta and the Montana Archaeological Society, Waterton Lakes National Park, Alberta, 2-6 May 1990) (Calgary: Archaeological Society of Alberta, 1993) 140 at 142.

241 During the consultation process described in *Husby, supra* note 234, the district manager of the Queen Charlotte Islands Forest District consulted with the Haida Nation over whether to issue Husby Forest Products road and cutting permits for a number of forested areas falling within Husby's forest licence on Graham Island. The Haida objected to issuance of permits for certain areas they categorize as "archaeological forests" and deem sacred (at para. 88). In their responses to the district manager, the Haida asserted both Aboriginal title and other Aboriginal rights in connection with the areas. Although the Haida made it plain that they consider the areas in question sacred, they did not, it seems, explicitly assert a specific Aboriginal right centred on their sacredness. The district manager decided against issuing the road and cutting permits for the areas in question. For subsequent events, see *supra* note 234.

242 Section 35(1) of the *Constitution Act, 1982* now bars Parliament from unilaterally extinguishing Aboriginal rights (*Van der Peet, supra* note 30 at 538).

243 It might be thought that the chambers judges' decisions in *Halfway River* and *Kelly Lake Cree* belie my claim, as the chambers judges in both cases addressed the infringement-justification issue. It must be kept in mind, however, that that the chambers judge in *Halfway River* applied the *Sparrow* infringement-justification analysis to treaty rights rather than Aboriginal rights. She found that the Crown had unjustifiably infringed the Halfway River people's treaty right to hunt. It must also be kept in mind that while the chambers judge in *Kelly Lake Cree Nation* found that the Crown had justifiably infringed the Saulteau First Nation's treaty rights, he did not decide whether it had justifiably infringed their Aboriginal spiritual and religious rights. The most he determined was that if the Saulteau people's Aboriginal rights were proved to be *as they asserted them to be*, the Crown would have justifiably infringed them.

244 *Haida Nation (Part 1), supra* note 29 at para. 51. BC's *Provincial Policy for Consultation with First Nations, supra* note 233 at 11 and 25, ignores Lambert J.A.'s use of the word "potential" and speaks only of consultation and accommodation being proportional to the soundness of the claim. The difference is explainable. Lambert's focus was on what a chambers judge would and would not normally determine on judicial review. Since a chambers judge would normally leave the task of deciding whether to accept or reject a First Nation's claim to an Aboriginal right to a trial court, he or she would normally calculate only the potential for or chances of the claim succeeding at trial. Simply put, the chambers judge decides whether the claim's chances of succeeding at trial suffice to engage the Crown's duties to consult and seek accommodation, while the trial judge decides whether it should succeed. The provincial government's consultation policy ignores the word "potential" because it (in the pair of passages previously referred to) focuses on what a trial court would ultimately hold. Its policy does, nonetheless, require its decision makers to assess the soundness of a First Nation's claim to an Aboriginal right in the sense of its chances of succeeding at trial if it came to trial (*Provincial Policy, ibid.* at 27ff).

The potential soundness of a First Nation's claim to an Aboriginal right may not, it should be noted, be definable simply as the chances of its claim succeeding at trial, for a court may accept some portions of the claim and reject others. A First Nation's claim does not, then, have to be articulated in the final form adopted by a court in order to count as potentially sound or simply sound. The province's recent consultation policy gives no indication that the provincial Crown is alive to this possibility. Its emphasis is on the need for its decision makers to assess the probability or possibility of asserted Aboriginal rights being proved in court (*ibid.* at 27-30).

245 As I observed in *supra* note 233 the Crown may bear some responsibility for assembling evidence in support of a First Nation's claim for Aboriginal rights independently of its consultations with First Nations.

246 See Chapter 2, note 59.

247 In *Halfway River (BCCA), supra* note 91 at para. 182, Madam Justice Huddart had this to say:

> Once the District Manager has set up an adequate opportunity to consult, the First Nation is required to co-operate fully with that process and to offer the relevant information to aid in determining the exact nature of the right in question. The First

Nation must take advantage of this opportunity as it arises. It cannot unreasonably refuse to participate ... In my view, a First Nation should not be permitted to provide evidence on judicial review it has had an opportunity to provide to the decision-maker, to support a petition asserting a failure to respect a treaty right.

Of course, if the Crown failed either to initiate consultation or to provide adequate consultation, the Crown rather than the First Nation would likely be found at fault. In such cases, it seems likely that reviewing courts would, should they deem it necessary, allow First Nations to make submissions about Aboriginal rights they would have asserted had they been given the opportunity.

248 Although such an argument was available to the Saulteau First Nation in the Twin Sisters case, there is no indication that it was ever raised. For the basis for my claim that such an argument was available, see pages 112ff., this volume.

249 For her discussion, see above page 134, this volume.

250 Except in those presumably rare instances in which the *Sparrow* infringement-justification analysis is applied, reviewing courts will likely either rely on a modified notion of *prima facie* infringement or substitute a less strict notion of interference. By a modified notion of *prima facie* infringement, I have in mind something like *prima facie infringement of an asserted Aboriginal right*.

  When one begins to speculate on these matters, it becomes apparent how prescient Madam Justice Huddart was when, in *Halfway River (BCCA)*, supra note 91 at para. 191, she stated: "Having [consulted and ascertained the nature and scope of the treaty right at issue] ... and having determined the effect of the proposed non-aboriginal use, he [the district manager] then makes a determination as to whether the proposed use is compatible with the treaty right. If it is he must seek to accommodate the uses to each other. *It will be that accommodation the court reviews within the contours of a justificatory standard yet to be determined*" [emphasis added].

251 If, e.g., a court should find that a serious diminishment of a site's sacredness translates into a denial of a First Nation's preferred means of exercising its asserted associated Aboriginal right, the inference of *prima facie* infringement would be automatic. Huddart J.A.'s remarks along these lines (see pages 137-38, this volume.) merit rereading.

252 Courts would likely, one hopes, show caution in making such findings. For it is not always clear, especially to outsiders, who has authority to speak or act for a particular First Nation when it comes to sacred sites.

253 The *Taku River* and *Haida* cases may even themselves have involved use of the strategy in the broad sense. For my justification for saying this, see Chapter 4, note 90.

254 *Taku River Tlingit First Nation v. British Columbia (Project Assessment Director)*, 2004 SCC 74.

255 *Haida Nation v. British Columbia (Minister of Forests)*, 2004 SCC 73.

256 *Taku River, supra* note 254 at para. 24.

257 *Haida Nation, supra* note 255 at para. 18.

258 *Ibid.* at para. 50.

Chapter 5: How First Nations Sacred Sites Have Fared in Canada's Courts

1 For my reasons for saying that their position is ethically compromised, see pages 164-65, this volume.

2 The sacredness of certain sites within the Gitksan and Wet'suwet'en traditional territories was occasionally mentioned or alluded to in the main *Delgamuukw* action. I have included the *Westar* case in my discussion because the Court of Appeal's decision therein has strongly influenced people's understanding of the *Meares Island* case and hence has definitively shaped the Meares strategy.

3 For details, see Chapter 3, note 83.

4 See Chapter 4, note 145.

5 See pages 62-63, this volume.

6 Granted that the courts have shown some openness to claims of sacredness by First Nations, one may still question how open they have been. The analysis that follows demonstrates that they have been less than fully open.

7 The Hindmarsh Island affair affords an instructive example of the assumption at work. There, a conglomeration of Australian politicians, government officials, anthropologists, journalists, and others – presumably, largely unthinkingly – adopted the assumption, with tragic results for the indigenous community involved. See Margaret Simons, *The Meeting of the Waters: The Hindmarsh Island Affair* (Sydney, Australia: Hodder, 2003).

8 I have more to say on this matter at page 172ff., this volume.

9 See Chapter 1, note 3.

10 Two statements can be logically consistent without one being logically deducible from the other.

11 Here is a more direct argument against the assumption. While the significance of a sacred site is paradigmatically expressed in descriptive ("is") statements, its ethic is paradigmatically expressed in normative ("ought") statements or rules. Granted that the widely accepted philosophical position that "ought" statements are not logically deducible from "is" statements, a sacred site's ethic cannot be logically deduced from its significance.

12 In the *Ure Creek* case, Macdonell J. concluded that the construction of the logging road into the Ure Creek area would not irreparably harm the Lil'wat. (See page 56, this volume.) Given that the Lil'wat had supplied ample evidence of the significance and status of the area as a sacred place, his conclusion that any harm they might suffer would be compensable betrays a lack of appreciation for what it meant for them to speak of the area as sacred.

13 For what the trio of courts said, see above at 29, 55, and 166, respectively.

14 See above at 63, 103, and 107-9 respectively. In the earlier *Siska Creek* case, Smith J. (above at 109) acknowledged the First Nation's holistic approach to the Siska Valley but held that its evidence had failed to prove that the soon-to-be-constructed logging road would irreparably harm the band's intangible interests. Despite Smith J.'s stated acknowledgment, his basis for holding that the evidence failed to prove irreparable harm was his finding that the road would not interfere with "any site-specific interests of the Band." His finding suggests that he misunderstood the Siska Band's holistic perspective (not to mention the sacred site's ethic).

15 Such was the view of the Ministry of Forests and Canfor in their appeal of Madam Justice Dorgan's decision in the *Halfway River* case. Here is how Finch J.A., in *Halfway River First Nation v. British Columbia (Ministry of Forests)*, [1999] B.C.J. No. 1880 at para. 97 (B.C.C.A.) (QL) [*Halfway River (BCCA)*], summed up their complaints: "The appellants say that the learned chambers judge erred when she held that any interference with the petitioners' right to hunt was a breach of Treaty 8, *and say further that she erred in basing her decision on the petitioners' 'holistic perspective'* and in holding that they had the right to exercise their 'preferred means' of hunting in an 'unspoiled wilderness'" [emphasis added].

16 See page 51, this volume.

17 See page 66, this volume.

18 In *Chapman v. Luminis Pty. Ltd.* (No. 5), [2001] F.C.A. 1106 at para. 333, a case involving Hindmarsh Island, Justice von Doussa of the Federal Court of Australia forcefully expressed the general point:

> To the eurocentric mind accustomed to the open exchange of information, the late disclosure of an important claim or explanation which supports the interests of the discloser will be viewed with suspicion. However, it is now well recognized in this Court and I think widely in the community, that under Aboriginal custom not all information is open. Much cultural information is surrounded by restrictions on disclosure. Some cultural knowledge relating to sacred beliefs is highly secret. Some, though sacred, may be revealed in part. The concept of graded secrecy, that is layers of knowledge is recognised, where outer layers may be widely known, but inner layers, including knowledge as to the significance of the belief to the culture may be known to only a very small number of senior people in the clan who are considered to be its custodians. The transmission of restricted cultural knowledge is likely to be strictly governed by traditional customs and a system of respect which delineate by whom, to whom and in what circumstances the knowledge may be revealed. The phenomenon of eleventh

hour disclosure when all means short of disclosure have failed to protect an Aboriginal tradition is also recognized.

On Hindmarsh Island, see Simons, *supra* note 7.

19 In the *Lower Tsitika Valley* case, the Tlowitsis-Mumtagila spoke of the road building and logging as a *desecration* (see pages 49-50, this volume.) In a case related to the *Ure Creek* case, the Lil'wat also spoke of the road building and logging as a *desecration*. See *International Forest Products v. Pascal*, [1991] B.C.J. No. 718 & No. 719 at 3 (B.C.S.C.) (QL). In the *High Falls* case, the Poplar Point Ojibway spoke of the hydroelectric dam as a *desecration* (see page 59, this volume.) In the earlier *Siska Creek* case, the Siska Band claimed that the logging would *permanently damage* their spiritual practices in the area (see page 108, this volume. Lastly, in the *Twin Sisters* case, the Saulteau First Nation and Kelly Lake Cree Nation spoke of the exploratory gas well as a *defilement*. See *Kelly Lake Cree Nation v. Canada (Ministry of Energy and Mines)*, [1998] B.C.J. No. 2471 at paras. 192 and 197 (B.C.S.C.) (QL).

20 See page 55, this volume.

21 See page 124, this volume.

22 See page 137, this volume. Perhaps Huddart J.A.'s position was anticipated by Seaton J.A. in the *Meares Island* case, where he observed that Nuu-chah-nulth society is interwoven with Meares Island, its heritage sites, and its resources. For Seaton J.A.'s remarks, see Chapter 3, this volume, at 32. Locke J.A., in his dissent in the *Westar* case, expanded slightly on Seaton J.A.'s observation in his discussion of whether the relationship of the Gitksan and Wet'suwet'en to the Shedin indicated uniqueness sufficient to warrant interim protection. For Locke J.A.'s remarks, see page 46, this volume.

23 See page 119, this volume.

24 The clearest statement I have found is a remark by Hall J.A. in *Kitkatla* implying that a site serving sustenance purposes is more important than a site serving spiritual or religious purposes. For his remark and the reference, see Chapter 4, note 227.

25 See page 138, this volume.

26 James Tully describes various ways in which the presumption has found expression in relations between Aboriginal peoples and Canadians since the nineteenth century:

> During the nineteenth century a different relationship was imposed over the Aboriginal peoples without their consent and despite their active resistance. Their status as equal, coexisting, and self-governing nations was denied. Their governments were displaced, and they were forcibly subjected to the Canadian political system by the establishment of a structure of domination administered through a series of Indian acts. This colonial regime has gone through several phases. Aboriginal peoples have been treated as obstacles to Canadian settlement and expansion who could be removed from their territories, relocated on Crown reserves, and governed by the Indian Act; they have been treated as primitive wards incapable of consent whose religions, languages, cultures, and governments could be eliminated and who could be coerced into the superior Canadian ways by their civilised guardians; they have been treated as disappearing races who could be marginalised and left to die out; and they have been treated as burdens on the Crown who could be off-loaded and assimilated to Canadian citizenship by extinguishing or superseding their Aboriginal and treaty rights. More recently, they have been treated as minorities with a degree of legal autonomy, self-government, and claims to land within the Canadian political system. *What has remained constant through these phases is the colonial assumption that Aboriginal peoples are subordinate and subject to the Canadian government,* rather than equal, self-governing nations subject to the agreements reached through the treaty system. [emphasis added]

See James Tully's "A Just Relationship between Aboriginal and Non-Aboriginal Peoples of Canada," in Curtis Cook and Juan D. Lindau, eds., *Aboriginal Rights and Self-Government: The Canadian and Mexican Experience in North American Perspective* (Montreal and Kingston: McGill-Queens University Press, 2000) 39 at 41-42.

The courts play the crucial role in Canada's self-justifying discourse of First Nations subordination, presenting their subordination as a brute legal fact. For example, Lamer C.J.C., in *R. v. Van der Peet,* [1996] 2 S.C.R. 507 at 539 writing about s. 35(1) of the *Constitution Act, 1982,* said: "[W]hat s. 35(1) does is provide the constitutional framework through which the fact that aboriginals lived on the land in distinctive societies, with their own practices, traditions and cultures, is acknowledged and *reconciled with the sovereignty of the Crown* ... the aboriginal rights recognized and affirmed by s. 35(1) must be directed towards *the reconciliation of the pre-existence of aboriginal societies with the sovereignty of the Crown*" [emphasis added]. Lamer C.J.C.'s words echo the earlier statement by the Court in *R. v. Sparrow,* [1990] 1 S.C.R. 1075 at 1103: "It is worth recalling that while British policy towards the native population was based on respect for their right to occupy their traditional lands, a proposition to which the *Royal Proclamation of 1763* bears witness, there was from the outset never any doubt that sovereignty and legislative power, and indeed the underlying title, to such lands vested in the Crown." According to the Supreme Court of Canada, then, sovereignty over First Nations peoples and lands is an indisputable political/legal fact to which First Nations must become reconciled. For an illuminating critique of these pretensions, see Michael Asch and Patrick Macklem, "Aboriginal Rights and Canadian Sovereignty: An Essay on *R. v. Sparrow*" (1991) 29 Alta. L.R. 498.

27 Underlying the lack of collective consent is often a lack of individual consent. For example, Patricia Monture-Angus voices the sentiments of many: "I do not think of myself as a Canadian as all of those state relations have been forced on Haudenausonee people. ... Consent is the central issue that requires resolution before I could consider myself to be both Kanien'kehaka and Canadian." See her *Journeying Forward: Dreaming First Nations Independence* (Halifax: Fernwood, 1999), n. 1 at 152.

28 John Borrows poses the legally salient question – to which, I might add, there is no legally satisfying answer: "If Aboriginal peoples have prior rights to land and participatory governance, how did the Crown and court gain their right to adjudicate here?" See his *Recovering Canada: The Resurgence of Indigenous Law* (Toronto: University of Toronto Press, 2002) at 59.

29 It is a weak objection to argue that because First Nations have voluntarily taken their fight to protect their sacred sites to the courts, the courts have thereby acquired legitimate authority to measure their interests in their sacred sites. The objection ignores the more basic fact that the overall social/political context in which First Nations peoples carry their fight to the courts rests on coercion rather than consent.

30 For this statement to be true of First Nations sacred sites, "spirituality and religion" must not be limited to practical religious use of sacred sites but must also include associated theological/cosmological beliefs. For, as the *Twin Sisters* case shows, a First Nations sacred site need not have a practical religious use. As Brian Edward Brown demonstrates, US courts have shown an unfortunate propensity to limit Native American religious interests in their sacred sites to their practical religious use. He argues that the courts' propensity betrays "a shallow and confined understanding of sacred presence intrinsic not only to Native American traditions but to the plurality of human religious experience." See his *Religion, Law, and the Land: Native Americans and the Judicial Interpretation of Sacred Land* (Westport, CT: Greenwood Press, 1999) at 174-75.

31 The distinction between spiritual and religious interests on the one hand and other interests on the other is not a denial that the other interests may have spiritual and religious dimensions. It would not be unusual for a First Nation's sustenance or environmental interests in a sacred site, for instance, to be existentially inseparable from its spiritual and religious interests. The conceptual distinction does not imply existential separation.

32 See page 69, this volume.

33 *Haida Nation v. British Columbia (Minister of Forests),* [2002] B.C.J. No. 378 at para. 26 (B.C.C.A.) (QL) [*Haida Nation (Part 1)*].

34 Lambert J.A.'s remarks in *Haida Nation v. British Columbia (Minister of Forests),* [2002] B.C.J. No. 1882 at para. 62 (B.C.C.A.) (QL) [*Haida Nation (Part 2)*], are particularly apropos. Speaking of the Crown's fiduciary duty, he wrote: "The fiduciary duty of the Crown, federal or provincial, is a duty to behave towards the Indian people with utmost good faith

and to put the interests of the Indian people under the protection of the Crown so that, in cases of conflicting rights, the interests of the Indian people, to whom the fiduciary duty is owed, must not be subordinated by the Crown to competing interests of other persons to whom the Crown owes no fiduciary duty." In the same vein, see also Madam Justice Hansen's earlier remarks in *Mikisew Cree First Nation v. Canada (Minister of Canadian Heritage)*, [2001] F.C.J. No. 1877 at paras. 115-22 (F.C.T.D.) (QL), rev'd on other grounds 2004 F.C.A. 66 [*Mikisew Cree*], and Tysoe J.'s later remarks in *Gitxsan First Nation v. British Columbia (Minister of Forests)*, [2002] B.C.J. No. 2761 at para. 85 (B.C.S.C.) (QL).

35 See page 36, this volume. Craig J.A.'s view partly mirrored Gibbs J.'s in his earlier judgment in the same case. For Gibbs J.'s view, see page 29, this volume.

36 See pages 50 and 64, respectively.

37 See page 61, this volume.

38 See pages 41 and 44, respectively.

39 See page 102, this volume. Although he did not disagree with the chambers judge's conclusion that the Crown's approval of Canfor's cutting permit constituted a *prima facie* infringement of the Halfway River First Nation's treaty rights, Finch J.A., in *Halfway River (BCCA), supra* note 15 at para. 140, took issue with her description of the Tusdzuh as "unspoiled wilderness": "The Tusdzuh was not unspoiled wilderness in 1996 when the District Manager approved C.P.212, nor was it unspoiled wilderness in 1982 when treaty rights received constitutional protection. This was wilderness criss-crossed with seismic lines, where oil and gas exploration and mining had taken place."

40 From the points of view of many First Nations, the problem with this presupposition is admirably summed up in the words of a tribal elder who is quoted as saying: "You are talking about preserving the environment and the plants and animals that we see. I am worried about preserving the environment that we do not see – the places where the spirits live." For the quote and its reference, see Kimberley L. Lawson, "Cultural Interpretation in Times of Change" in George P. Nicholas and Thomas D. Andrews, eds., *At a Crossroads: Archaeology and First Peoples in Canada* (Burnaby, BC: Archaeology Press, 1997) 33 at 36.

41 A further problem is that Canadian sacred sites have never – very probably because they could never – become the loci of competing and (usually) conflicting interests in a way adequately comparable to First Nations sacred sites. A yet further problem is that few Canadian sacred sites are comparable. Unlike many First Nations sacred sites, most Canadian sacred sites serve practical religious and/or theological/cosmological functions that are easily separable from place. And so, whether, say, a church or a mosque is located in one or another part of a city has little to no effect on its practical religious and/or theological/cosmological functions.

42 A slightly different strategy of abstracting from sacred sites and comparing the courts' treatment of First Nations spirituality and religion with their treatment of Canadian spirituality and religion might determine whether the courts are biased specifically against First Nations spirituality and religion.

43 After surveying how the courts in Australia, Canada, New Zealand, and the United States have responded when given the final say on issues involving the accommodation of indigenous peoples' religious interests in their sacred sites, Robert Collins, in his "Sacred Sites and Religious Freedom on Government Land" (2003) 5 U. Pa. J. Const. L. 241 at 269, concluded: "Lacking a workable metric to determine the importance and authenticity of religious claims, judges rest their decisions almost entirely on the adequacy of secular justifications for denying religious claims, and most contested claims lose."

Chapter 6: *Tima Kwetsi* – Epilogue

1 See especially the Inter-American Court/Commission cases mentioned in Chapter 2, note 50.

2 See page 159, this volume.

3 The courts have not been alone in making such faulty assumptions. Expressing a similar mistaken view, Jane Hubert writes: "It may be difficult to define what is meant by 'sacred' among different peoples and in varying contexts, but when the land comes under threat then the sacred sites, sacred places and sites of special significance become identifiable,

even to outsiders, by the extent to which the communities concerned will fight to preserve and protect them from disturbance, interference or destruction." See her "Sacred
Beliefs and Beliefs of Sacredness" in David L. Carmichael, Jane Hubert, Brian Reeves, Audhild Schanche, eds., *Sacred Sites, Sacred Places* (London: Routledge, 1994) 9 at 18.

4 The courts should avoid priding themselves overmuch on their efforts to obtain a better
understanding of First Nations' perspectives. Criticizing recent Supreme Court of Canada
decisions, Patricia Monture-Angus says: "Colonialism has not changed, just shifted, and
it is now wearing the judicial robes of respect for 'perspective.'" See her *Journeying Forward: Dreaming First Nations Independence* (Halifax: Fernwood, 1999) at 134.

5 I follow the BC two-stage view. See Chapter 3, note 6.

6 I picture the basic reasoning proceeding as follows: (1) The proposed activity is either a
serious or a minor violation of the sacred site's ethic. (2) If the proposed activity is a serious violation of the site's ethic, the consequent harm is irreparable. (3) If the consequent
harm is irreparable, the sacred site is sufficiently unique to qualify as an exception to the
general rule favouring Canadian economic interests. If, despite my argument above,
courts feel a need for a middle term to justify the inference of sufficient uniqueness from
irreparable harm, they might consider the site's status within the First Nation's culture.
High status would then serve to warrant the inference.

7 For a helpful discussion of why this is so, see Patrick Macklem, *Indigenous Difference and
the Constitution of Canada* (Toronto: University of Toronto Press, 2001) at 107-31.

8 Speaking of the limits of the Supreme Court of Canada's ability to lead public opinion,
Cole Harris says: "It can lead public opinion, but probably not by much. Whatever the
rights of the matter, a radical decision of the Supreme Court in favour of Native people is
not feasible. It would not be enforced, and the court would probably have undermined
itself, if not the country." See his *Making Native Space: Colonialism, Resistance, and Reserves
in British Columbia* (Vancouver: UBC Press, 2002) at 297. John Borrows argues, however,
that such a position looks at the issue only from one side:

> Aboriginal people and others puzzled by the wide effect of Crown assertions might
> develop a greater respect for the judiciary if the courts ruled according to principles
> of law. They would consider such a conclusion [i.e., that the unilateral exercise of
> Crown sovereignty over Aboriginal peoples is legally invalid] reasonable, practical,
> realistic, sensible, and demonstrative of an understanding of the law and history of
> Aboriginal rights. They would see that a rejection of Crown assertions of sovereignty
> could help reduce the suffering of Aboriginal peoples arising from their alienation
> from their own land and organizing institutions. Such a decision could even enhance
> the reputation of the administration of justice, as the court would be seen to be
> applying the law in accordance with its highest principles. The courts' questioning of
> unilateral Crown assertions of sovereignty would be a substantial development of
> Canada's legal order. It would highlight the guarantee to every Canadian of an impar-
> tial and independent judiciary, which has been described as "the most important
> benefit of civilization."

See his *Recovering Canada: The Resurgence of Indigenous Law* (Toronto: University of
Toronto Press, 2002) at 121.

Selected Bibliography

Articles and Books

Alfred, Taiaiake. "Deconstructing the British Columbia Treaty Process" (Paper prepared for the Assembly of First Nations, August 2000). The Delgamuukw/Gisday'wa National Process, online: <http://www.delgamuukw.org/research/bctreatyprocess.pdf>, last accessed 14 May 2004.

Asch, Michael, and Patrick Macklem. "Aboriginal Rights and Canadian Sovereignty: An Essay on *R. v. Sparrow*" (1991) 29 Alta. L.R. 498.

Battiste, Marie, and James (Sa'ke'j) Youngblood Henderson. *Protecting Indigenous Knowledge and Heritage: A Global Challenge* (Saskatoon: Purich, 2000).

"B.C. Wants Private Sector to Run Heritage Sites" *Globe and Mail* (8 August 2002) A9A.

Bell, Catherine. "Protecting Indigenous Heritage Resources in Canada: A Comment on *Kitkatla v. British Columbia*" (2001) 10 Int'l J. Cult. Prop. 246.

Borrows, John. *Recovering Canada: The Resurgence of Indigenous Law* (Toronto: University of Toronto Press, 2002).

Brown, Brian Edward. *Religion, Law, and the Land: Native Americans and the Judicial Interpretation of Sacred Land* (Westport, CT: Greenwood Press, 1999).

Carmichael, David L., Jane Hubert, and Brian Reeves. "Introduction" in David L. Carmichael, Jane Hubert, Brian Reeves, and Audhild Schanche, eds., *Sacred Sites, Sacred Place* (London: Routledge, 1994) 1.

Collins, Richard B. "Sacred Sites and Religious Freedom on Government Land" (2003) 5 U. Pa. J. Const. L. 241.

Friends of Clayoquot Sound. "Friends of Clayoquot Time-Line," online: Friends of Clayoquot Sound <http://www.focs.ca/1clayoquot/timeline.htm>, last accessed 14 May 2004.

–. *Meares Island* (pamphlet) (Tofino: Friends of Clayoquot Sound, n.d.).

–. *Meares Island: Protecting a Natural Paradise* (Tofino: Friends of Clayoquot Sound, 1985).

Gulliford, Andrew. *Sacred Objects and Sacred Places: Preserving Tribal Traditions* (Boulder: University Press of Colorado, 2000).

Harris, Cole. *Making Native Space: Colonialism, Resistance, and Reserves in British Columbia* (Vancouver: UBC Press, 2002).

Hubert, Jane. "Sacred Beliefs and Beliefs of Sacredness" in David L. Carmichael, Jane Hubert, Brian Reeves, and Audhild Schanche, eds., *Sacred Sites, Sacred Places* (London: Routledge, 1994) 9.

Hunter, John J.L. "Advancing Aboriginal Title Claims after Delgamuukw: The Role of the Injunction" (Paper presented at the Continuing Legal Education Conference on Litigating Aboriginal Title, June 2000) 1.3.13, online: Davis and Company <http://www.davis.ca/publications/2000-06_advancing_aboriginal_title_claims_injunctions.pdf>, last accessed 14 May 2004.

Isaac, Thomas. *Aboriginal and Treaty Rights in the Maritimes: The* Marshall *Decision and Beyond* (Saskatoon: Purich, 2001).

Kymlicka, Will. *Finding Our Way: Rethinking Ethnocultural Relations in Canada* (Oxford: Oxford University Press, 1998).

Lawson, Kimberley L. "Cultural Interpretation in Times of Change" in George P. Nicholas and Thomas D. Andrews, eds., *At a Crossroads: Archaeology and First Peoples in Canada* (Burnaby, BC: Archaeology Press, 1997) 33.

Macklem, Patrick. *Indigenous Difference and the Constitution of Canada* (Toronto: University of Toronto Press, 2001).

–. "Recent Developments in Aboriginal Rights: A Thematic Overview" in *Aboriginal Law Conference 2002: Determining, Defining and Proving Aboriginal Rights and Title* (Materials prepared for the Continuing Legal Education seminar *Aboriginal Law Conference 2002*, Vancouver, 1 March 2002) (Vancouver: Continuing Legal Education Society of BC, 2002) 1.1.01.

Milton, John. "Results of Hamilton's Negotiations with the Haudenosaunee Council," Hamilton Independent Media Center (18 February 2004), online: Hamilton Independent Media Center <http://hamilton.indymedia.org/feature/display/5714/index.php>, last accessed 18 October 2004.

Mohs, Gordon. "Sto:lo Sacred Ground" in David L. Carmichael, Jane Hubert, Brian Reeves, and Audhild Schanche, eds., *Sacred Sites, Sacred Places* (London: Routledge, 1994) 184.

Monture-Angus, Patricia. *Journeying Forward: Dreaming First Nations Independence* (Halifax: Fernwood, 1999).

Quinn, Frank. "As Long as the Rivers Run: The Impacts of Corporate Water Development on Native Communities in Canada" (1991) 11 Canadian Journal of Native Studies 137.

Ray, Arthur J. "Treaty 8: A British Columbia Anomaly" (1999) 123 BC Studies 5.

Reynolds, James I. "The Royal Proclamation 1763 and Section 35 of the Constitution Act 1982 – Solid Base or Shifting Sands?" in *Aboriginal Law Conference 2002: Determining, Defining and Proving Aboriginal Rights and Title* (Materials prepared for the Continuing Legal Education seminar *Aboriginal Law Conference 2002*, Vancouver, 1 March 2002) (Vancouver: Continuing Legal Education Society of BC, 2002) 2.1.01, online: Ratcliff and Company <http://www.ratcliff.com/business/doc-reynolds.htm>, last accessed 12 February 2002.

Simons, Margaret. *The Meeting of the Waters: The Hindmarsh Island Affair* (Sydney, Australia: Hodder, 2003).

Staples, Lindsay, and Nick Poushinsky. *Determining the Impact of the Tulsequah Chief Mine Project on the Traditional Land Use of the Taku River Tlingit First Nation* (Report prepared for the Environmental Assessment Office, August 1997), online: BC Environmental Assessment Office <http://www.eao.gov.bc.ca>, last accessed 14 May 2004.

Stogre, Michael. *That the World May Believe: The Development of Papal Social Thought on Aboriginal Rights* (Sherbrooke, QC: Editions Paulines, 1992).

Timmons, Rebecca S. "Kootenai – Ksanka – Kunaitupii" in Brian O.K. Reeves and Margaret A. Kennedy, eds., *Kunaitupii: Coming Together on Native Sacred Sites: Their Sacredness, Conservation and Interpretation* (Proceedings of the First Joint Meeting of the Archaeological Society of Alberta and the Montana Archaeological Society, Waterton Lakes National Park, Alberta, 2-6 May 1990) (Calgary: Archaeological Society of Alberta, 1993) 140.

Tully, James. "A Just Relationship between Aboriginal and Non-Aboriginal Peoples of Canada" in Curtis Cook and Juan D. Lindau, eds., *Aboriginal Rights and Self-Government: The Canadian and Mexican Experience in North American Perspective* (Montreal and Kingston: McGill-Queen's University Press, 2000) 39.

–. "Reconsidering the B.C. Treaty Process" in *Speaking Truth to Power II: A Treaty Forum* (Vancouver, BC: British Columbia Treaty Commission, 2001) 3.

Venditti, Pat. "Siska First Nation Blockade Begins to Stop Watershed Destruction," Forest Action Network (6 October 1999), online: Forests.org <http://www.forests.org/archive/canada/siskafir.htm>, last accessed 17 May 2004.

Waldram, James B. *As Long as the Rivers Run: Hydroelectric Development and Native Communities in Western Canada* (Winnipeg: University of Manitoba Press, 1988).

White-Harvey, Robert. "Reservation Geography and the Restoration of Native Self-Government" (1994) 17 Dal. L.J. 587.

York, Geoffrey, and Loreen Pindera. *People of the Pines: The Warriors and the Legacy of Oka* (Toronto: Little, Brown, 1991).

Legislation

British Columbia Treaty Commission Agreement (21 September 1992), online: BC Treaty Commission <http://www.bctreaty.net>, last accessed 10 May 2004.

Canada National Parks Act, S.C. 2000, c. 32.

Canadian Charter of Rights and Freedoms, Part I of the *Constitution Act, 1982,* being Schedule B to the *Canada Act 1982* (U.K.), 1982, c. 11.

Cemeteries Act (Revised), R.S.O. 1990, c. C.4

Constitution Act, 1867 (U.K.), 30 & 31 Vict. c. 3, reprinted in R.S.C. 1985, App. II, No. 5 (formerly the *British North America Act, 1867*).

Constitution Act, 1982, being Schedule B to the *Canada Act 1982* (U.K.), 1982, c. 11.

Crown Proceedings Act, R.S.B.C. 1979, c. 86.

Crown Proceedings Act, R.S.B.C. 1996, c. 89.

Environmental Assessment Act, R.S.B.C. 1996, c. 119.

Executive Order 13007 (U.S.), "Protection and Accommodation of Access to 'Indian Sacred Sites'" (24 May 1996), 61 FR 26771; 29 May 1996.

Fisheries Act, R.S.C. 1970, c. F-14.

Forest Act, R.S.B.C. 1979, c. 140.

Forest Act, R.S.B.C. 1996, c. 157.

Heritage Conservation Act, R.S.B.C. 1979, c. 16.

Heritage Conservation Act, R.S.B.C. 1996, c. 187.

Indian Act, R.S.C. 1985, c. I-5.

Mi'kmaq-Nova Scotia-Canada Umbrella Agreement (June 2002), online: Government of Nova Scotia <http://www.gov.ns.ca/abor/pubs/ umbrella_june_2002.pdf>, last accessed 17 May 2004.

Nisga'a Final Agreement (Victoria: Ministry of Aboriginal Affairs, 1998).

Royal Proclamation of 1763 (U.K.), reprinted in R.S.C. 1985, App. II, No. 1. An accurate copy of the original is found in C.S. Brigham, ed., *British Proclamations Relating to America 1603-1783* in *Transactions and Collections of the American Antiquarian Society* (Worcester, MA: American Antiquarian Society, 1911) 212-18.

Sahtu Dene and Métis Comprehensive Land Claim Agreement (Ottawa: Ministry of Indian and Northern Affairs, 1993).

Supreme Court Rules (B.C. Reg. 221/90).

Government Documents

British Columbia. *Provincial Policy for Consultation with First Nations* (October 2002), online: Ministry of Sustainable Resource Management <http://www.gov.bc.ca/srm/>, last accessed 17 May 2004.

British Columbia, BC Treaty Commission. *Annual Report 2001* and *Annual Report 2002,* online: BC Treaty Commission <http://www.bctreaty.net>.

–. *Update* (May 2002), online: BC Treaty Commission <http://www.bctreaty.net>.

British Columbia, Ministry of Attorney General. *Report of the British Columbia Claims Task Force* (28 June 1991), online: Ministry of Attorney General, Treaty Negotiations Office <http://www.gov.bc.ca/tno/rpts/bcctf/toc.htm>, last accessed 17 May 2004.

British Columbia, Ministry of Forests, Ken Baker, Deputy Chief Forester. *Tree Farm Licence 39: Rationale for Allowable Annual Cut (AAC) Determination* (21 November 2001), online: B.C. Ministry of Forests <http://www.for.gov.bc.ca/hts/tfl/tfl39/tsr2/rationale.pdf>, last accessed 14 May 2004.

British Columbia, Ministry of Native Affairs. News Release 90:20, "Province Accepts Recommendations of Premier's Council on Native Affairs" (9 August 1990).

British Columbia, Ministry of Sustainable Resource Management. *Dawson Creek Land and Resource Management Plan,* online: Ministry of Sustainable Resource Management, Dawson

Creek Land and Resource Management Plan <http://srmwww.gov.bc.ca/rmd/lrmp/dawson/toc.htm#toc>, last accessed 14 May 2004.

British Columbia, Ministry of Sustainable Resource Management, Twin Sisters Special Management Committee. *Twin Sisters Special Management Committee Recommendations for Management Objectives and Strategies for the Special Management Zones and Proposed Protected Area* (21 October 1997), online: Ministry of Sustainable Resource Management, Dawson Creek Land and Resource Management Plan <http://srmwww.gov.bc.ca/lrmp/dawson/toc.htm#toc>, last accessed 14 May 2004.

British Columbia, Ministry of Sustainable Resource Management and Ministry of Energy and Mines. News Release 2002SRM0044-001098, "Strict Rules Key to Tulsequah Mine Approval" (13 December 2002), online: <http://www2.news.gov.bc.ca/nrm_news_releases/2002SRM0044-001098.htm#>, last accessed 28 April 2004.

British Columbia, Tulsequah Chief Project Committee. *Report and Recommendations of the Tulsequah Chief Project Committee with Respect to: A Decision on a Project Approval Certificate by the Minister of Environment, Lands and Parks and the Minister of Energy and Mines and Minister Responsible for Northern Development* (March 1998), online: Environmental Assessment Office <http://www.eao.gov.bc.ca>, last accessed 14 May 2004.

Canada, Department of Indian Affairs and Northern Development. *Basic Departmental Data – 2001* (Ottawa: Minister of Indian Affairs and Northern Development, 2002).

–. "Statement Made by the Honourable Jean Chrétien, Minister of Indian Affairs and Northern Development, on Claims of Indian and Inuit People" Communiqué 1-7339 (Ottawa: Department of Indian Affairs and Northern Development, 8 August 1973).

Canada, Department of Indian Affairs and Northern Development, and Intellectual Property Policy Directorate, Industry Canada. *Intellectual Property and Aboriginal People: A Working Paper* (Paper written for Research and Analysis Directorate by Simon Brascoupé and Karin Endemann) (Ottawa: Minister of Public Works and Government Services, 1999).

Canada, Ministry of Indian and Northern Affairs. Information Bulletin, "Nuu-Chah-Nulth, Canada, British Columbia Initial Agreement-in-Principle" (10 March 2001), online: Indian and Northern Affairs Canada <http://www.ainc-inac.gc.ca/nr/prs/j-a2001/ncn_e.pdf>, last accessed 14 May 2004.

–. News Release, "Kwakiutl First Nation Settlement Agreement Reached" (24 April 1997), online: Indian and Northern Affairs Canada <http://www.ainc-inac.gc.ca/nr/ rs.j-a1997/apr24.html>, last accessed 26 June 2002.

Canada. *Restructuring the Relationship,* Part 2, *Report of the Royal Commission on Aboriginal Peoples: Looking Forward, Looking Back,* vol. 2 (Ottawa: Canada Communication Group, 1996).

Taku River Tlingit First Nation. *Report and Recommendations of the Taku River Tlingit First Nation with Respect to a Decision on a Project Approval Certificate by the Minister of Environment, Lands and Parks and the Minister of Energy and Mines* (6 March 1998), online: BC Environmental Assessment Office <http://www.eao.gov.bc.ca>, last accessed 14 May 2004.

Jurisprudence
Attorney General of Manitoba v. Metropolitan Stores, [1987] 2 S.C.R. 110 (S.C.C.).
B.C. (A.G.) v. Wale, [1987] 2 W.W.R. 331 (B.C.C.A.).
B.C. (A.G.) v. Wale, [1991] 1 S.C.R. 62 (S.C.C.).
Calder v. Attorney General of British Columbia (1969), 8 D.L.R. (3d) 59 (B.C.S.C.).
Calder v. Attorney General of British Columbia (1970), 13 D.L.R. (3d) 64 (B.C.C.A.).
Calder v. Attorney General of British Columbia, [1973] S.C.R. 313 (S.C.C.).
Chapman v. Luminis Pty. Ltd. (No. 5), [2001] F.C.A. 1106 (Federal Court of Australia).
Clayoquot Indian Band v. British Columbia, [1986] B.C.J. No. 3169 (B.C.S.C.) (QL).
Delgam Uukw v. British Columbia (5 December 1986), Vancouver 006460 and 006495 (B.C.C.A.).
Delgamuukw v. British Columbia, [1991] 3 W.W.R. 97 (B.C.S.C.).
Delgamuukw v. British Columbia, [1997] 3 S.C.R. 1010 (S.C.C.).

Formula Contractors v. George (20 October 1988), Vancouver C884927 (B.C.S.C.).
Gitxsan First Nation v. British Columbia (Minister of Forests), [2002] B.C.J. No. 2761 (B.C.S.C.) (QL).
Guerin v. The Queen, [1984] 2 S.C.R. 335 (S.C.C.).
Gwoimt v. Westar and Formula (20 October 1988), Vancouver C885035 (B.C.S.C.).
Haida Nation v. British Columbia (Minister of Forests), [1995] B.C.J. No. 2411 (B.C.S.C.) (QL).
Haida Nation v. British Columbia (Minister of Forests), [1997] B.C.J. No. 2480 (B.C.C.A.) (QL).
Haida Nation v. British Columbia (Minister of Forests), [2002] B.C.J. No. 2427 (B.C.S.C.) (QL).
Haida Nation v. British Columbia (Minister of Forests), [2002] B.C.J. No. 378 (B.C.C.A.) (QL).
Haida Nation v. British Columbia (Minister of Forests), [2002] B.C.J. No. 1882 (B.C.C.A.) (QL).
Haida Nation v. British Columbia (Minister of Forests) 2004 SCC 73.
Halfway River First Nation v. British Columbia (Ministry of Forests), [1997] B.C.J. No. 1494 (B.C.S.C.) (QL).
Halfway River First Nation v. British Columbia (Ministry of Forests), [1999] B.C.J. No. 1880 (B.C.C.A.) (QL).
Heiltsuk Tribal Council v. British Columbia (Minister of Sustainable Resource Management), 2003 B.C.S.C. 1422.
House of Gwoimt v. Skeena Cellulose, [1995] B.C.J. No. 783 (B.C.S.C.) (QL).
House of Gwoimt v. Skeena Cellulose, [1995] B.C.J. No. 2967 (B.C.C.A.) (QL).
Hunt v. Halcan Log Services, [1987] 34 D.L.R. (4th) 504 (B.C.S.C.).
Husby Forest Products v. Minister of Forests, 2004 B.C.S.C. 142.
International Forest Products v. Pascal, [1991] B.C.J. No. 718 & No. 719 (B.C.S.C.) (QL).
Kelly Lake Cree Nation v. Canada (Ministry of Energy and Mines), [1998] B.C.J. No. 2471 (B.C.S.C.) (QL).
Kelly Lake Cree Nation v. Canada (Ministry of Energy and Mines), [1998] B.C.J. No. 3207 (B.C.S.C.) (QL).
Kelly Lake Cree Nation v. Canada, [1998] 2 F.C. 270 (F.C.T.D.) (QL).
Kelly Lake Cree Nation v. Canada, [2000] F.C.J. No. 1942 (F.C.T.D.) (QL).
Kitkatla Band v. British Columbia (Minister of Small Business, Tourism and Culture), [2002] 2 C.N.L.R. 143 (S.C.C.).
Lovelace v. Ontario, [2000] 1 S.C.R. 950 (S.C.C.).
MacMillan Bloedel v. Mullin, [1985] 2 C.N.L.R. 26 (B.C.S.C.).
MacMillan Bloedel v. Mullin, [1985] 2 C.N.L.R. 54 (B.C.C.A.).
Mary and Carrie Dann v. Unisted States (27 December 2002), Inter-Am. Comm. H.R., Case 11.140, Report No. 75/02, *Annual Report of the Inter–American Commision on Human Rights: 2002*, OEZ/Ser.L/V/II.117/doc. 1, rev. 1.
Maya Indigenous Communities of the Toledo District v. Belize (24 October 2003), Inter-Am. Ct. H.R., Case 12.053, Report No. 96/03.
Mayagna (Sumo) Awas Tingni Community v. Nicaragua (31 August 2001), Inter-Am. Ct. H.R. (Ser. C) No. 79.
McCrady v. Ontario, [1991] O.J. No. 1722 (Ont. Ct. Gen. Div.) (QL).
McCrady v. Ontario, [1992] O.J. No. 2321 (Ont. Ct. Gen. Div.) (QL).
Mikisew Cree First Nation v. Canada (Minister of Canadian Heritage), [2001] F.C.J. No. 1877 (F.C.T.D.) (QL).
Mikisew Cree First Nation v. Canada (Minister of Canadian Heritage) 2004 FCA. 66 (F.C.A.).
Mitchell v. M.N.R., [2001] 1 S.C.R. 911 (S.C.C.).
Mount Currie Indian Band v. International Forest Products, [1991] B.C.J. No. 703 (B.C.S.C.) (QL).
Nowegijick v. The Queen, [1983] 1 S.C.R. 29 (S.C.C.).
Paul v. British Columbia (Forest Appeals Commission), [2001] 89 B.C.L.R. (3d) 210 (B.C.C.A.).
Poplar Point Ojibway Nation v. Ontario, [1993] O.J. No. 601 Ont. Ct. (QL).
R. v. Adams, [1996] 3 S.C.R. 101 (S.C.C.)

R. v. Badger, [1996] 1 S.C.R. 771 (S.C.C.).

R. v. Catarat, [1998] S.J. No. 601 (Sask. Prov. Ct.) (QL).

R. v. Côté, [1996] 3 S.C.R. 139 (S.C.C.).

R. v. Kruger, [1978] 1 S.C.R. 104 (S.C.C.).

R. v. Marshall, [1999] 3 S.C.R. 456 (S.C.C.).

R. v. Sioui, [1987] R.J.Q. 1722.

R. v. Sioui, [1990] 1 S.C.R. 1025 (S.C.C.).

R. v. Sparrow, [1990] 1 S.C.R. 1075 (S.C.C.).

R. v. Van der Peet, [1996] 2 S.C.R. 507 (S.C.C.).

RJR MacDonald v. Canada (Attorney General), [1994] 1 S.C.R. 311 (S.C.C.).

Siska Indian Band v. British Columbia (Minister of Forests), [1998] B.C.J. No. 1661 (B.C.S.C.) (QL).

Siska Indian Band v. British Columbia (Minister of Forests), [1999] B.C.J. No. 2354 (B.C.S.C.) (QL).

Taku River Tlingit First Nation v. British Columbia (Project Assessment Director) 2004 SCC 74.

Taku River Tlingit First Nation v. Tulsequah Chief Mine Project, [1999] B.C.J. No. 984 (B.C.S.C.) (QL).

Taku River Tlingit First Nation v. Tulsequah Chief Mine Project, [1999] B.C.J. No. 1665 (B.C.S.C.) (QL).

Taku River Tlingit First Nation v. Tulsequah Chief Mine Project, [1999] B.C.J. No. 2204 (B.C.S.C.) (QL).

Taku River Tlingit First Nation v. Tulsequah Chief Mine Project, [2000] B.C.J. No. 2024 (B.C.C.A.) (QL).

Taku River Tlingit First Nation v. Tulsequah Chief Mine Project, [2002] B.C.J. No. 1301 (B.C.S.C.) (QL).

Taku River Tlingit First Nation v. Tulsequah Chief Mine Project, [2002] B.C.J. No. 155 (B.C.C.A.) (QL).

Tlowitsis-Mumtagila v. MacMillan Bloedel, [1990] B.C.J. No. 2499 (B.C.C.A.) (QL).

Tlowitsis-Mumtagila v. MacMillan Bloedel, [1991] 4 W.W.R. 83 (B.C.C.A.).

Tlowitsis Nation and Mumtagila Nation v. MacMillan Bloedel, [1991] 2 C.N.L.R. 164 (B.C.S.C.).

Westar Timber v. Gitksan Wet'suwet'en Tribal Council, [1990] 1 C.N.L.R. 151 (B.C.C.A.).

Westar Timber v. Ryan (20 October 1988), Vancouver C884927 (B.C.S.C.).

Websites

BC Environmental Assessment Office, <http://www.eao.gov.bc.ca>.

BC Ministry of Attorney General, Treaty Negotiations Office, <http://www.prov.gov. bc.ca/tno/>.

BC Ministry of Forests, <http://www.gov.bc.ca/bvprd/bc/channel.do?action=ministry &channelID=-8385&navId=NAV_ID_province>.

BC Ministry of Sustainable Resource Management, <http://www.gov.bc.ca/bvprd/bc/ channel.do?action=ministry&channelID=-8393&navId=NAV_ID_province>.

BC Treaty Commission, <http://www.bctreaty.net>.

Davis and Company, <http://www.davis.ca>.

Delgamuukw/Gisday'wa National Process, <http://www.delgamuukw.org>.

Forests.org, <http://forests.org>.

Friends of Clayoquot Sound, <http://www.focs.ca>.

Government of Nova Scotia, <http://www.gov.ns.ca>.

Hamilton Independent Media Center, <http://hamilton.indymedia.org.>

Indian and Northern Affairs Canada, <http://www.ainc-inac.gc.ca>.

Native Law Centre of Canada, <http://www.usask.ca/nativelaw>.

Nuxalk Nation, <http://www.nuxalk.org>.

Ontario's Living Legacy, <http://www.ontariolivinglegacy.com>.

Organization of American States, <http://www.oas.org>.

Ratcliff and Company, <www.ratcliff.com>.

Settlers in Support of Indigenous Sovereignty, <http://sisis.nativeweb.org>.

Union of BC Indian Chiefs, <http://www.ubcic.bc.ca>.

Index

LAW AND SOCIETY

Law and Society Series
W. Wesley Pue, General Editor

Gerald Kernerman
*Multicultural Nationalism: Civilizing Difference, Constituting
Community* (2005)

Pamela A. Jordan
*Defending Rights in Russia: Lawyers, the State, and Legal Reform
in the Post-Soviet Era* (2005)

Anna Pratt
Securing Borders: Detention and Deportation in Canada (2005)

Kirsten Johnson Kramar
Unwilling Mothers, Unwanted Babies: Infanticide in Canada (2005)

W.A. Bogart
*Good Government? Good Citizens? Courts, Politics, and Markets
in a Changing Canada* (2005)

Catherine Dauvergne
*Humanitarianism, Identity, Nation: Migration Laws of Australia
and Canada* (2005)

Michael Lee Ross
First Nations Sacred Sites in Canada's Courts (2005)

Andrew Woolford
Between Justice and Certainty: Treaty Making in British Columbia (2005)

John McLaren, Andrew Buck, and Nancy Wright (eds.)
Despotic Dominion: Property Rights in British Settler Societies (2004)

Georges Campeau
From UI to EI: Waging War on the Welfare State (2004)

Alvin J. Esau
*The Courts and the Colonies: The Litigation of Hutterite Church
   Disputes* (2004)

Christopher N. Kendall
Gay Male Pornography: An Issue of Sex Discrimination (2004)

Roy B. Flemming
Tournament of Appeals: Granting Judicial Review in Canada (2004)

Constance Backhouse and Nancy L. Backhouse
*The Heiress vs the Establishment: Mrs. Campbell's Campaign for Legal
   Justice* (2004)

Christopher P. Manfredi
*Feminist Activism in the Supreme Court: Legal Mobilization and
   the Women's Legal Education and Action Fund* (2004)

Annalise Acorn
Compulsory Compassion: A Critique of Restorative Justice (2004)

Jonathan Swainger and Constance Backhouse (eds.)
People and Place: Historical Influences on Legal Culture (2003)

Jim Phillips and Rosemary Gartner
Murdering Holiness: The Trials of Franz Creffield and George Mitchell (2003)

David R. Boyd
Unnatural Law: Rethinking Canadian Environmental Law and Policy (2003)

Ikechi Mgbeoji
*Collective Insecurity: The Liberian Crisis, Unilateralism, and Global
   Order* (2003)

Rebecca Johnson
*Taxing Choices: The Intersection of Class, Gender, Parenthood,
   and the Law* (2002)

John McLaren, Robert Menzies, and Dorothy E. Chunn (eds.)
Regulating Lives: Historical Essays on the State, Society, the Individual, and the Law (2002)

Joan Brockman
Gender in the Legal Profession: Fitting or Breaking the Mould (2001)